How To Draw
101
Cute Stuff
For Kids

I0479235

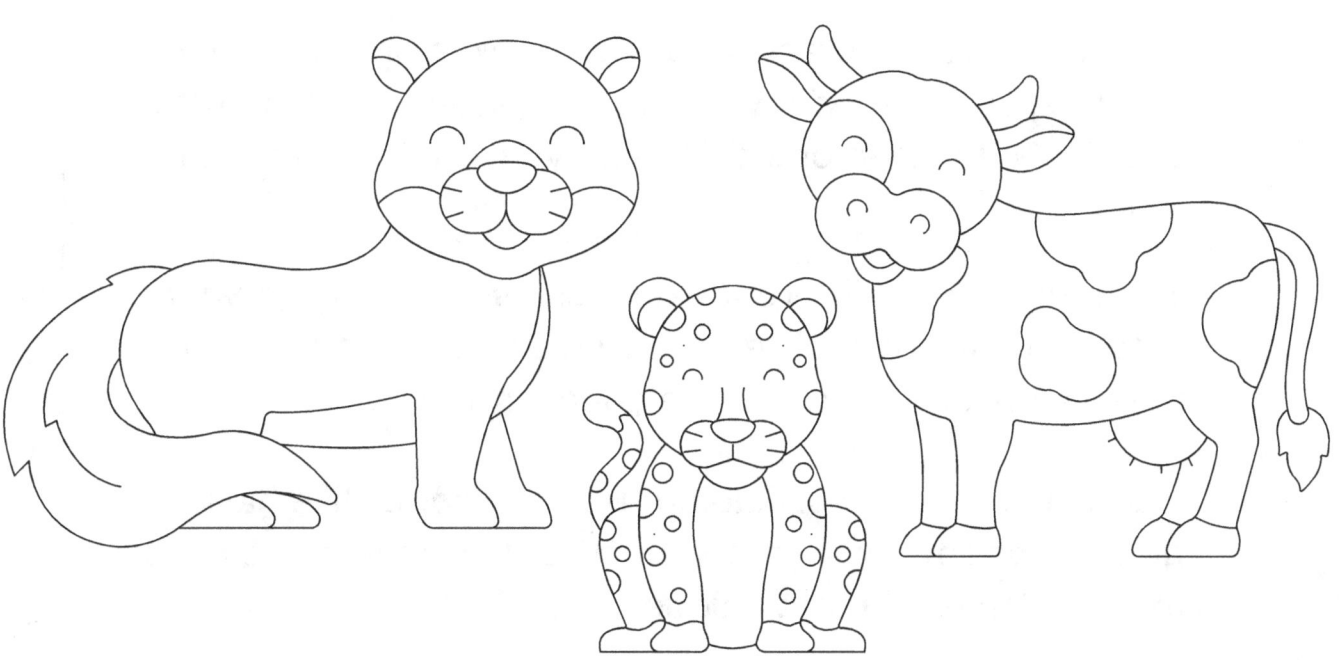

Tips
How to use this Book

1. Use reference images: If you're struggling to come up with ideas, or if you're having trouble getting a certain feature right, look up reference images to guide you.

2. Practice, practice, practice: Drawing takes practice, so don't be discouraged if your first few attempts don't turn out perfectly. Keep practicing and you'll get better with time.

3. Experiment with different expressions: Try drawing your cute character with different facial expressions to give it personality and make it more appealing to kids.

4. Add cute accessories: Adding fun accessories like hats, glasses, or bows can take your cute character to the next level and make it more unique.

5. Have fun: Above all, drawing should be fun! Don't stress too much about making your drawing perfect, just enjoy the process and let your creativity flow.

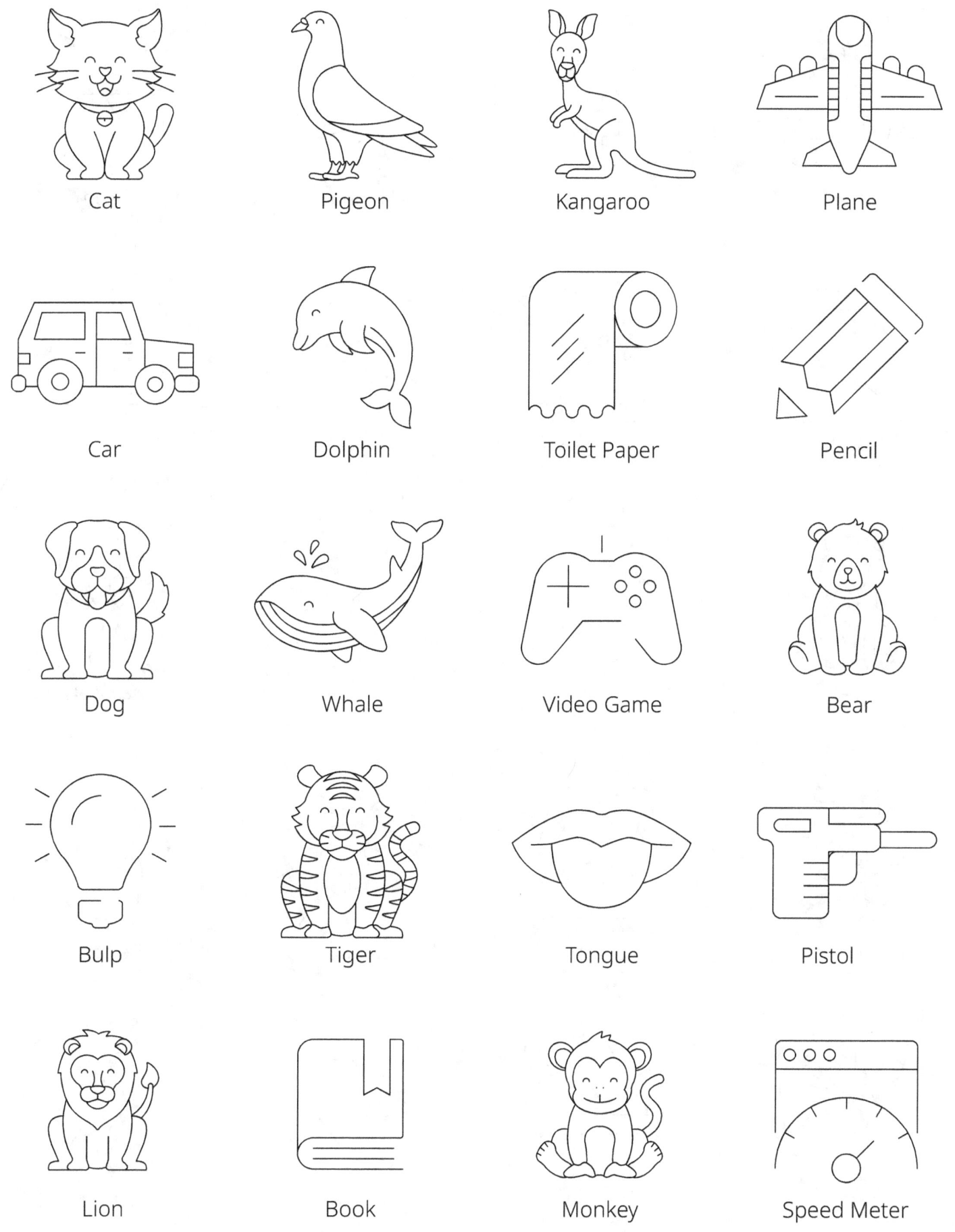

Cat	Pigeon	Kangaroo	Plane
Car	Dolphin	Toilet Paper	Pencil
Dog	Whale	Video Game	Bear
Bulp	Tiger	Tongue	Pistol
Lion	Book	Monkey	Speed Meter

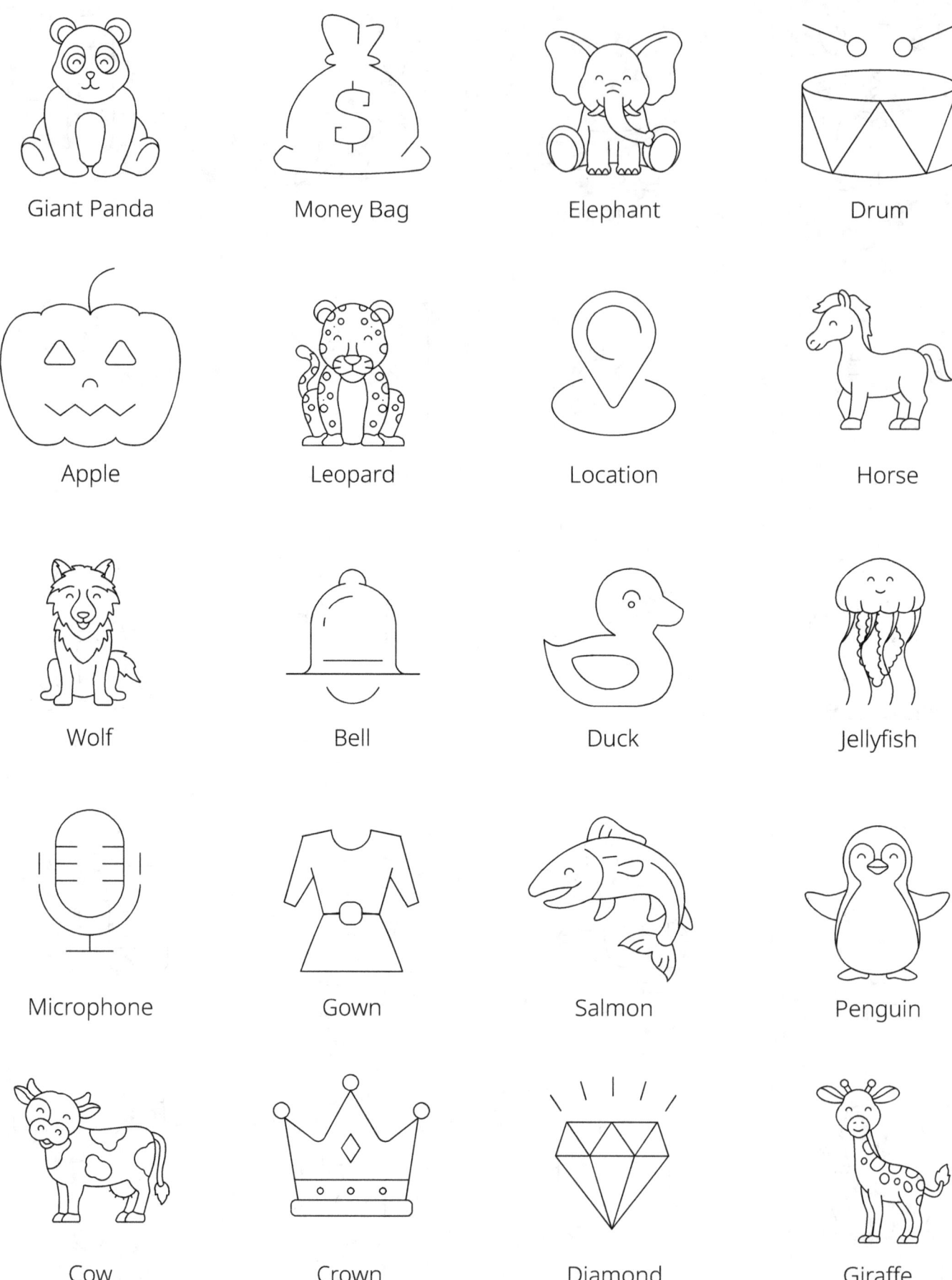

Giant Panda	Money Bag	Elephant	Drum
Apple	Leopard	Location	Horse
Wolf	Bell	Duck	Jellyfish
Microphone	Gown	Salmon	Penguin
Cow	Crown	Diamond	Giraffe

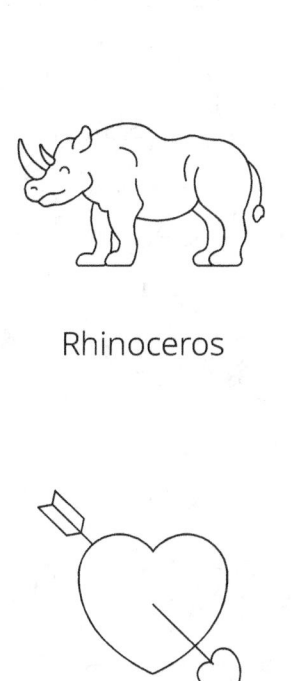

Rhinoceros

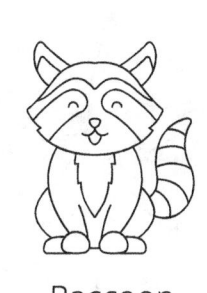

Cute Sun

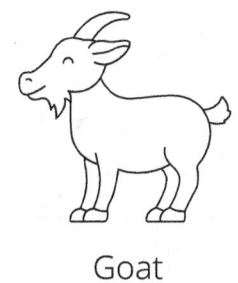

Jug

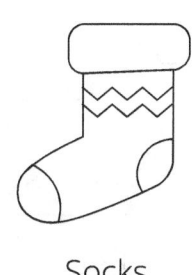

Otter

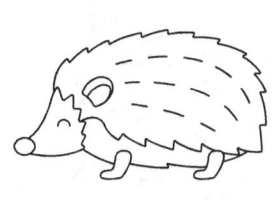

Love

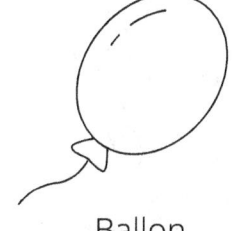

Raccoon

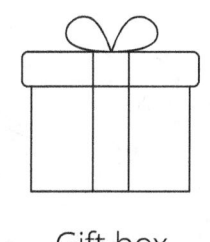

Goat

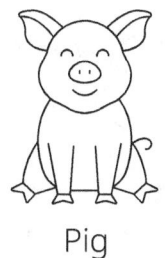

Socks

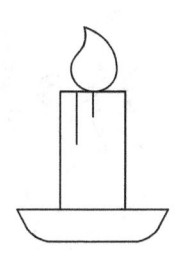

Hedgehog

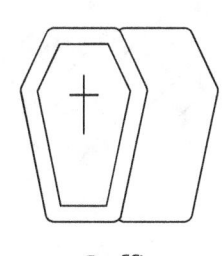

Ballon

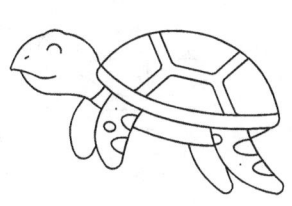

Gift box

Pig

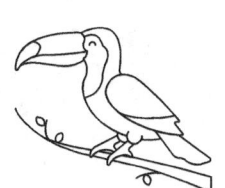

Candle

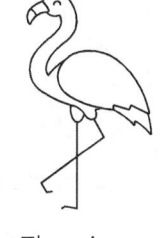

Coffin

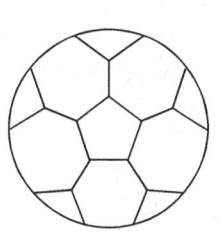

Tortoise

Lollipop

Toucan

Flamingo

Football

Madel

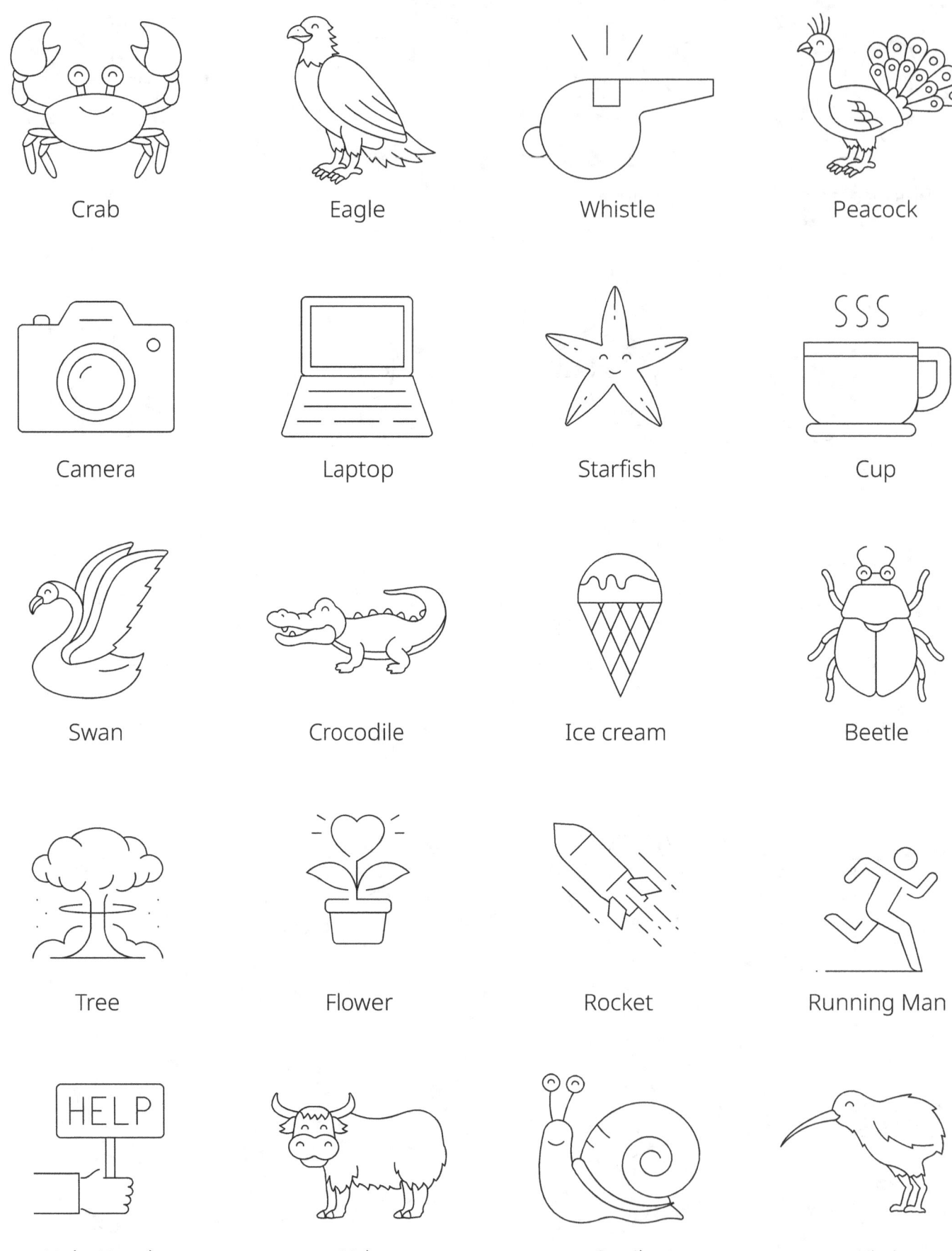

Crab	Eagle	Whistle	Peacock
Camera	Laptop	Starfish	Cup
Swan	Crocodile	Ice cream	Beetle
Tree	Flower	Rocket	Running Man
Help Hand	Yak	Snail	Kiwi

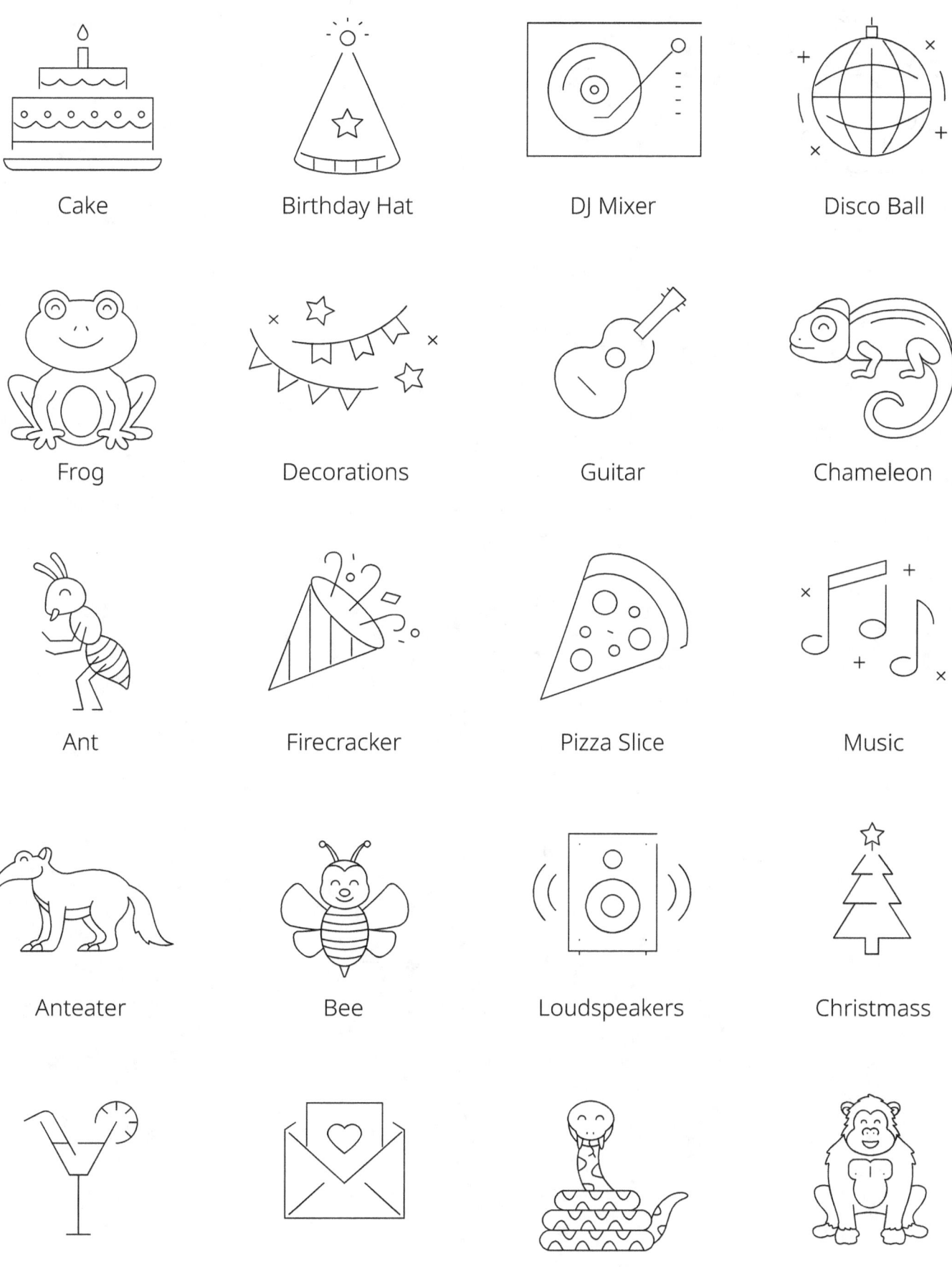

Cake	Birthday Hat	DJ Mixer	Disco Ball
Frog	Decorations	Guitar	Chameleon
Ant	Firecracker	Pizza Slice	Music
Anteater	Bee	Loudspeakers	Christmass
Cocktail	Valentine's Day	Snake	Gorilla

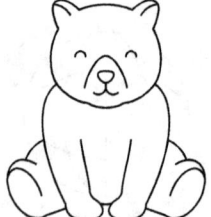

Polar Bear

Cat

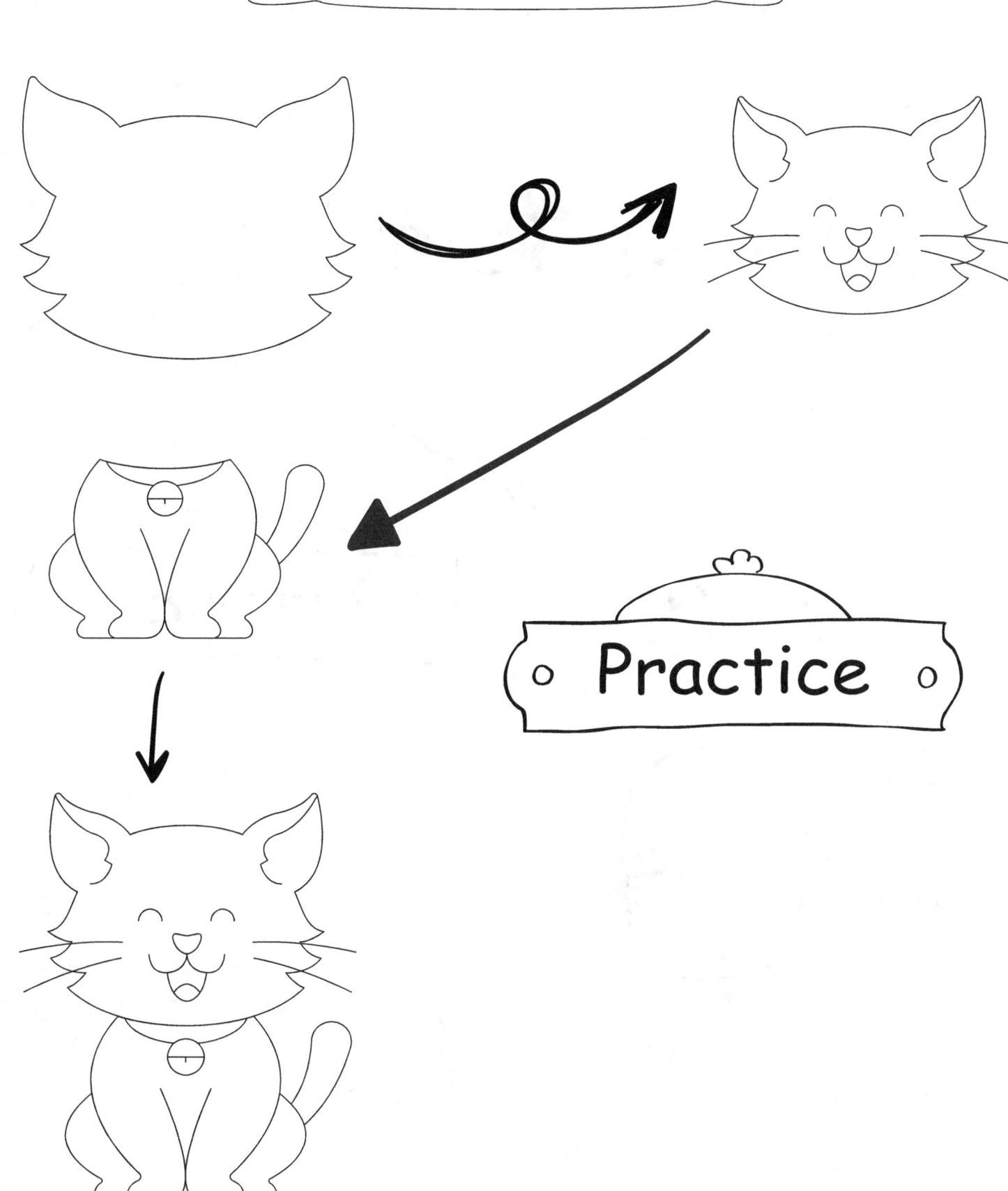

Practice

Pigeon

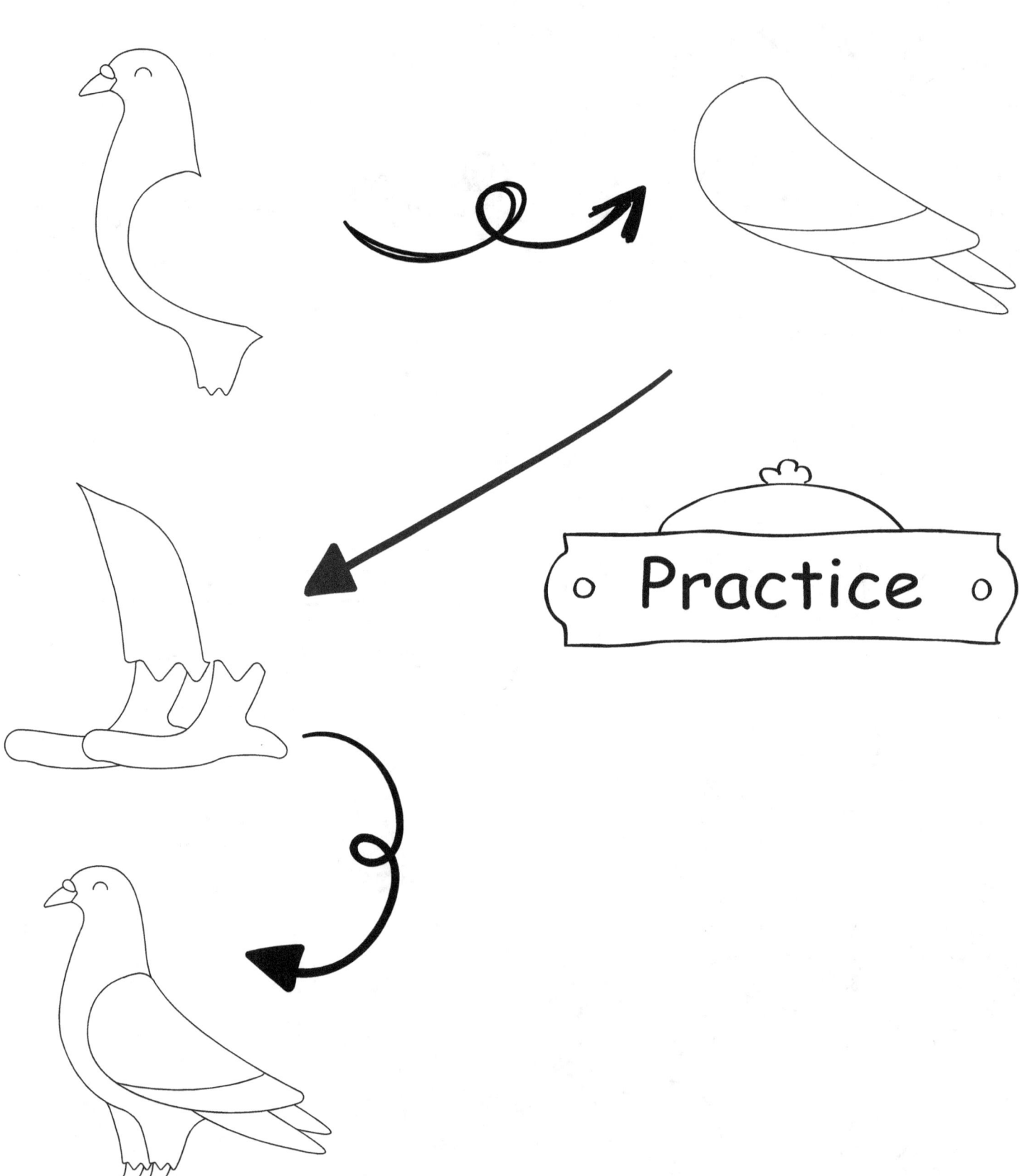

Practice

Kangaroo

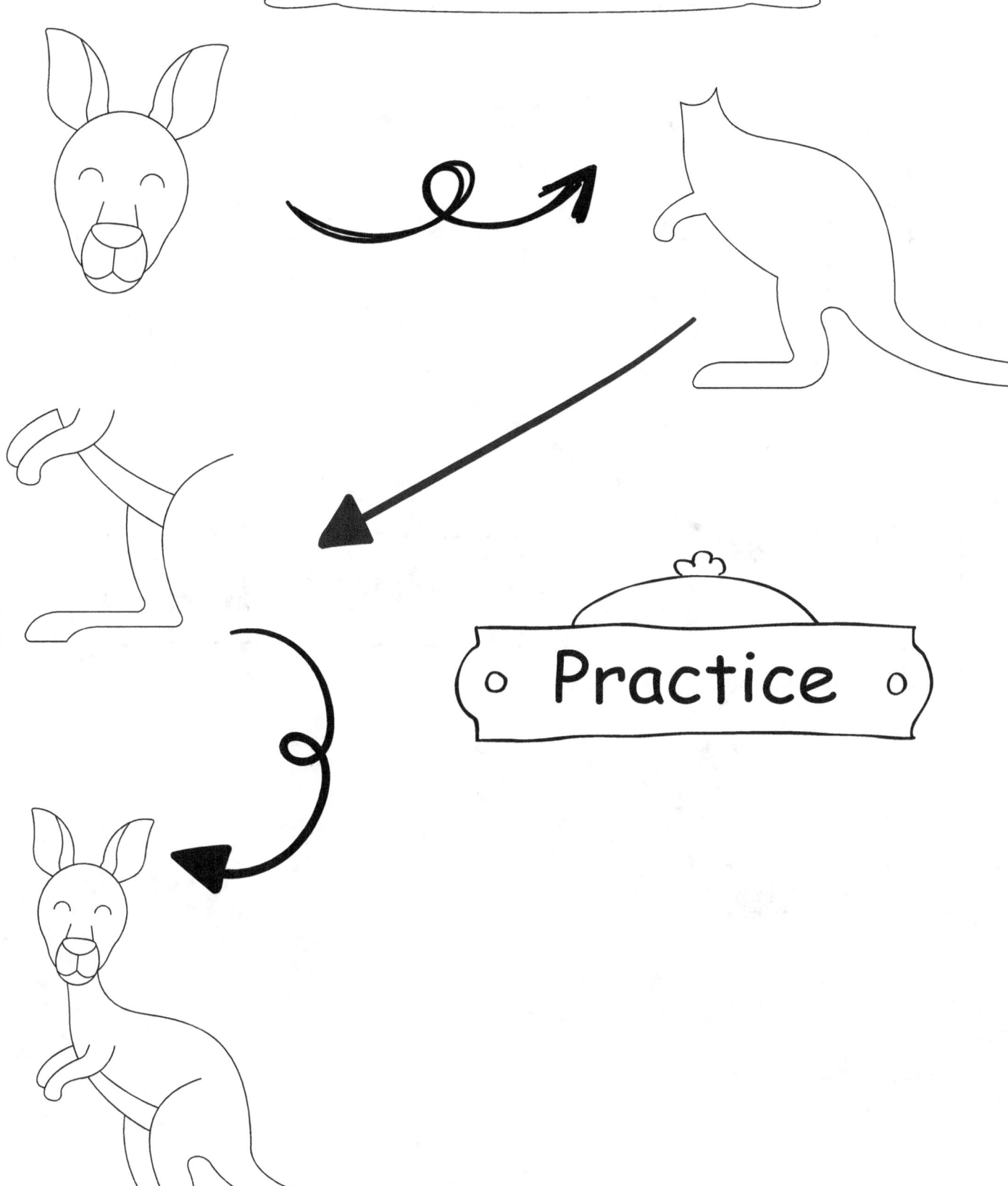

Practice

Plane

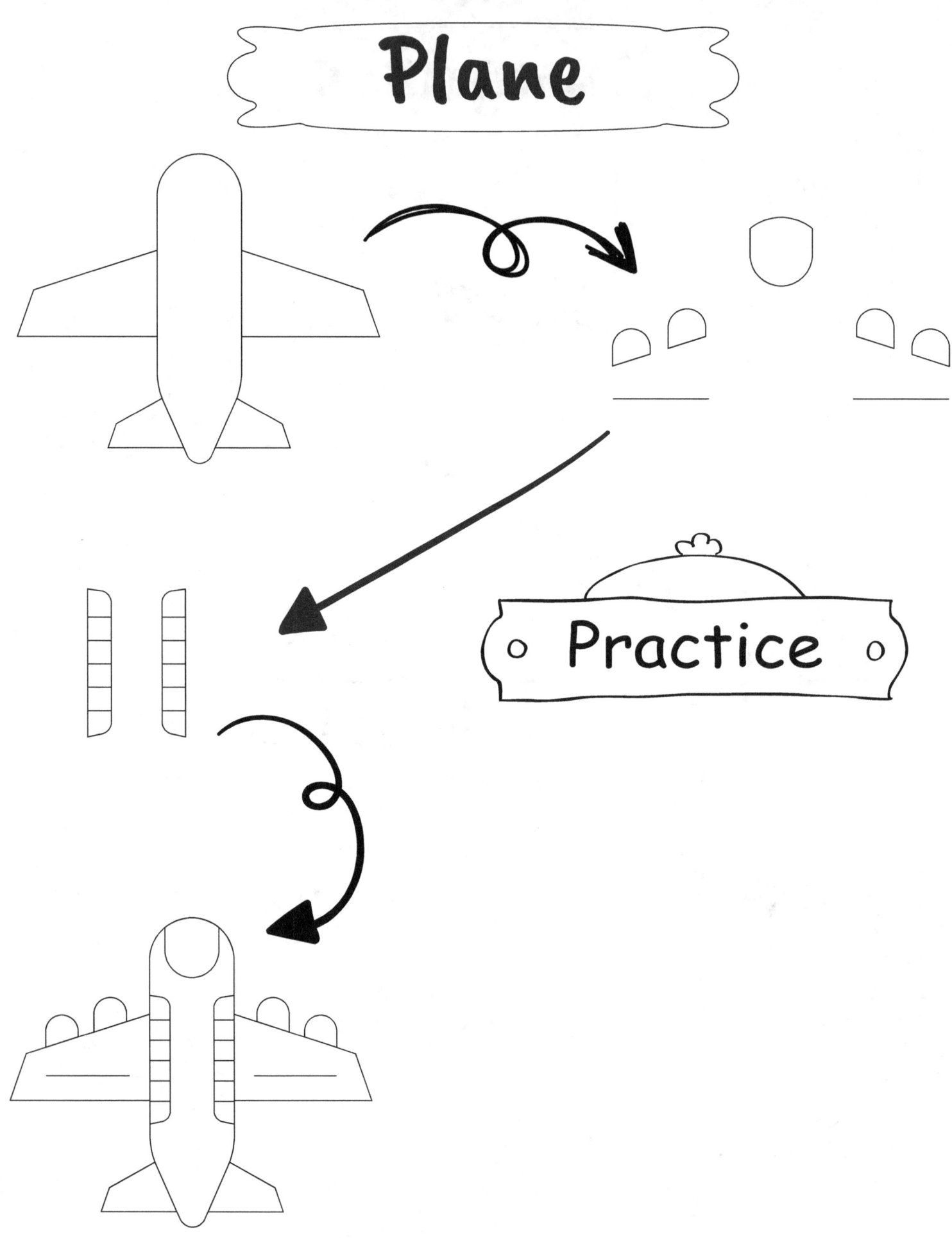

Car

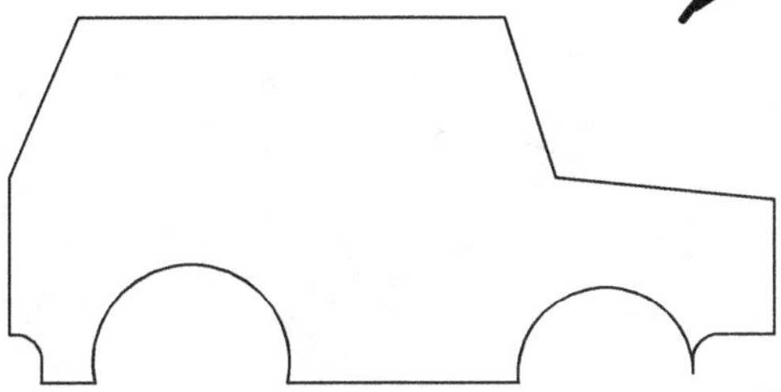

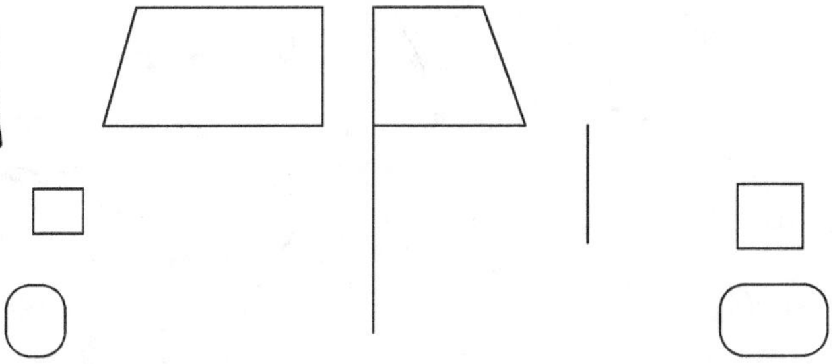

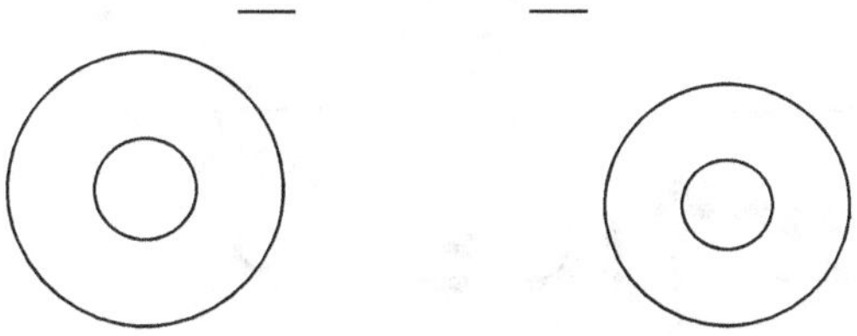

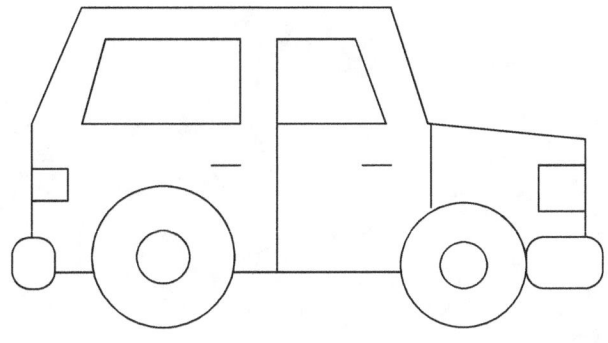

Practice

Dolphin

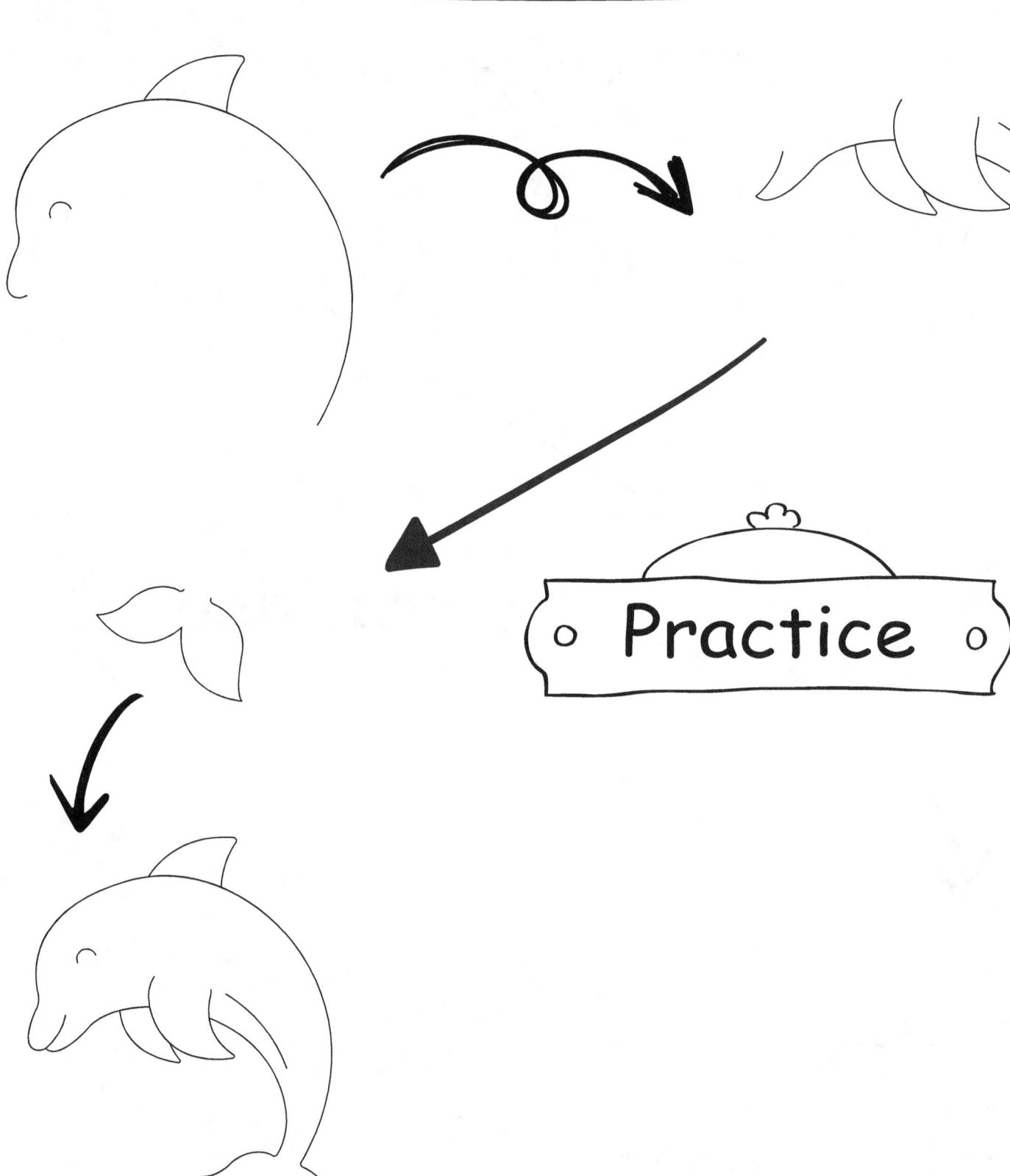

Practice

Toilet Paper

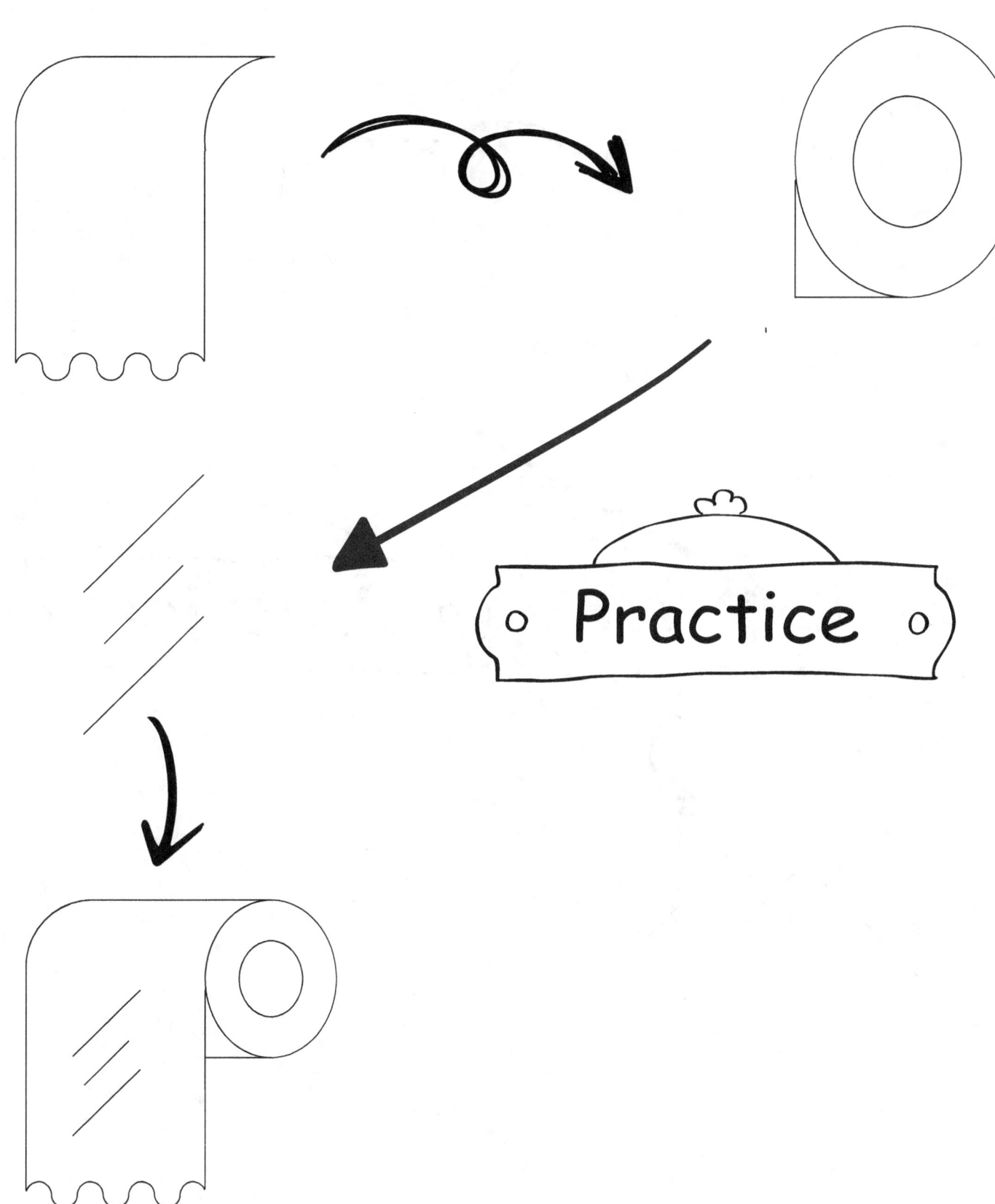

Practice

Pencil

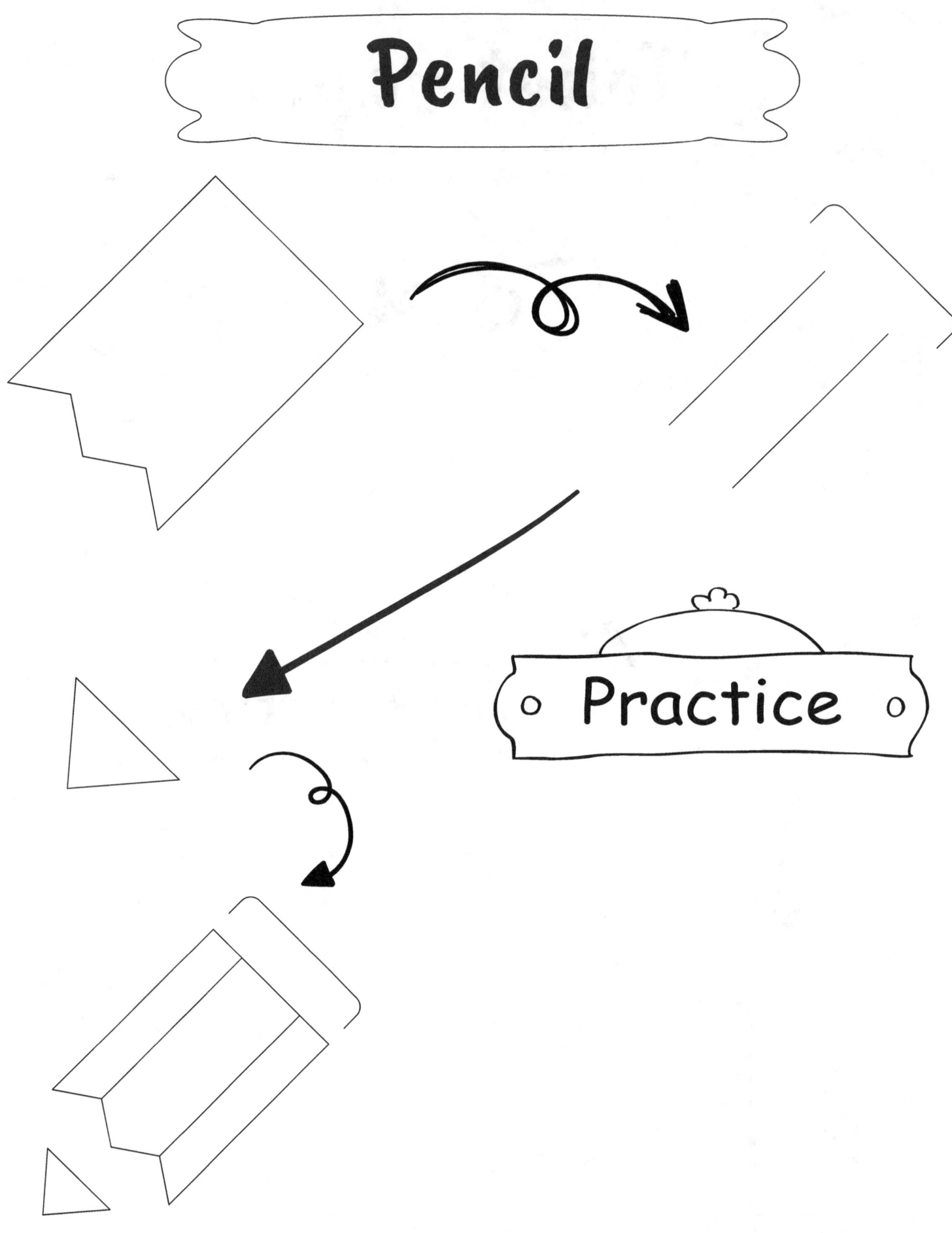

Practice

Dog

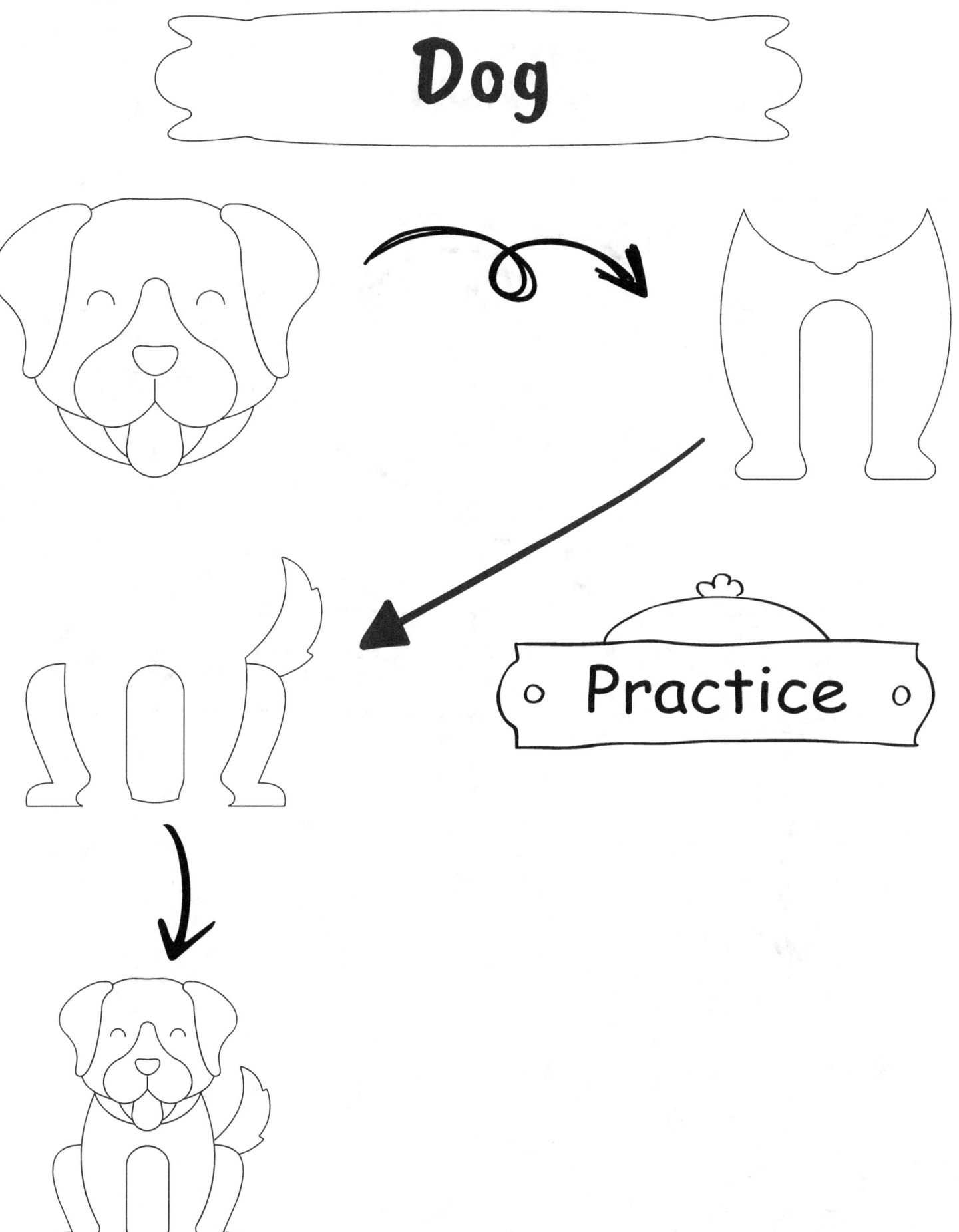

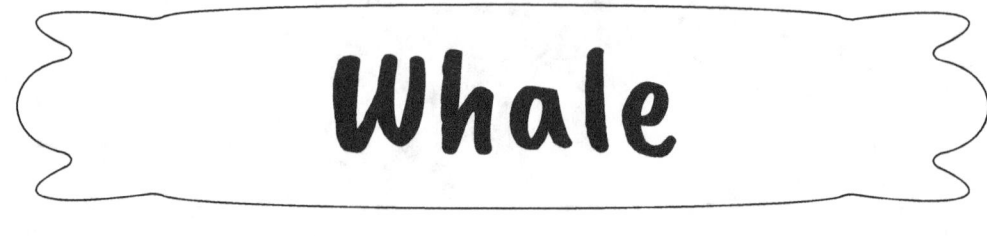

Whale

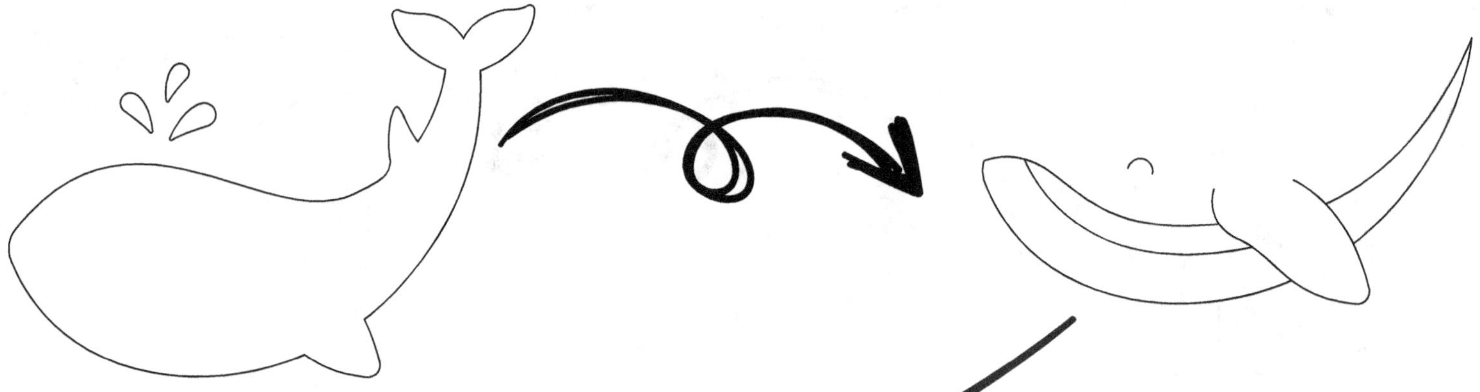

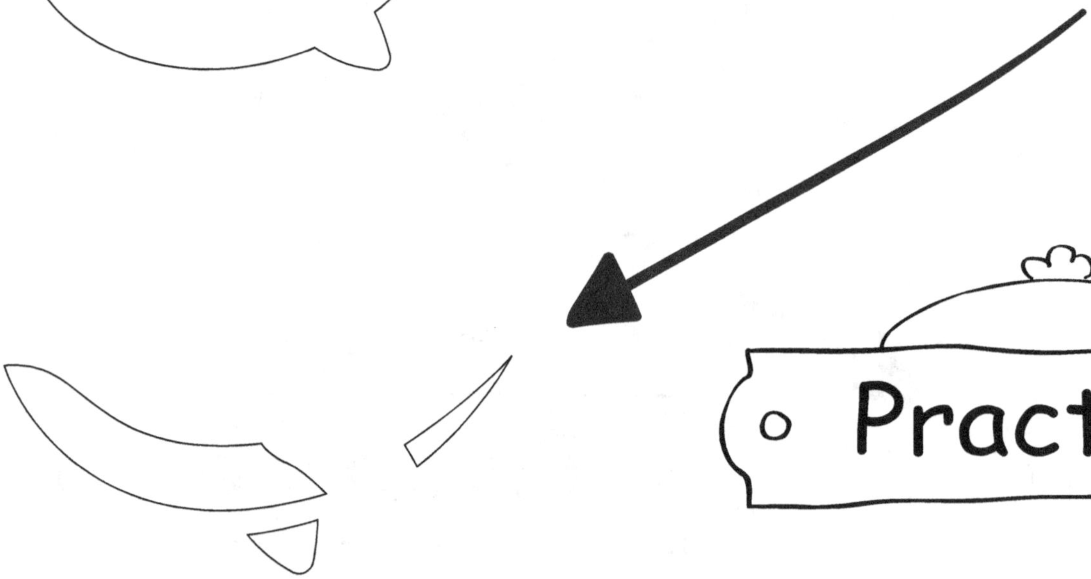

Practice

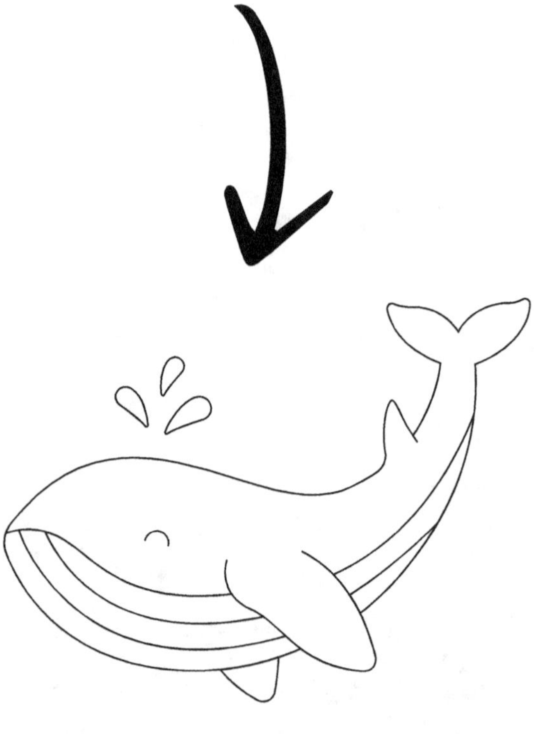

Video Game

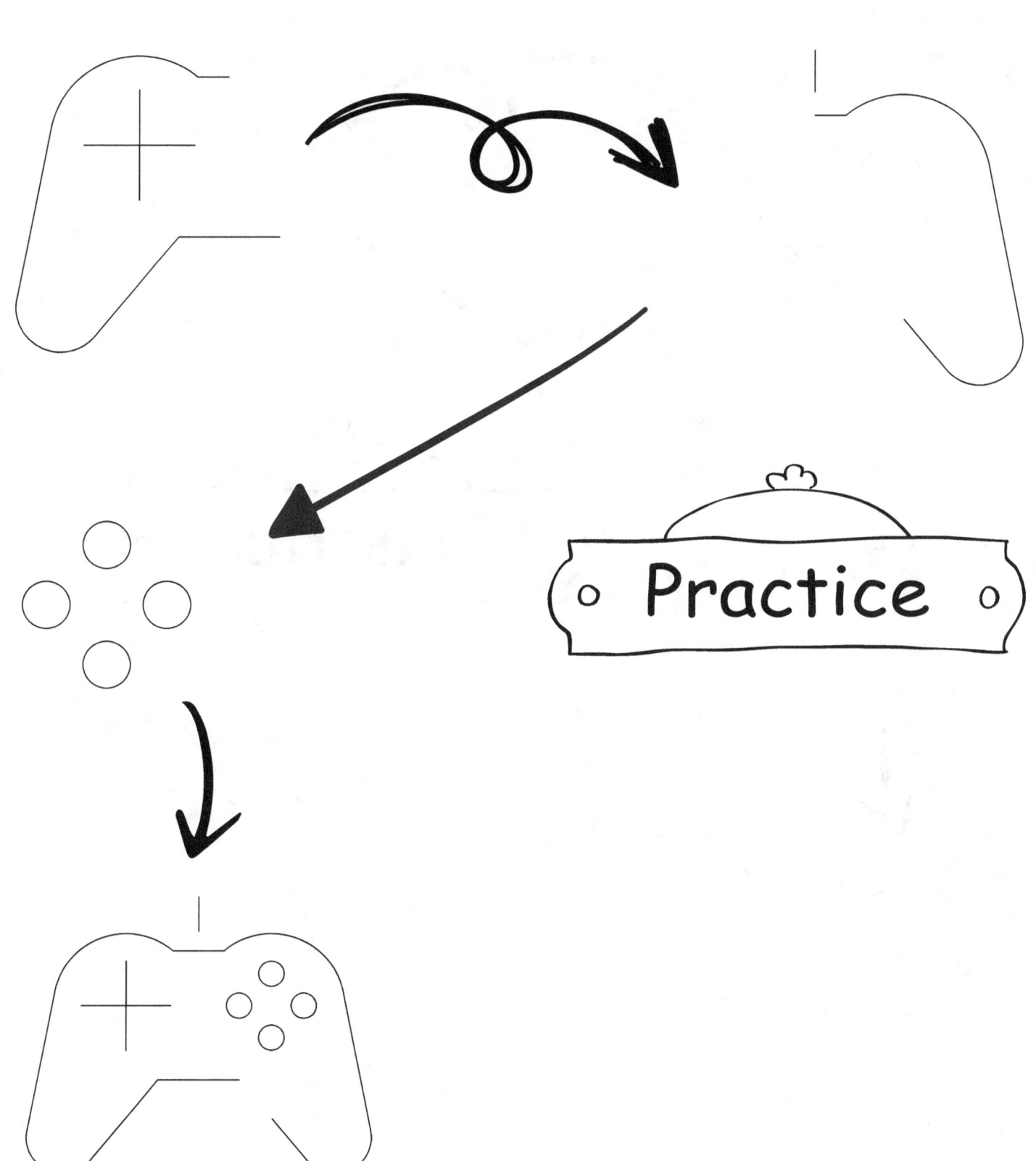

Practice

Bear

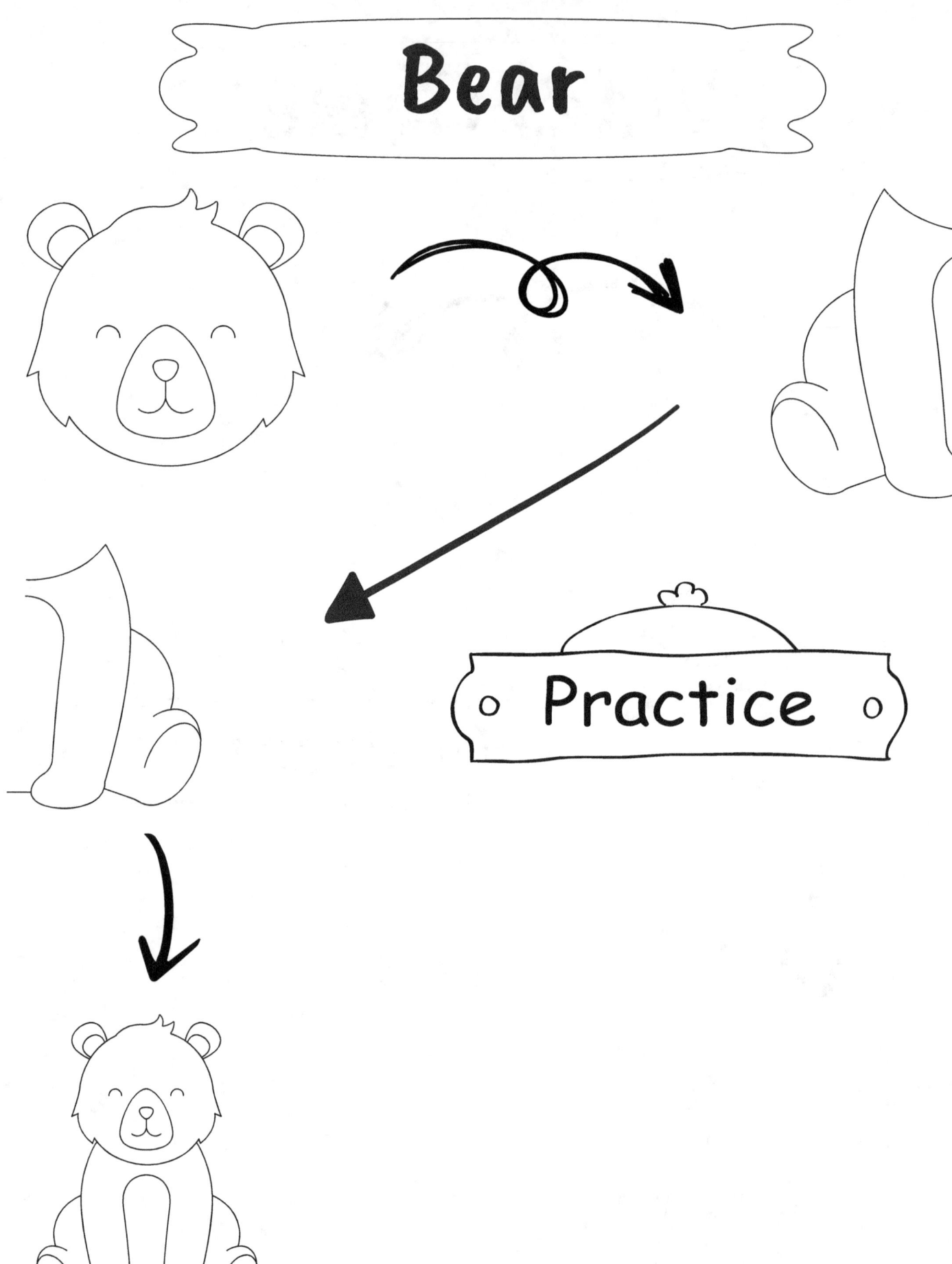

Practice

Bulp

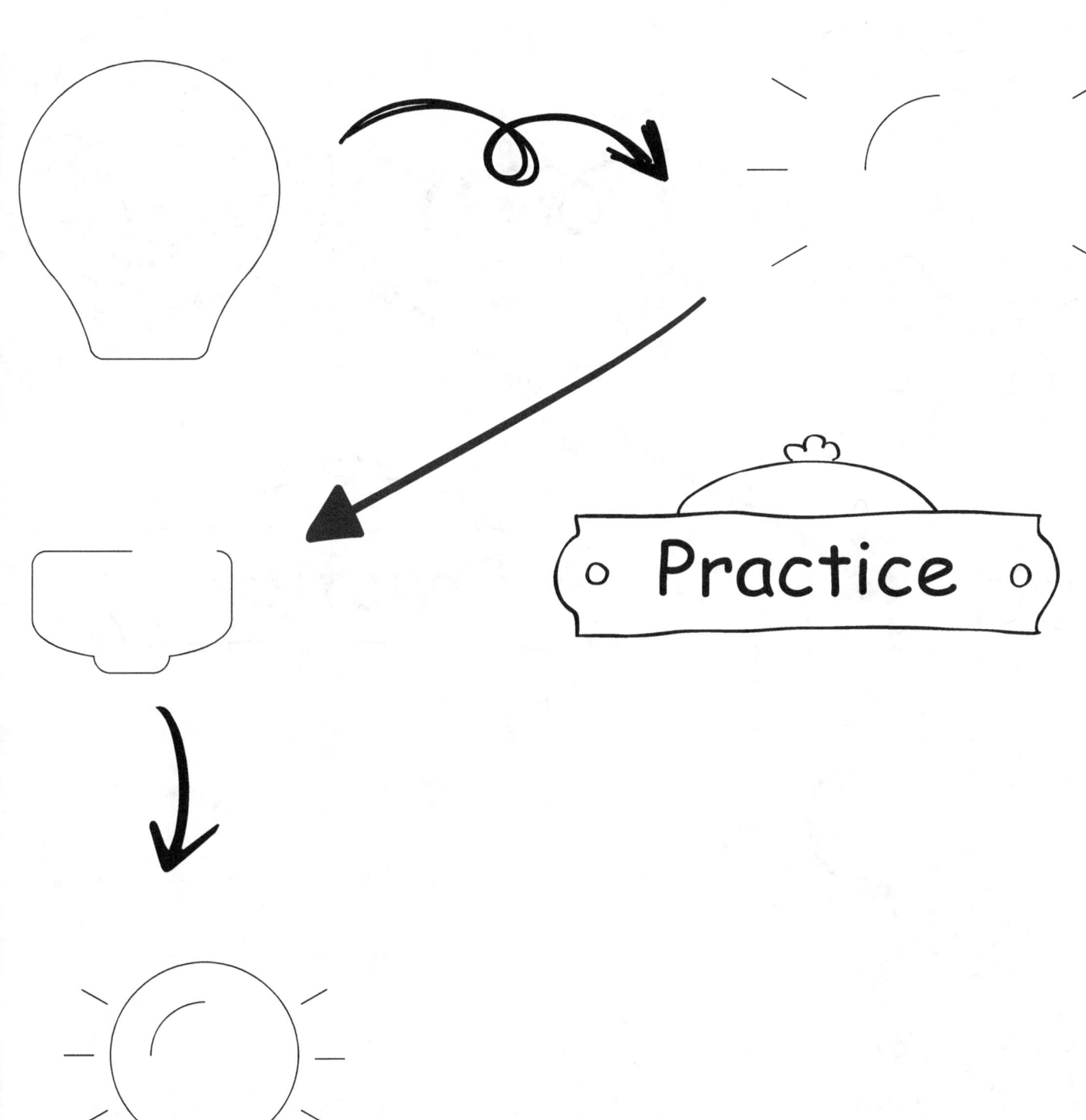

Practice

Tiger

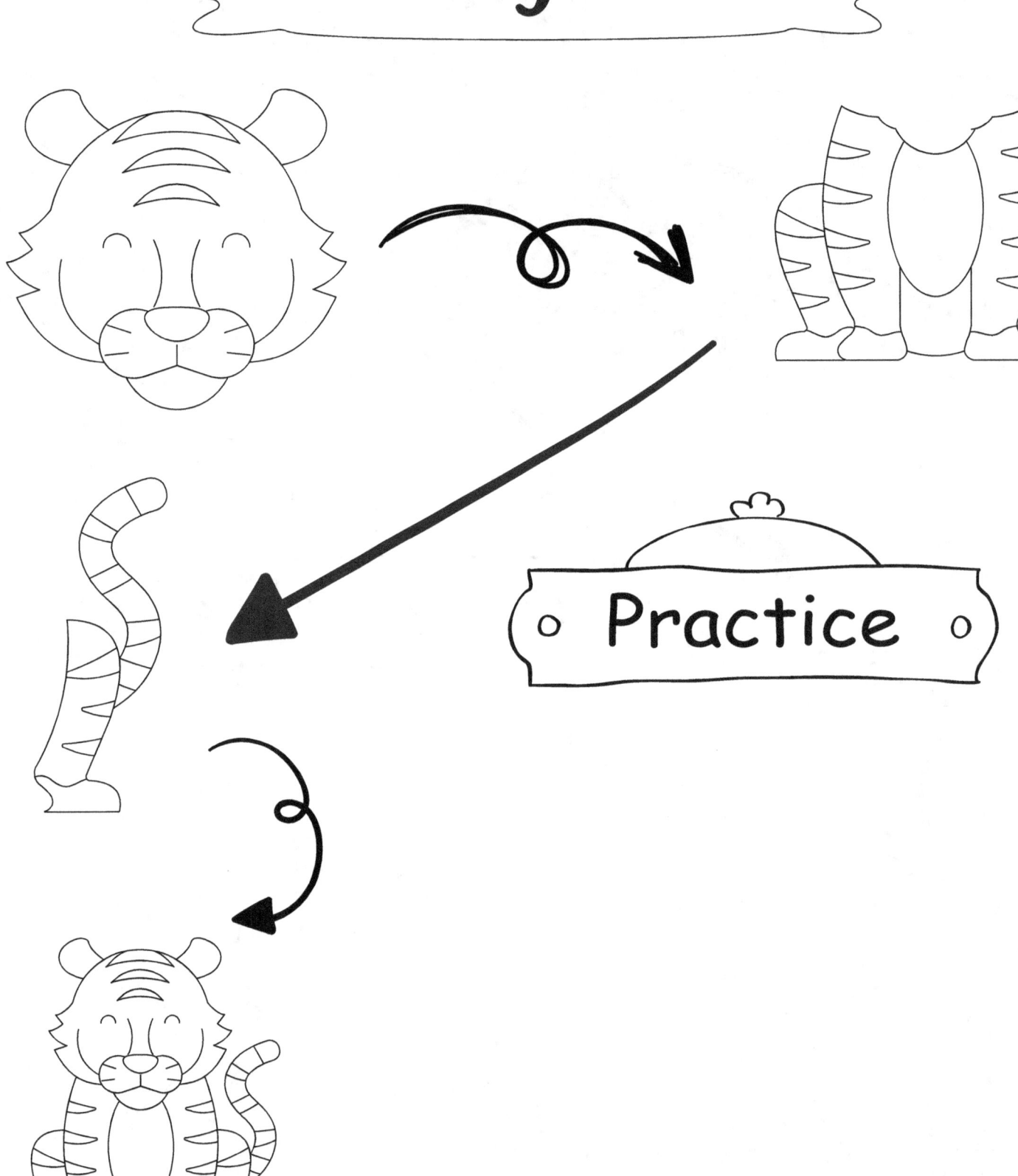

Practice

Tongue

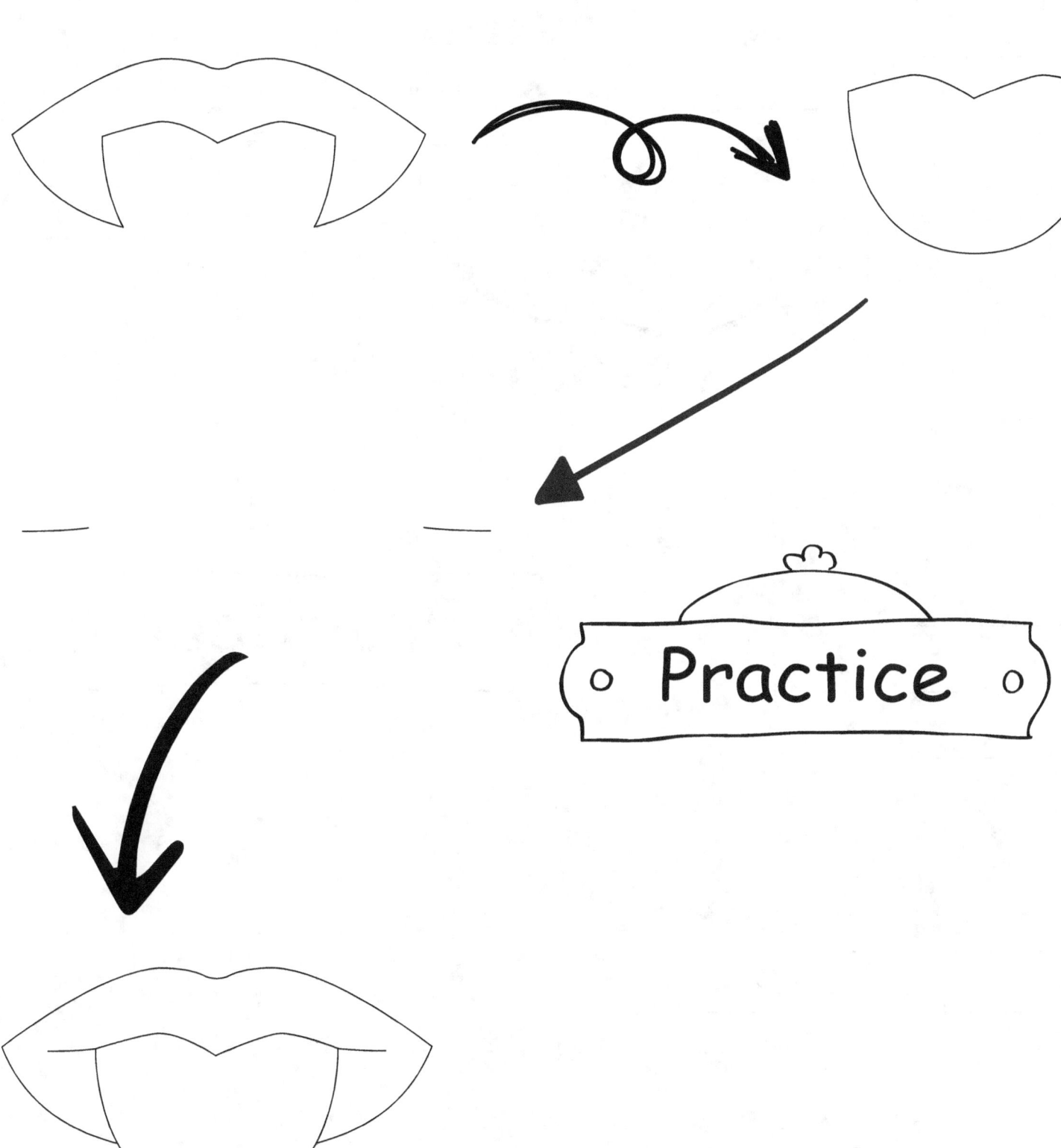

Pistol

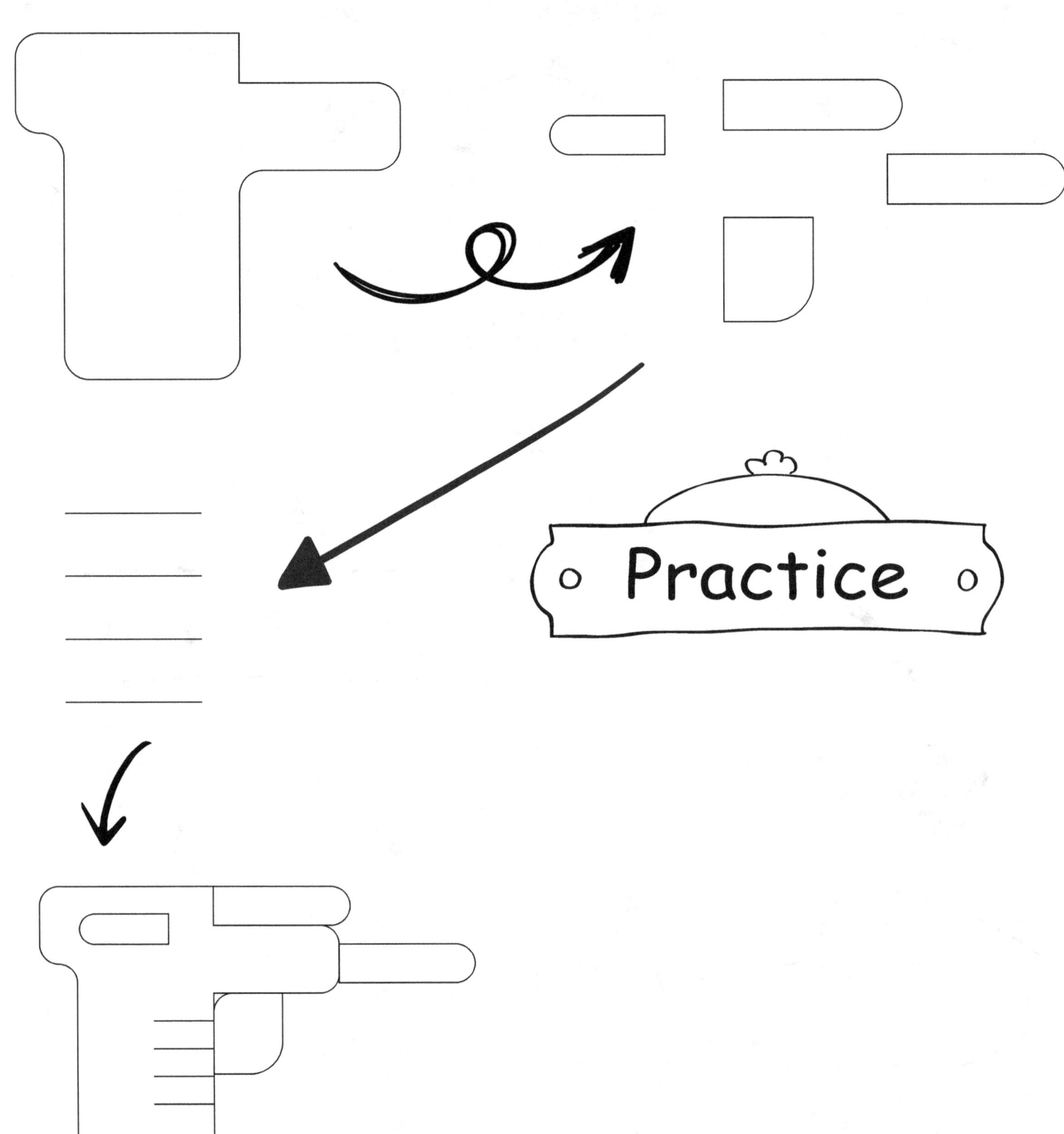

Practice

Lion

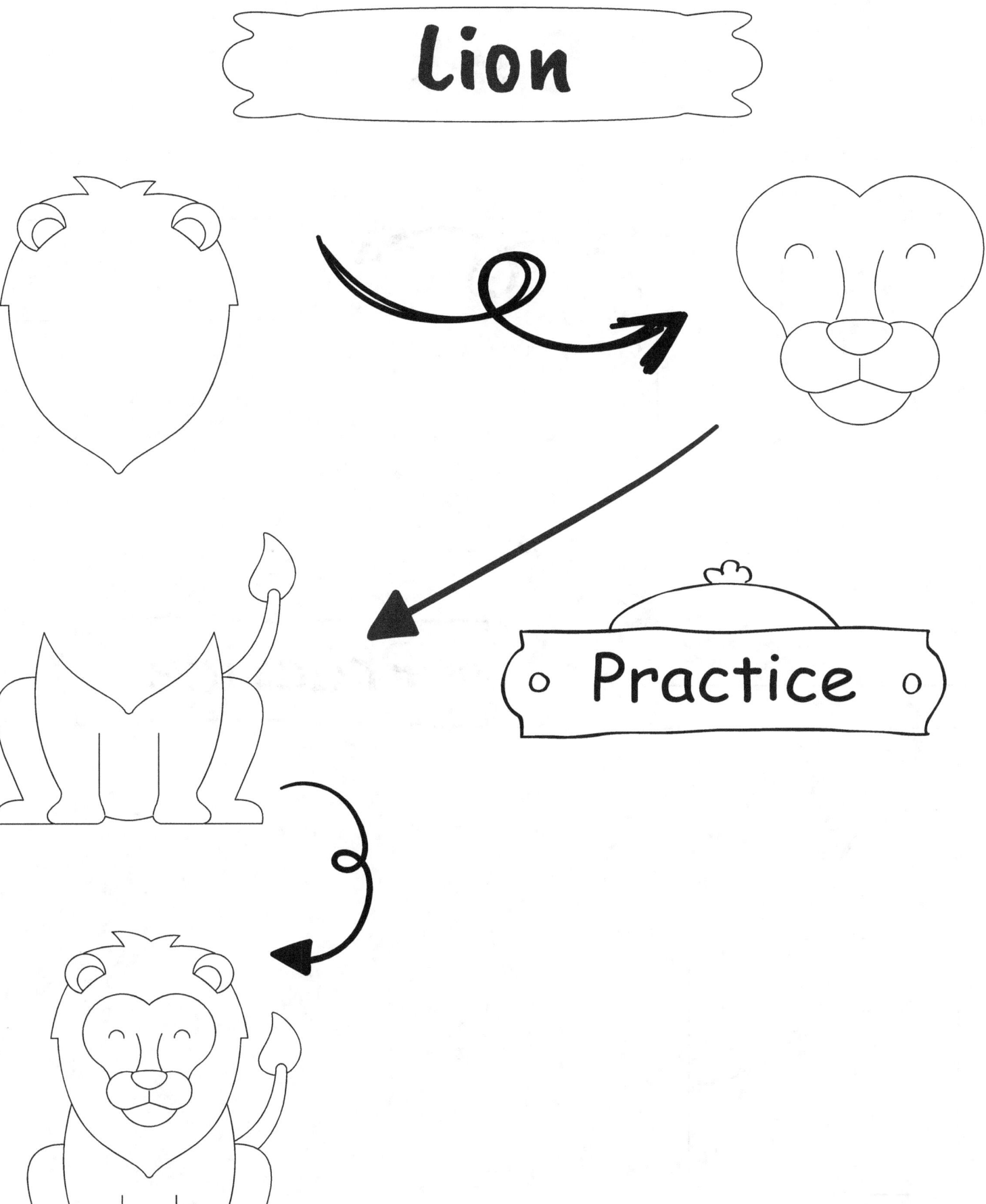

Practice

Book

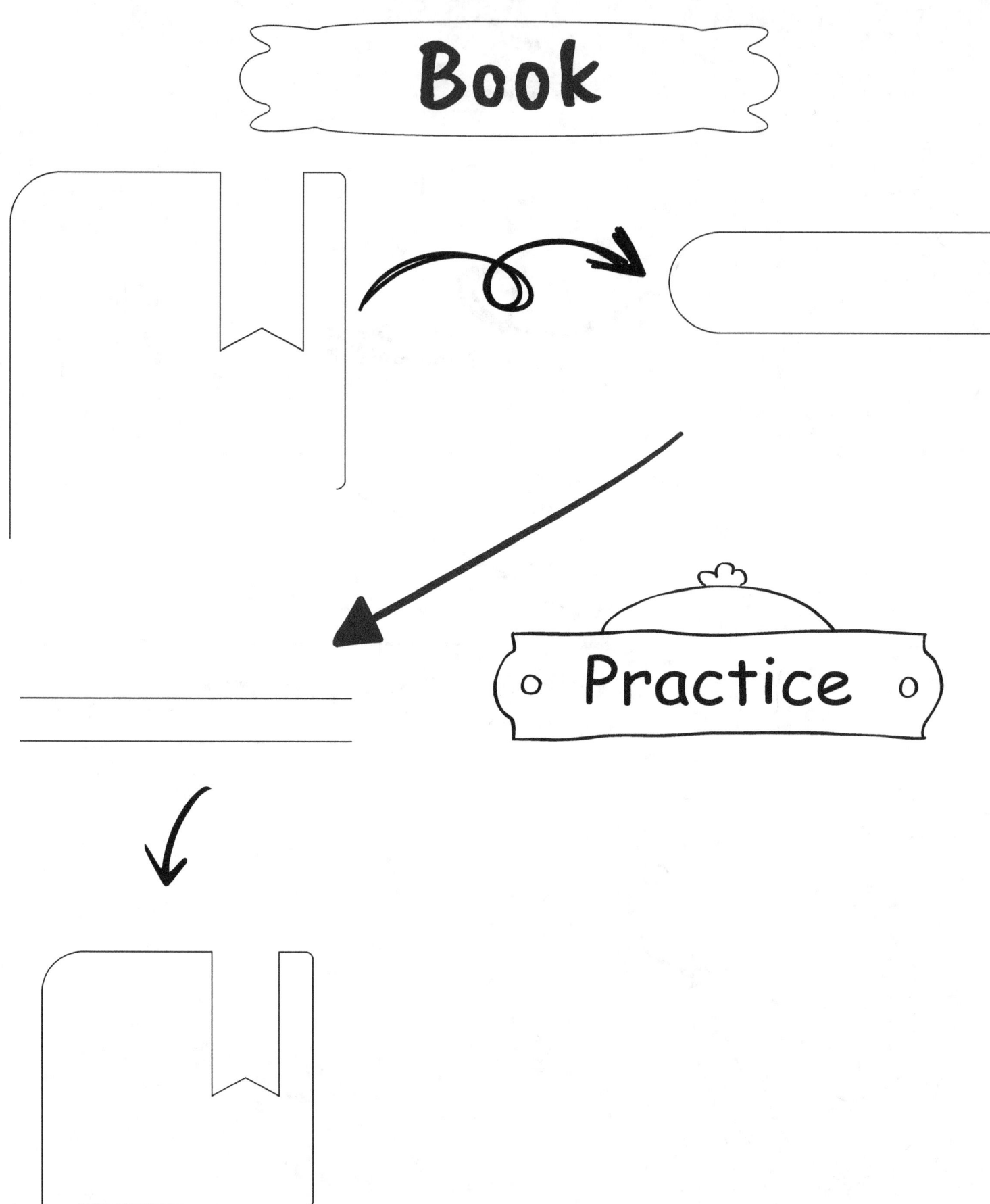

Practice

Monkey

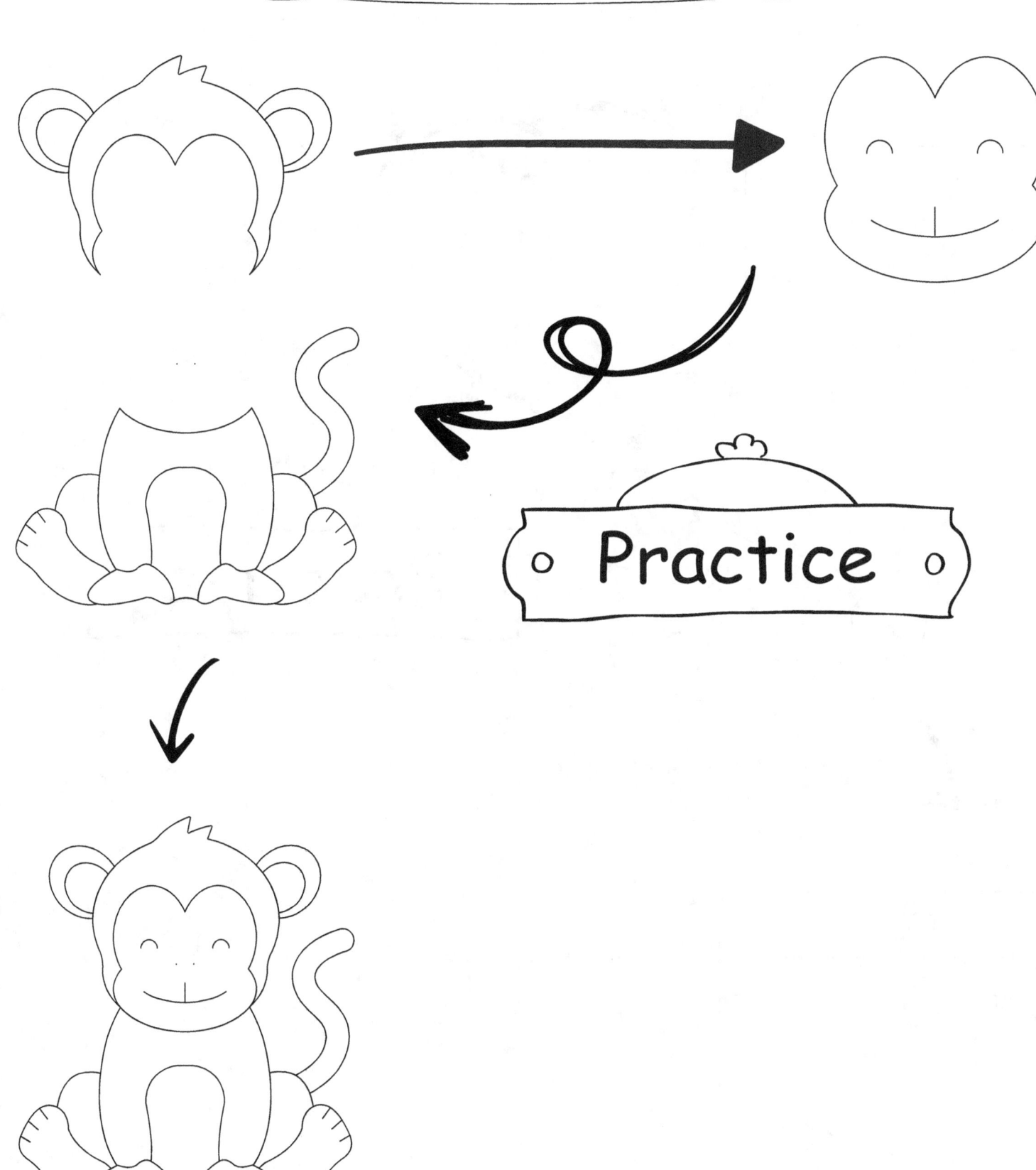

Practice

Speed Meter

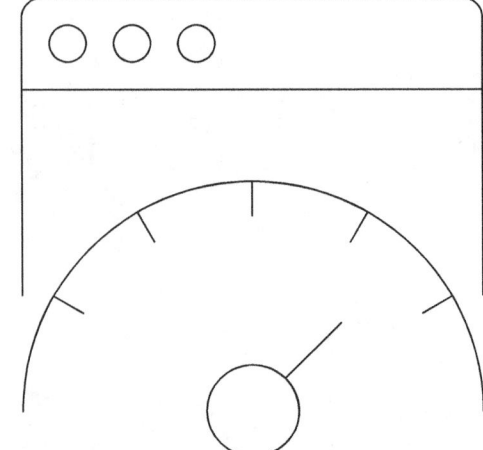

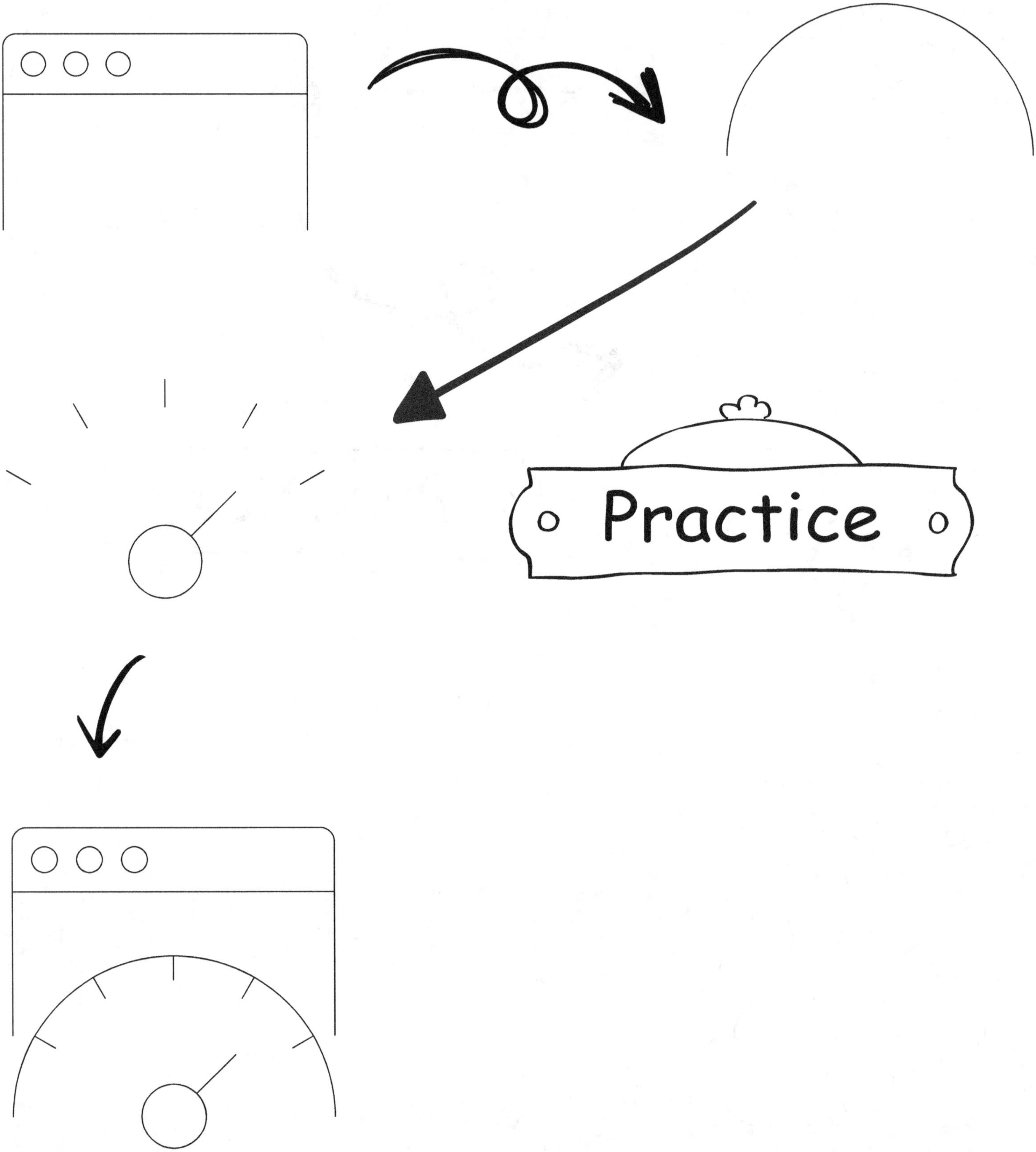

Practice

Giant Panda

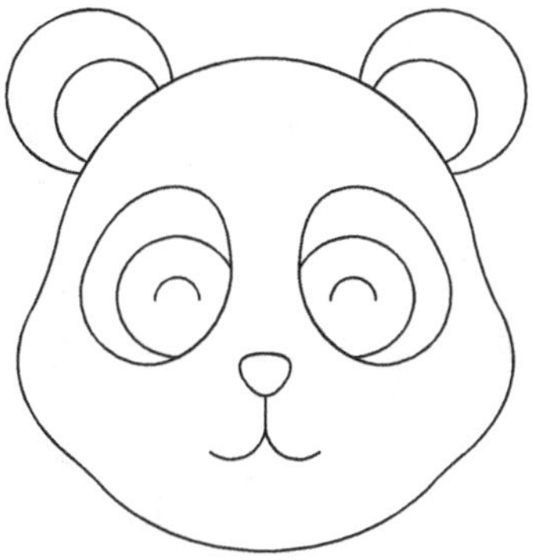

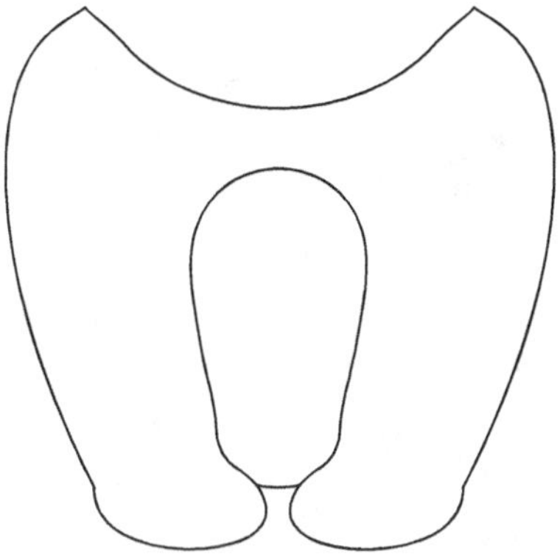

Practice

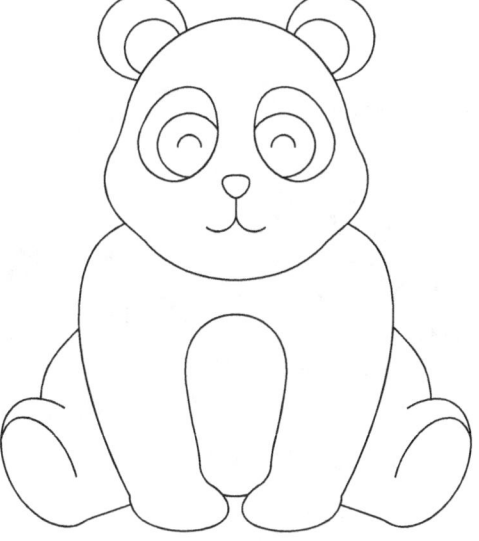

Money Bag

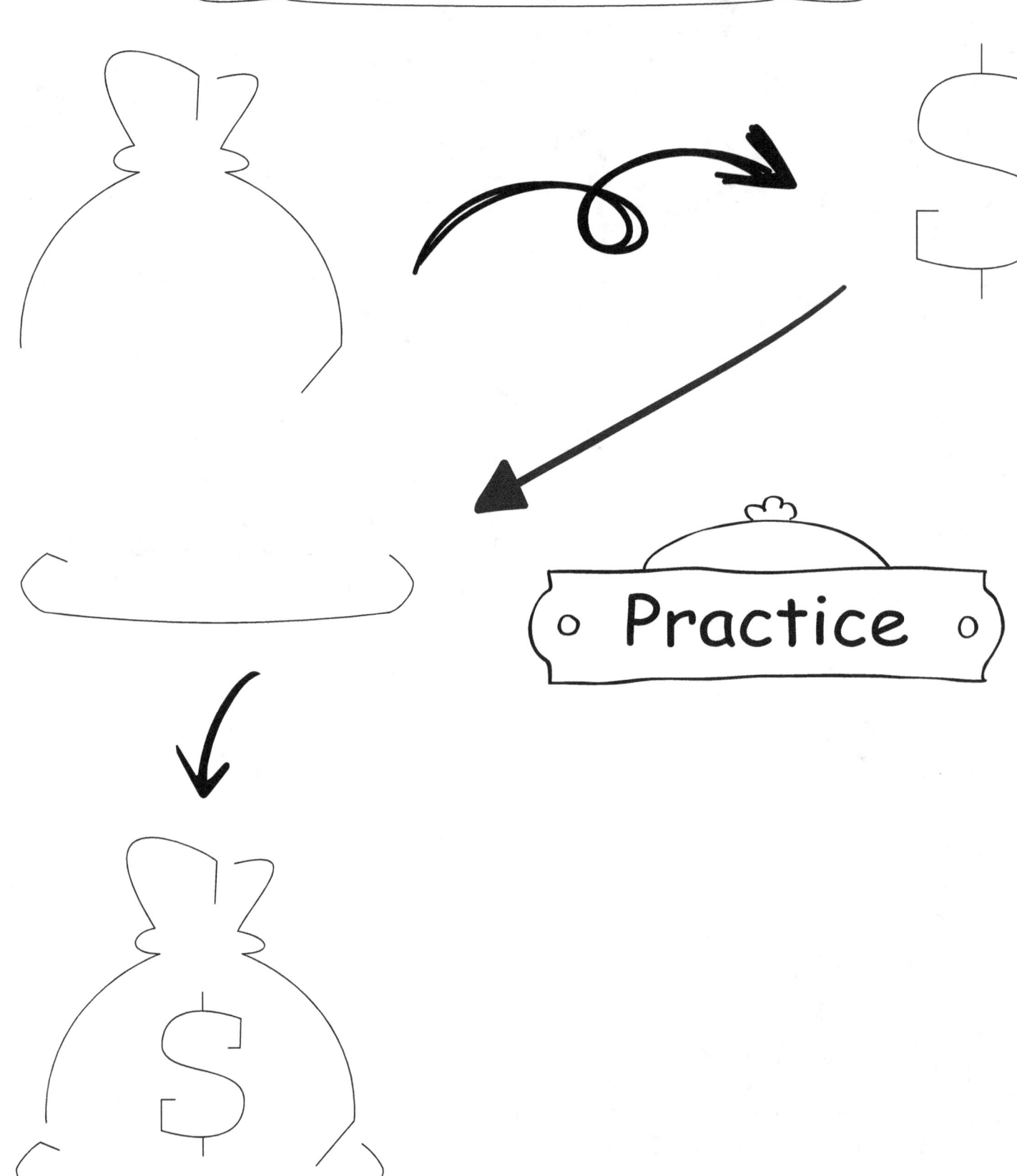

Elephant

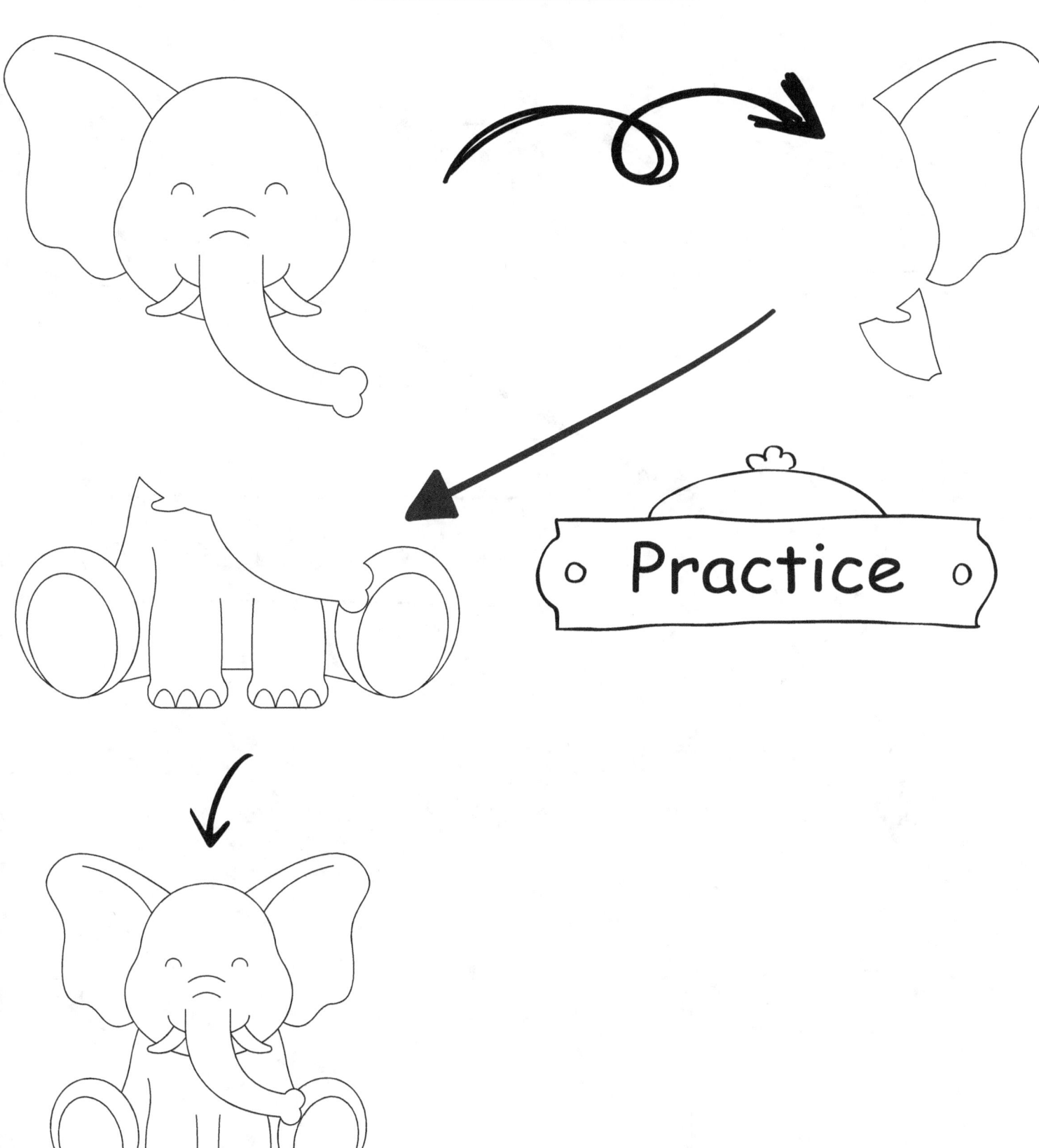

Practice

Drum

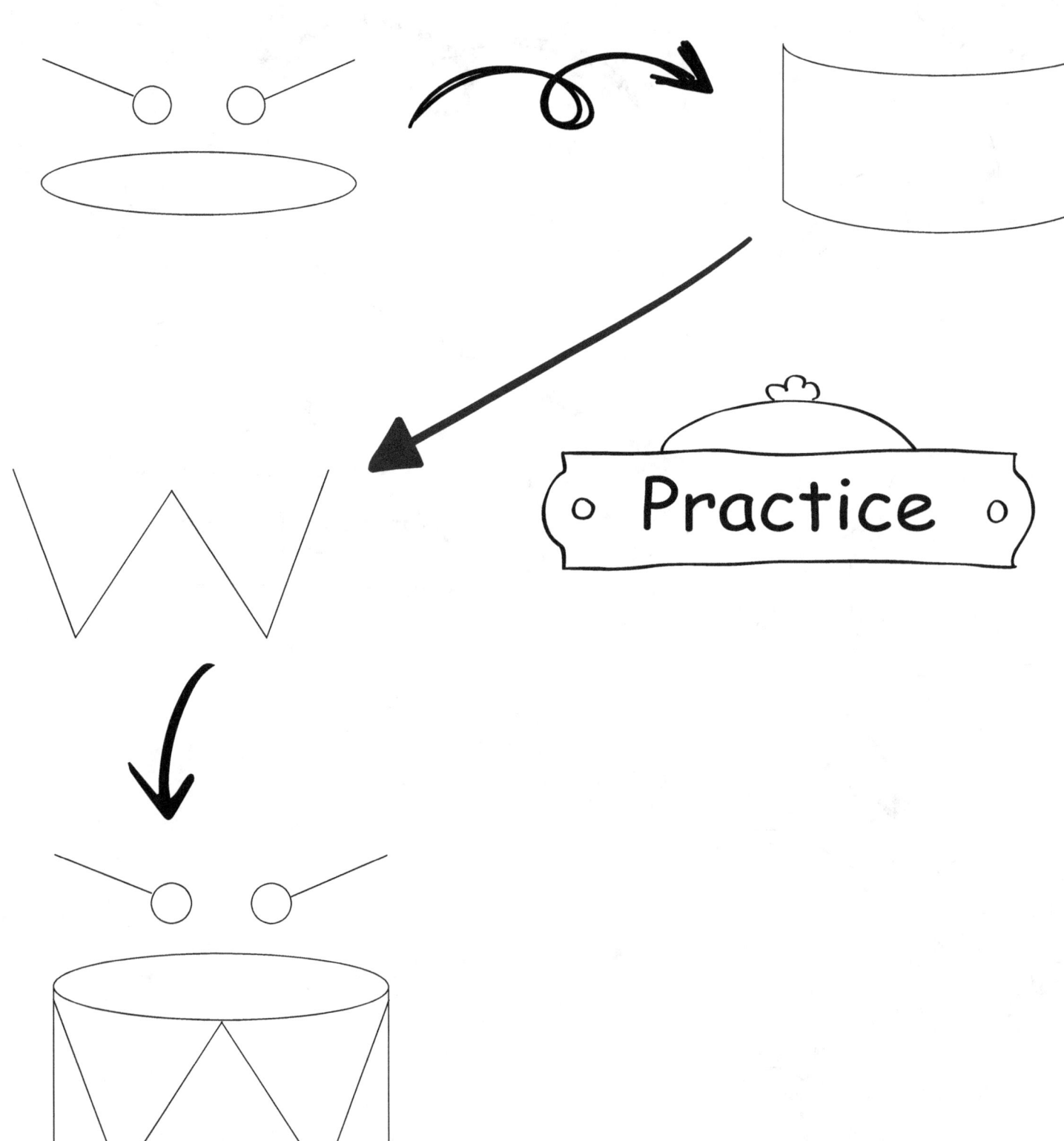

Practice

Apple

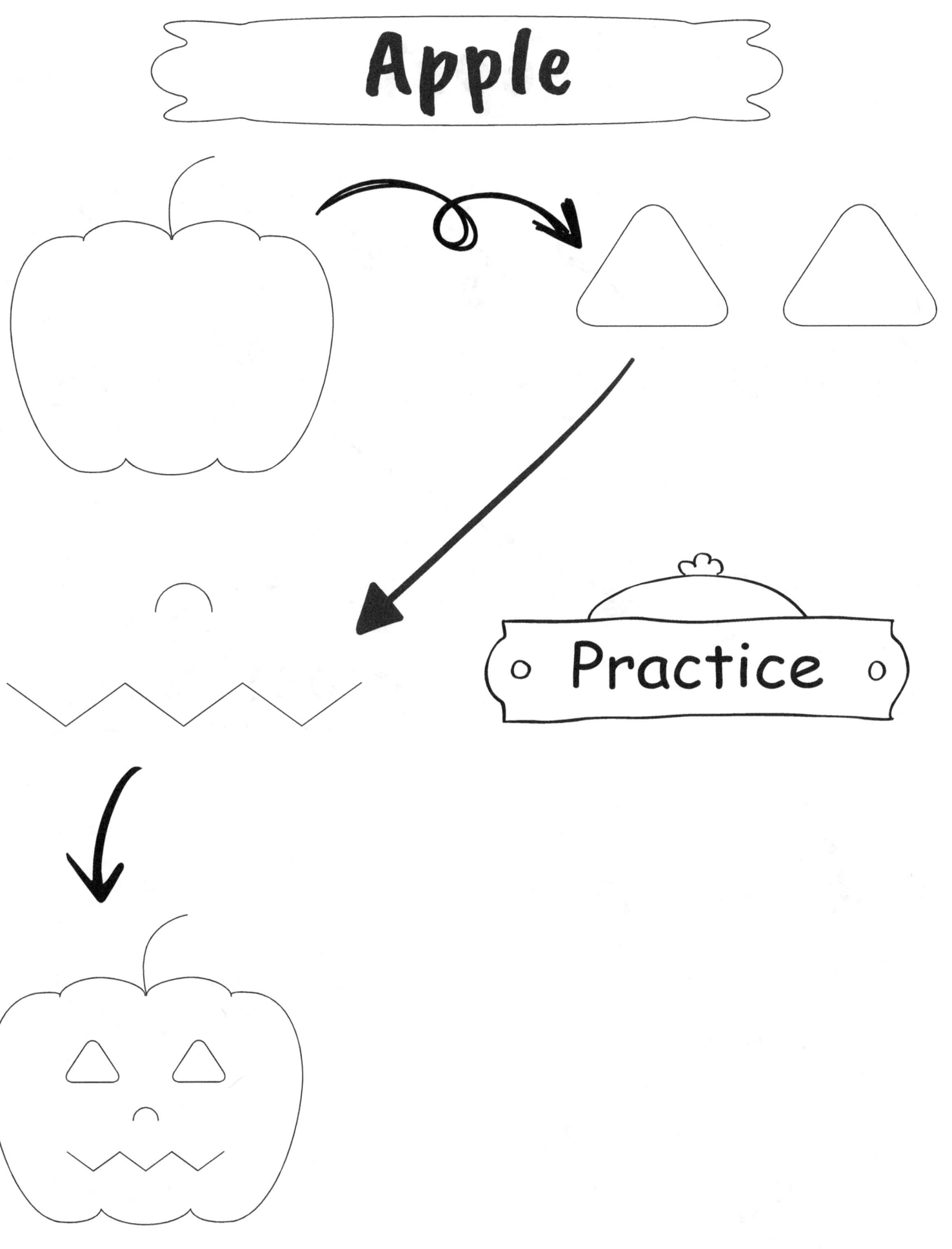

Practice

Leopard

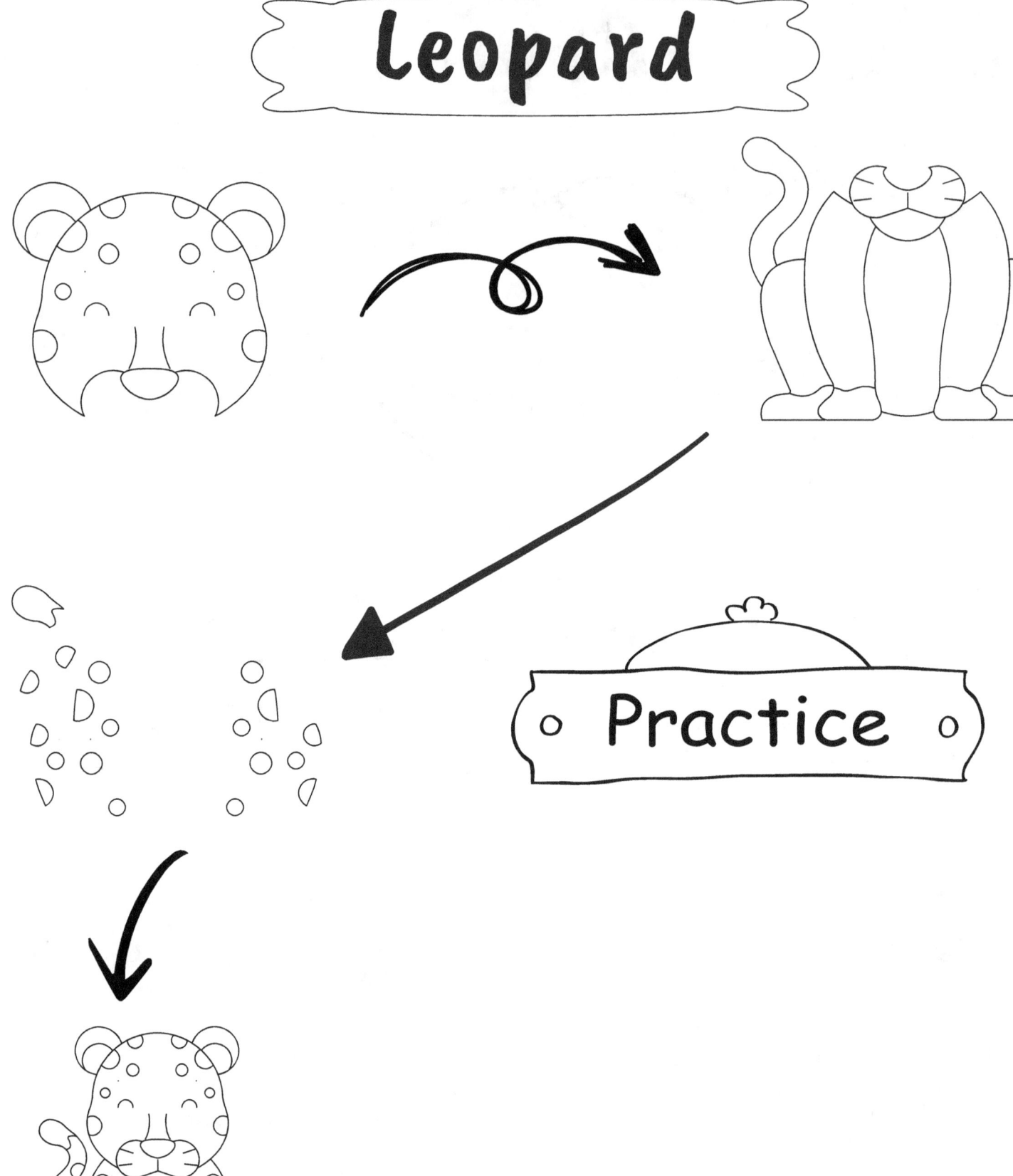

Practice

Location

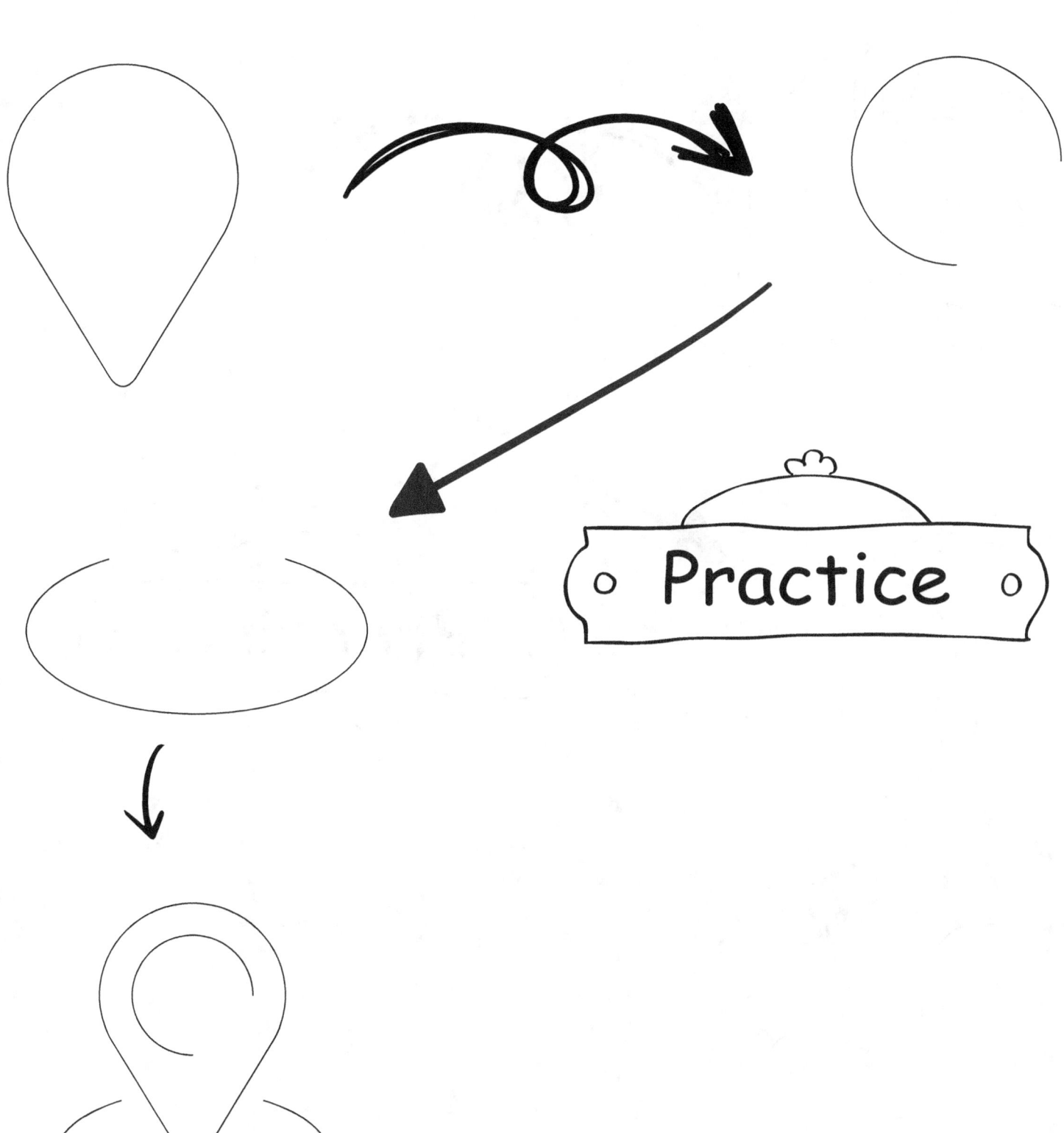

Horse

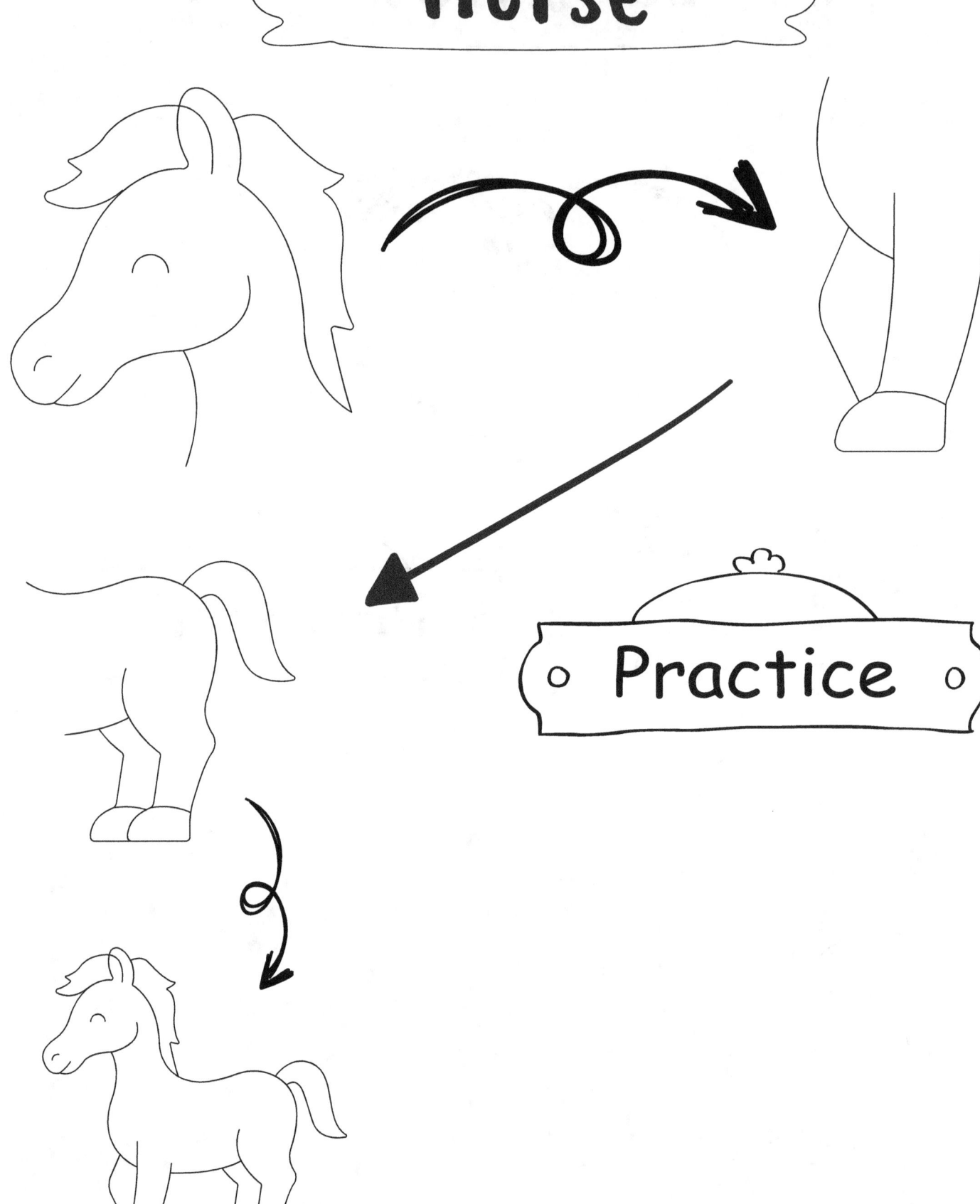

Practice

Wolf

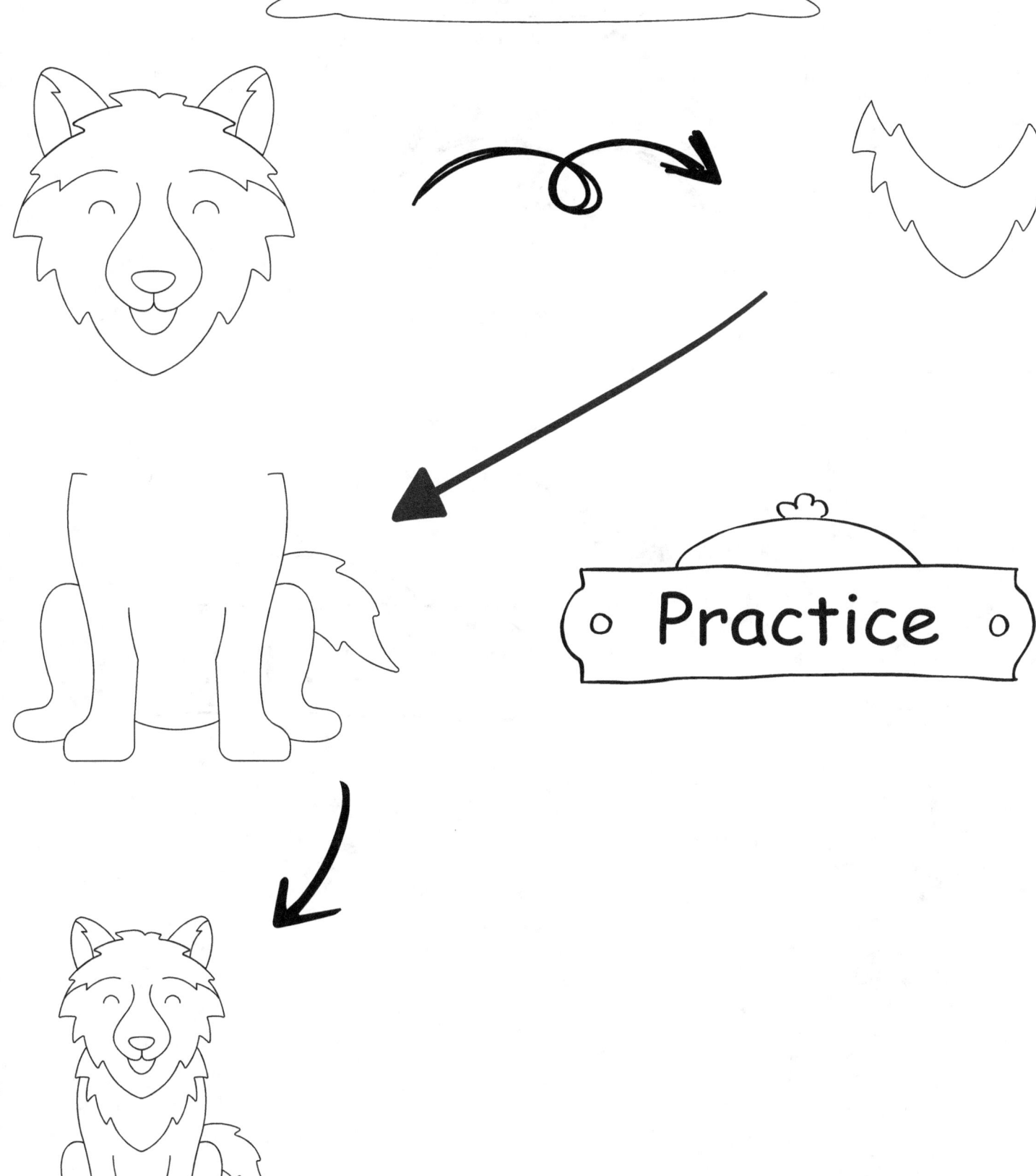

Bell

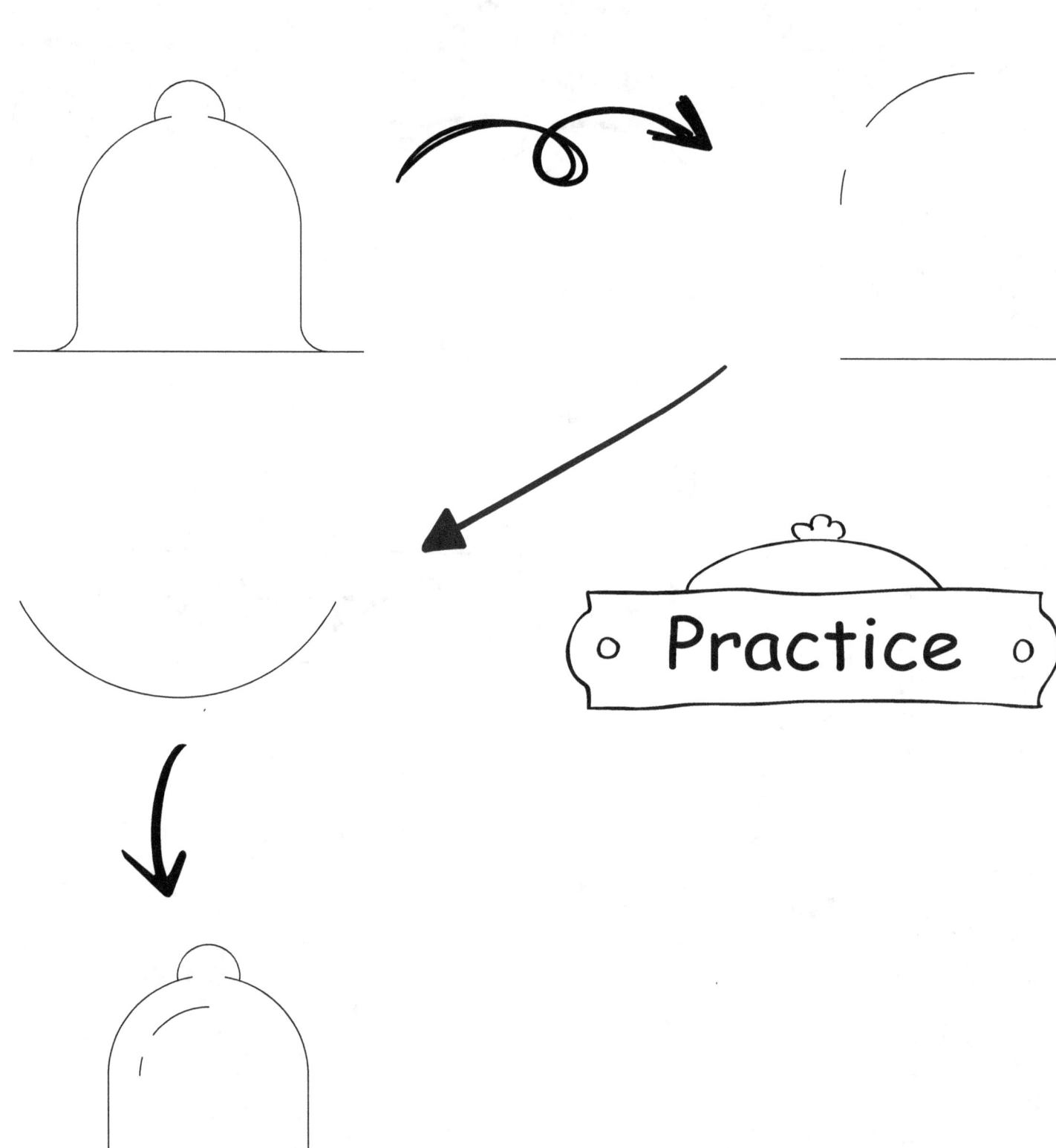

Practice

Duck

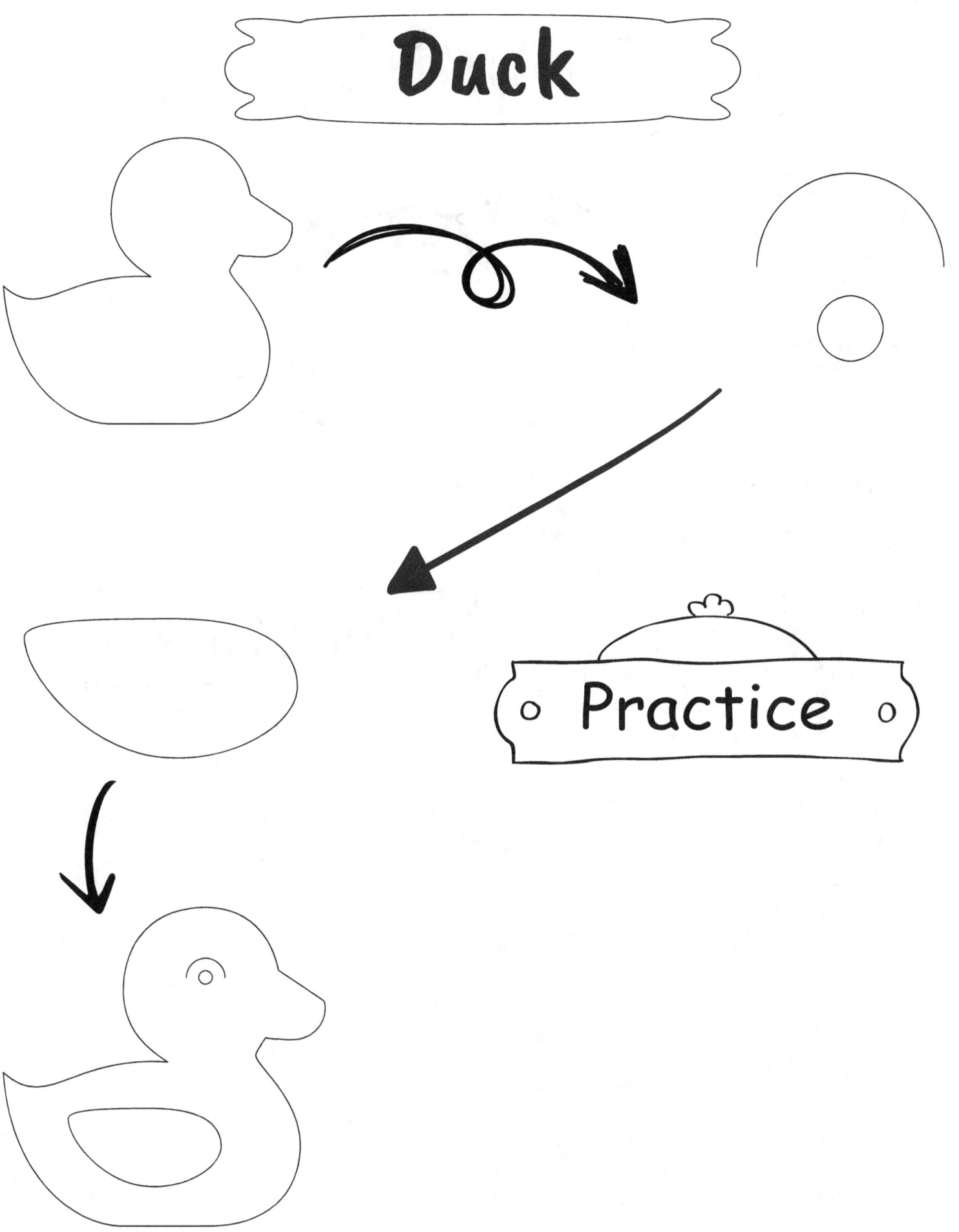

Practice

Jellyfish

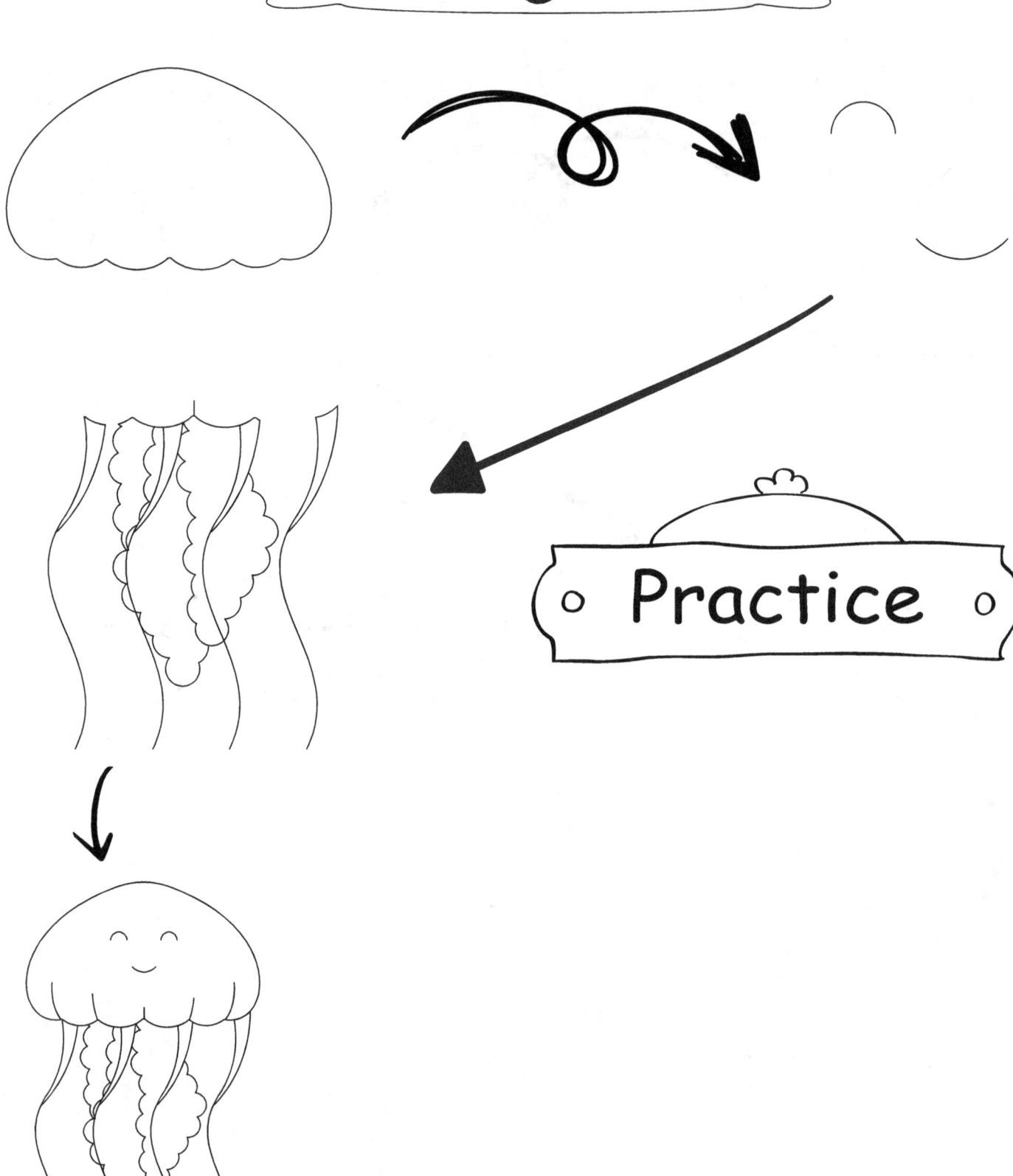

Practice

Microphone

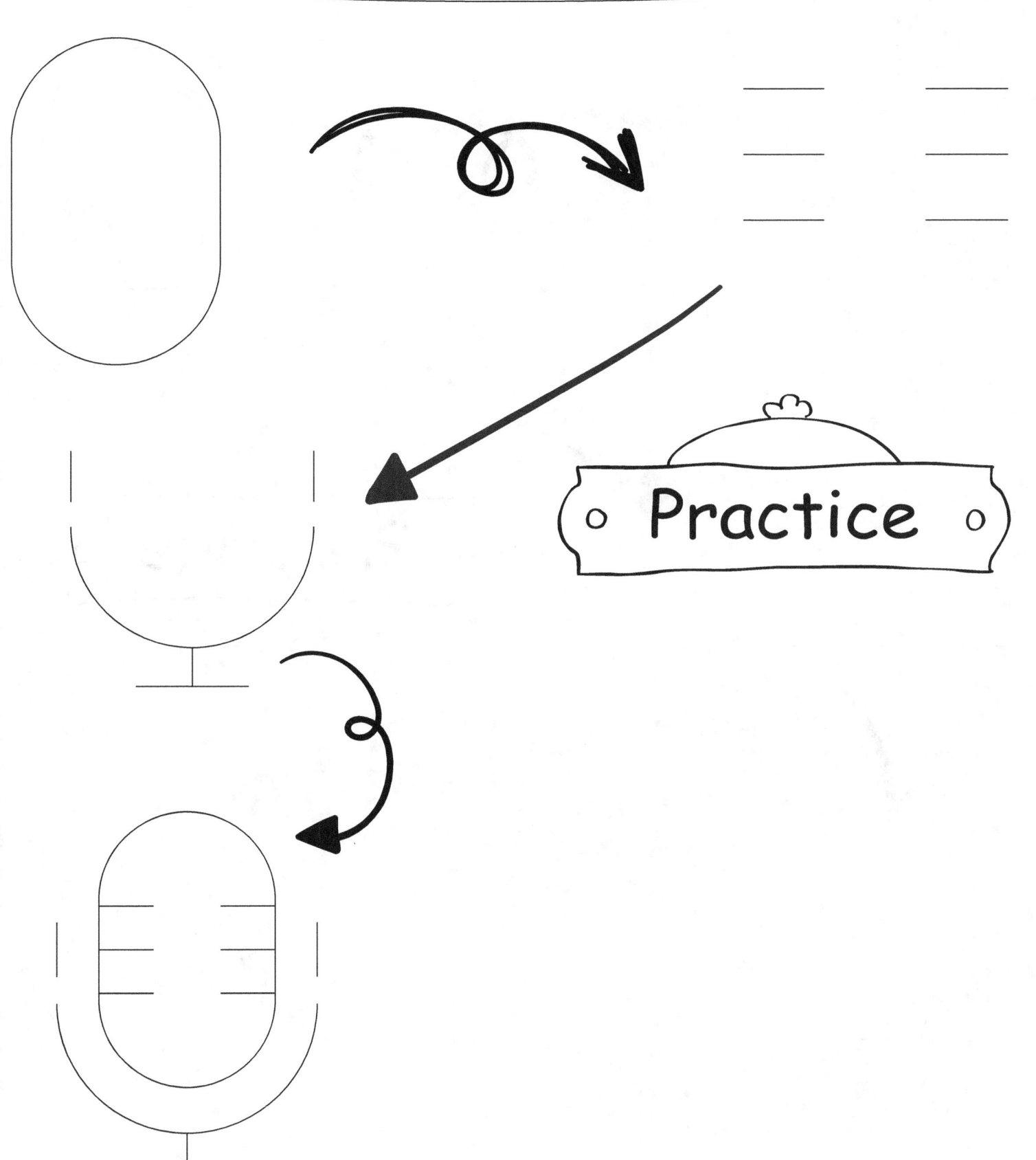

Practice

Gown

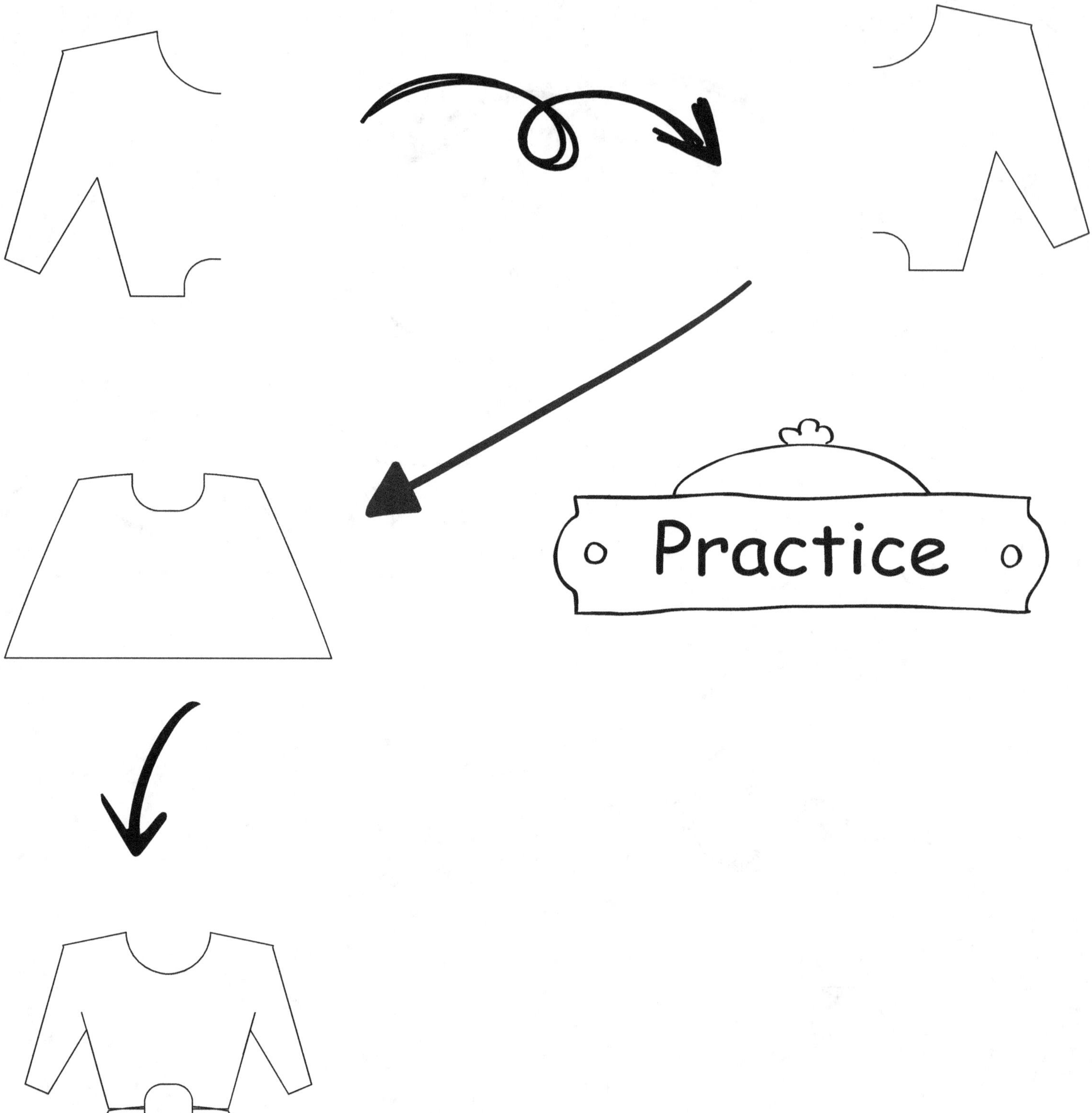

Practice

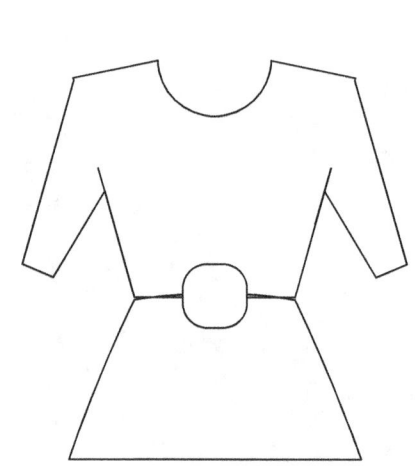

Salmon

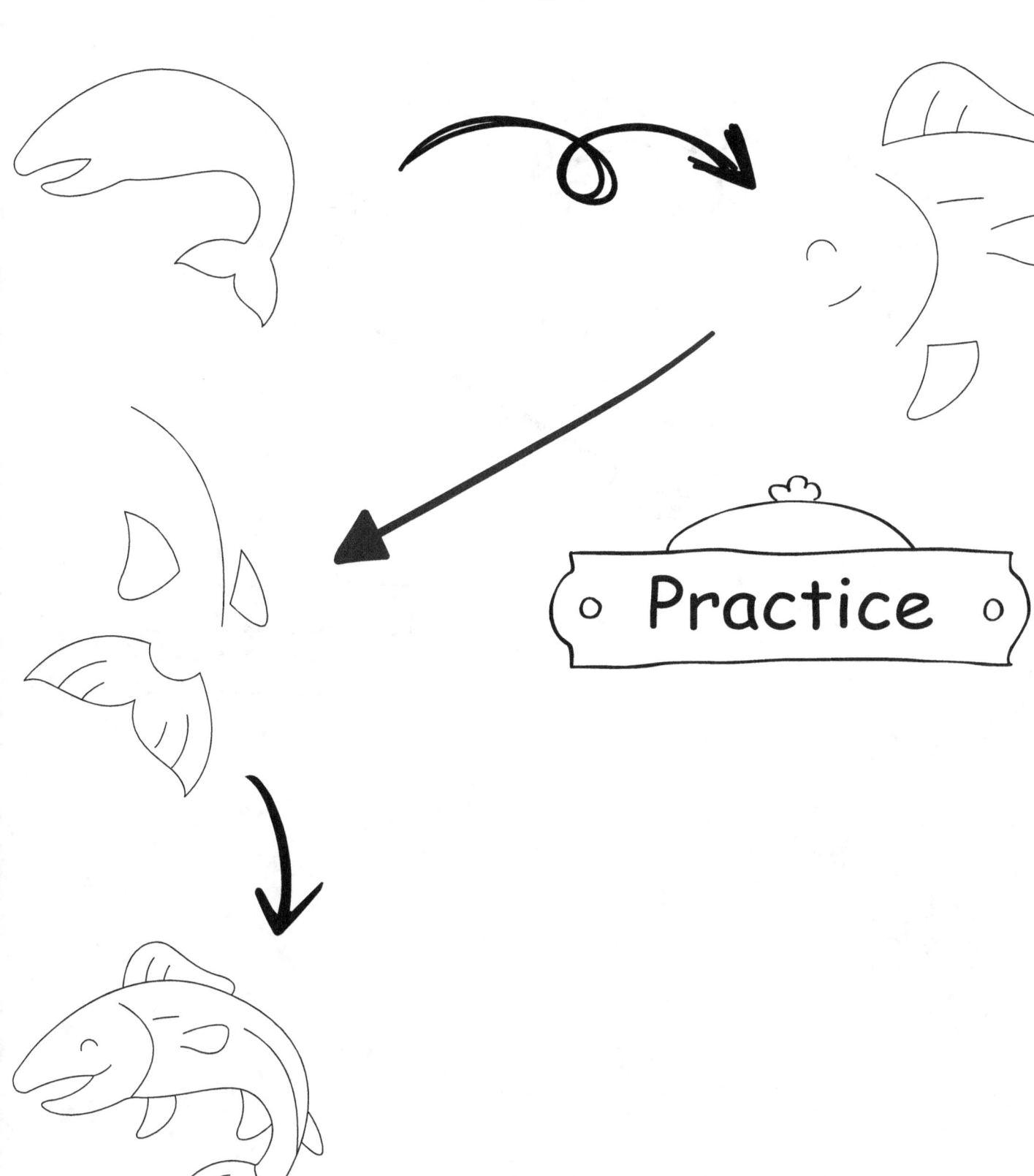

Practice

Penguin

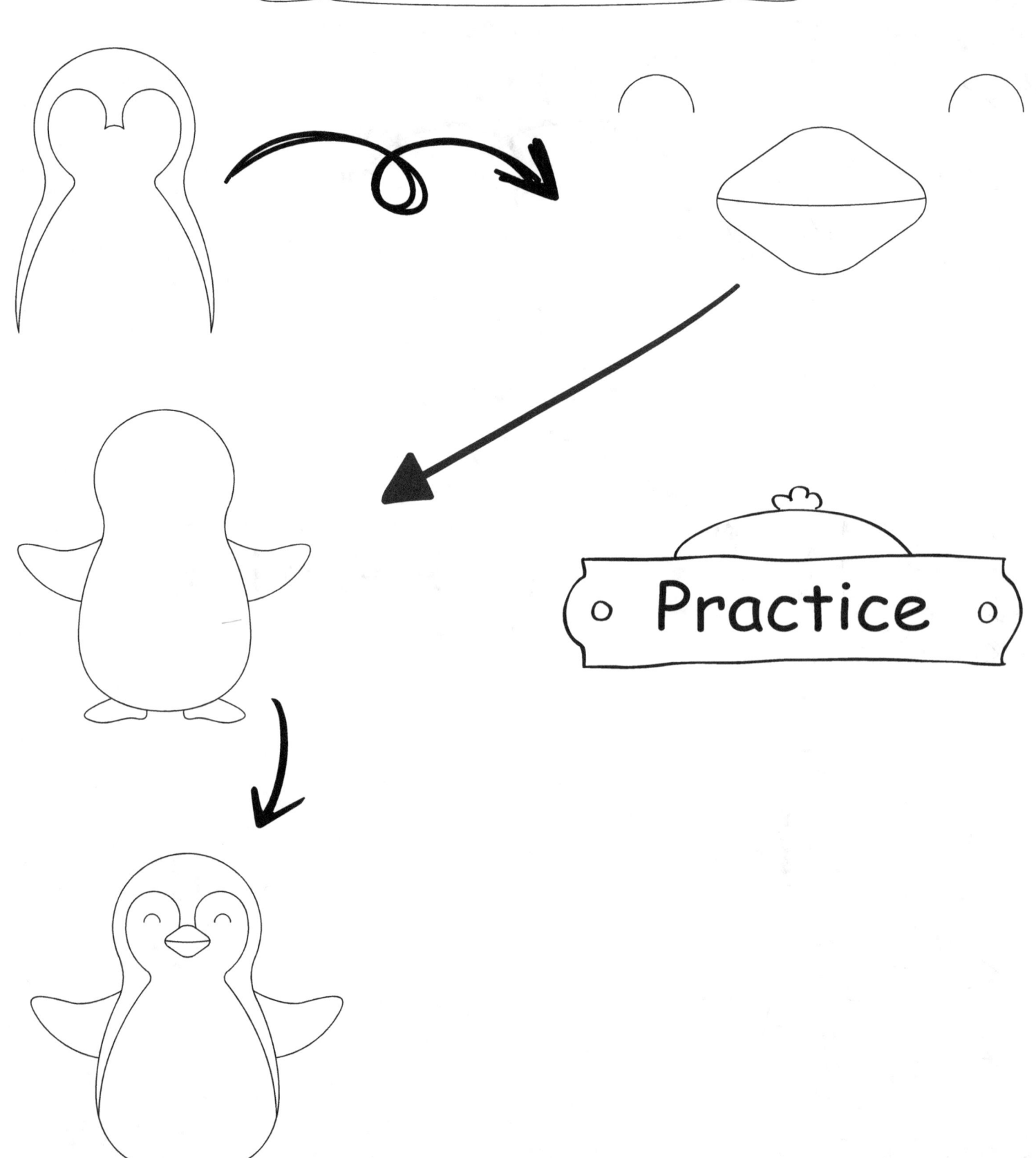

Cow

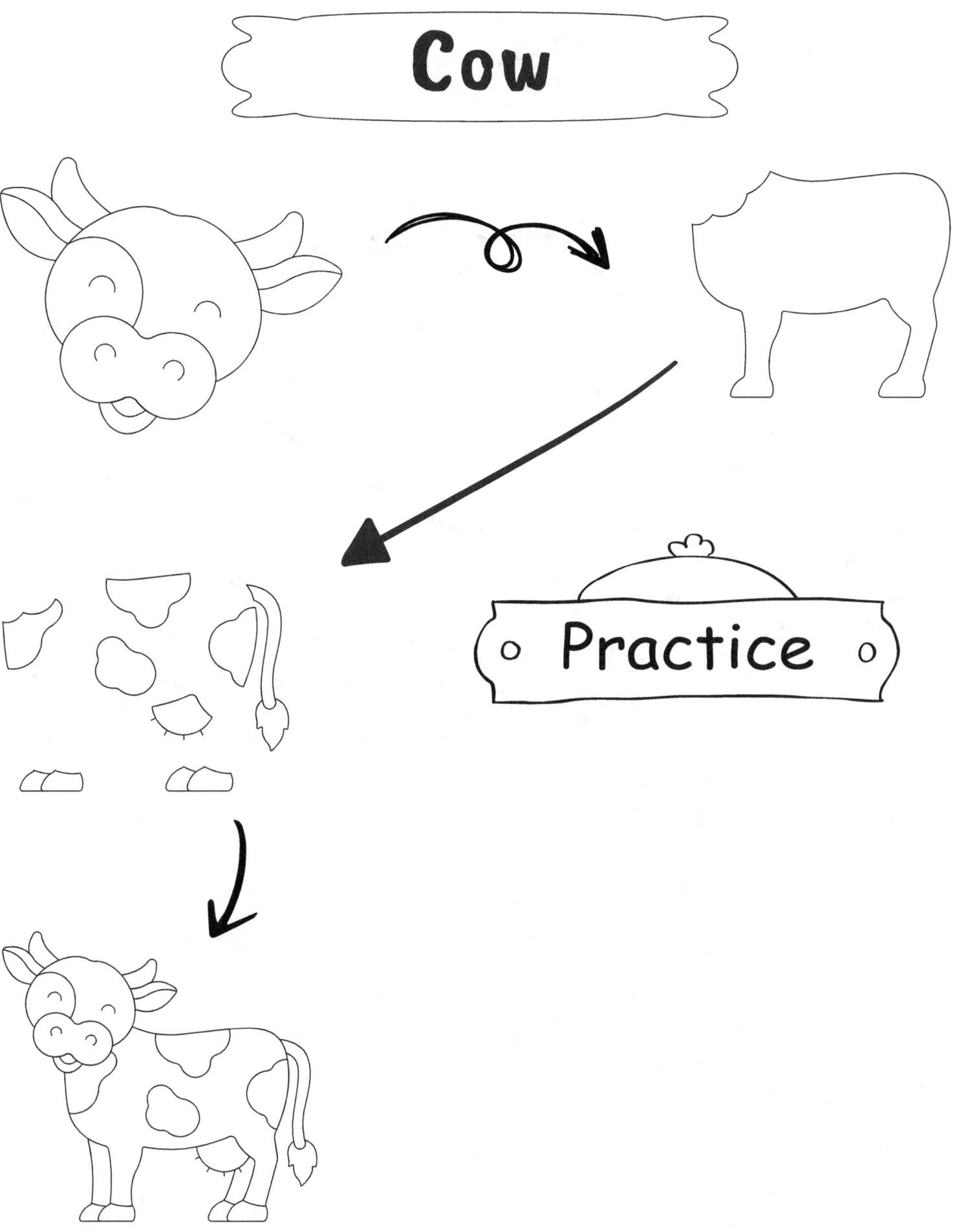

Practice

Crown

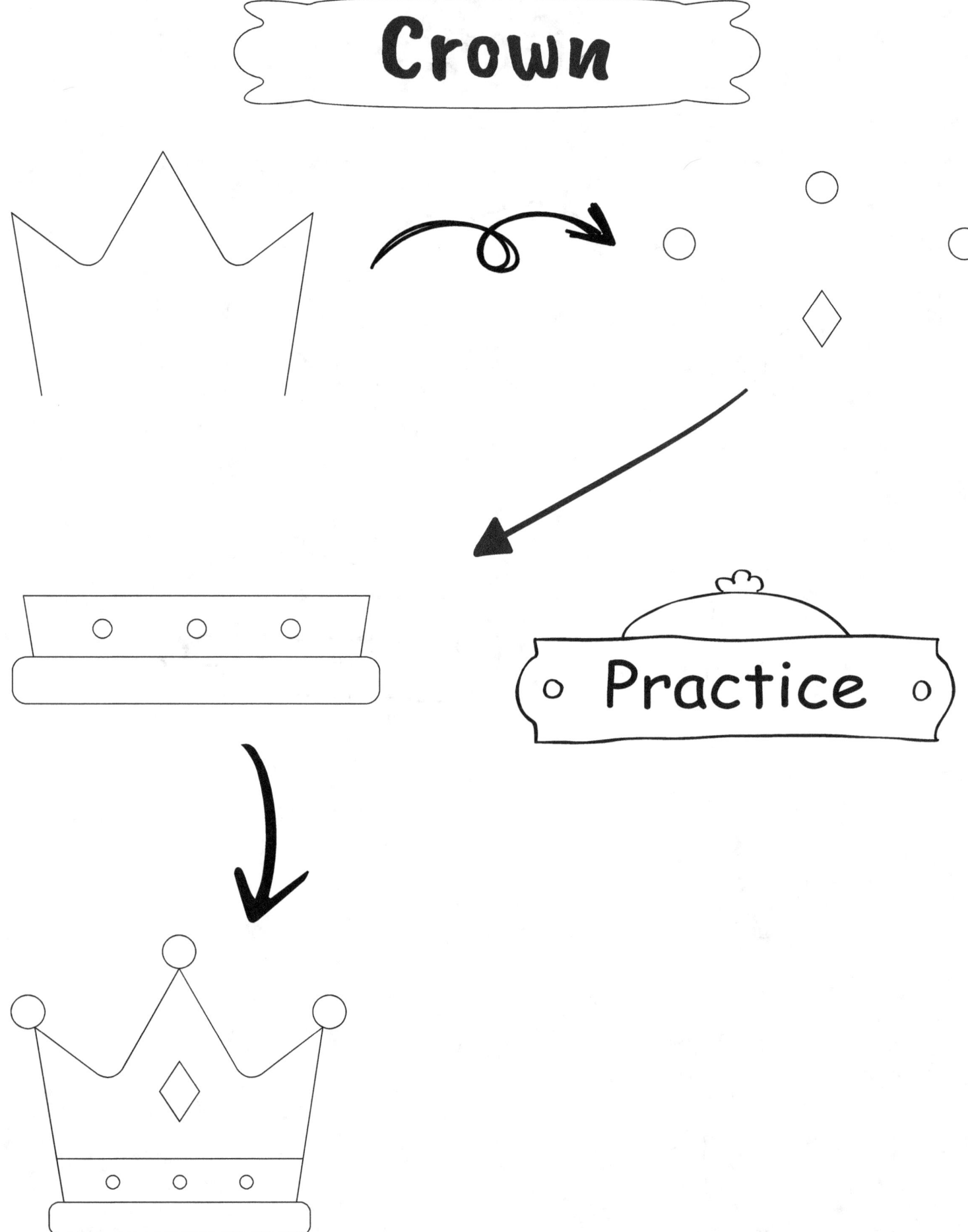

Practice

Diamond

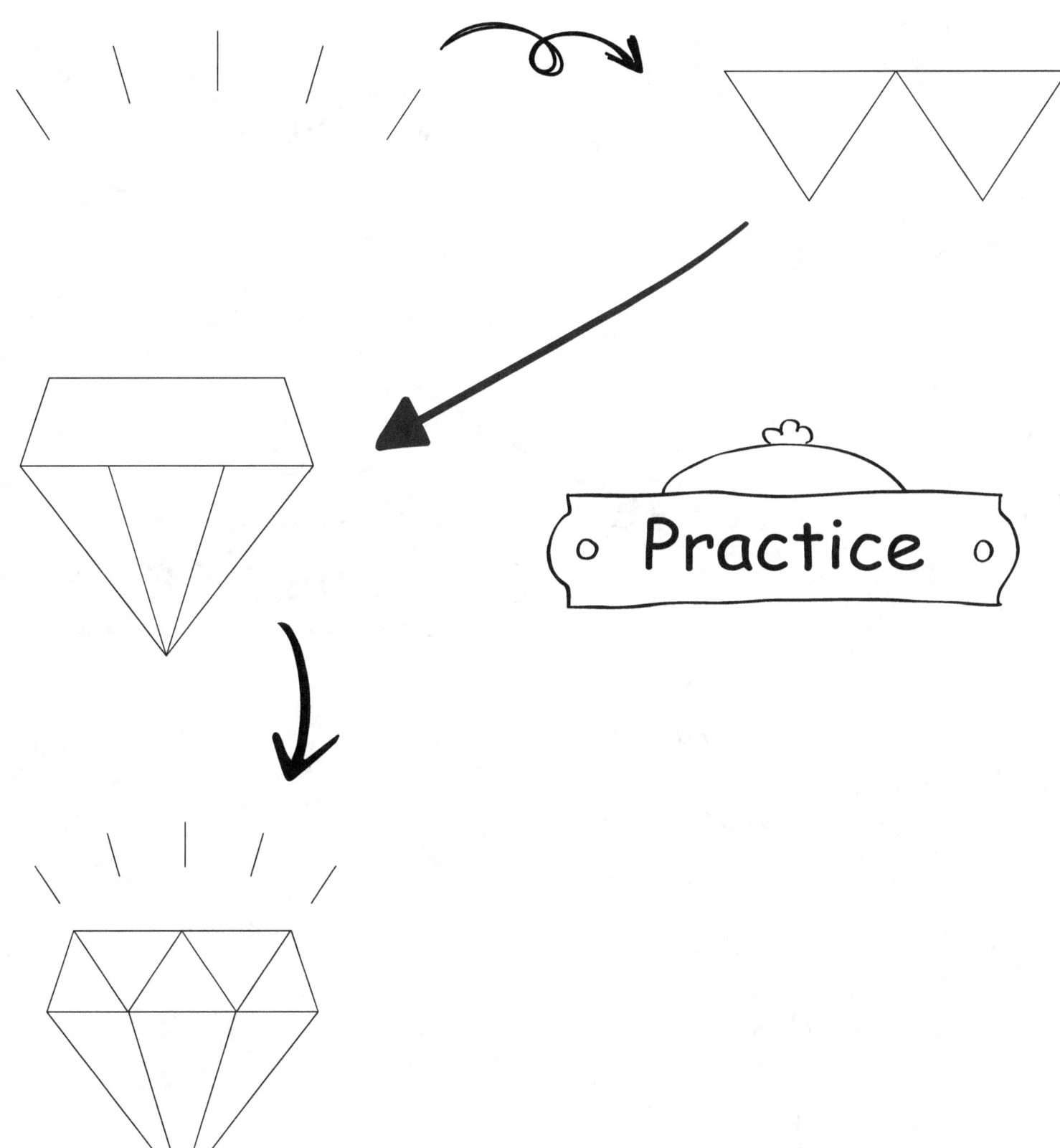

Practice

Giraffe

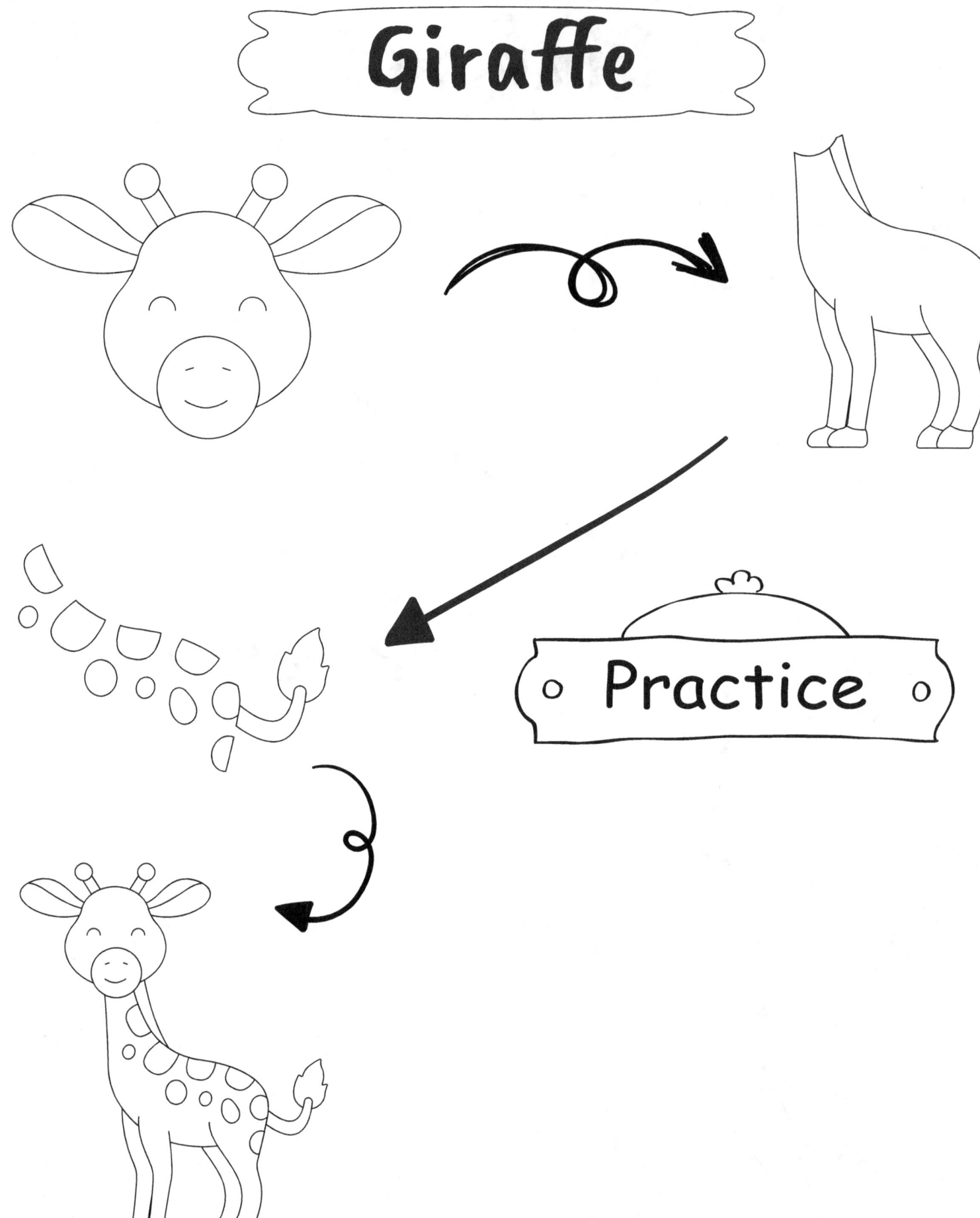

Practice

Rhinoceros

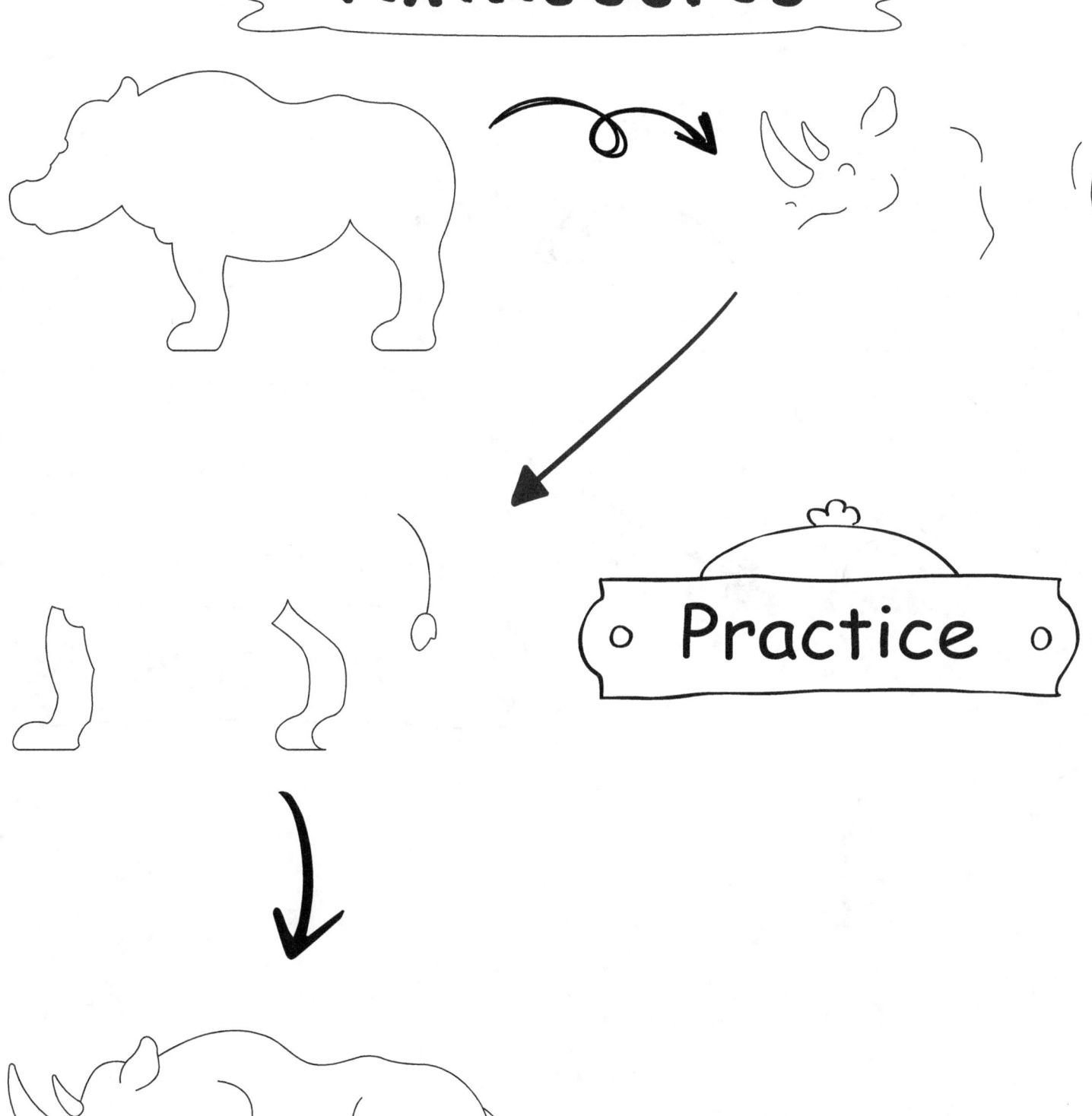

Practice

Cute Sun

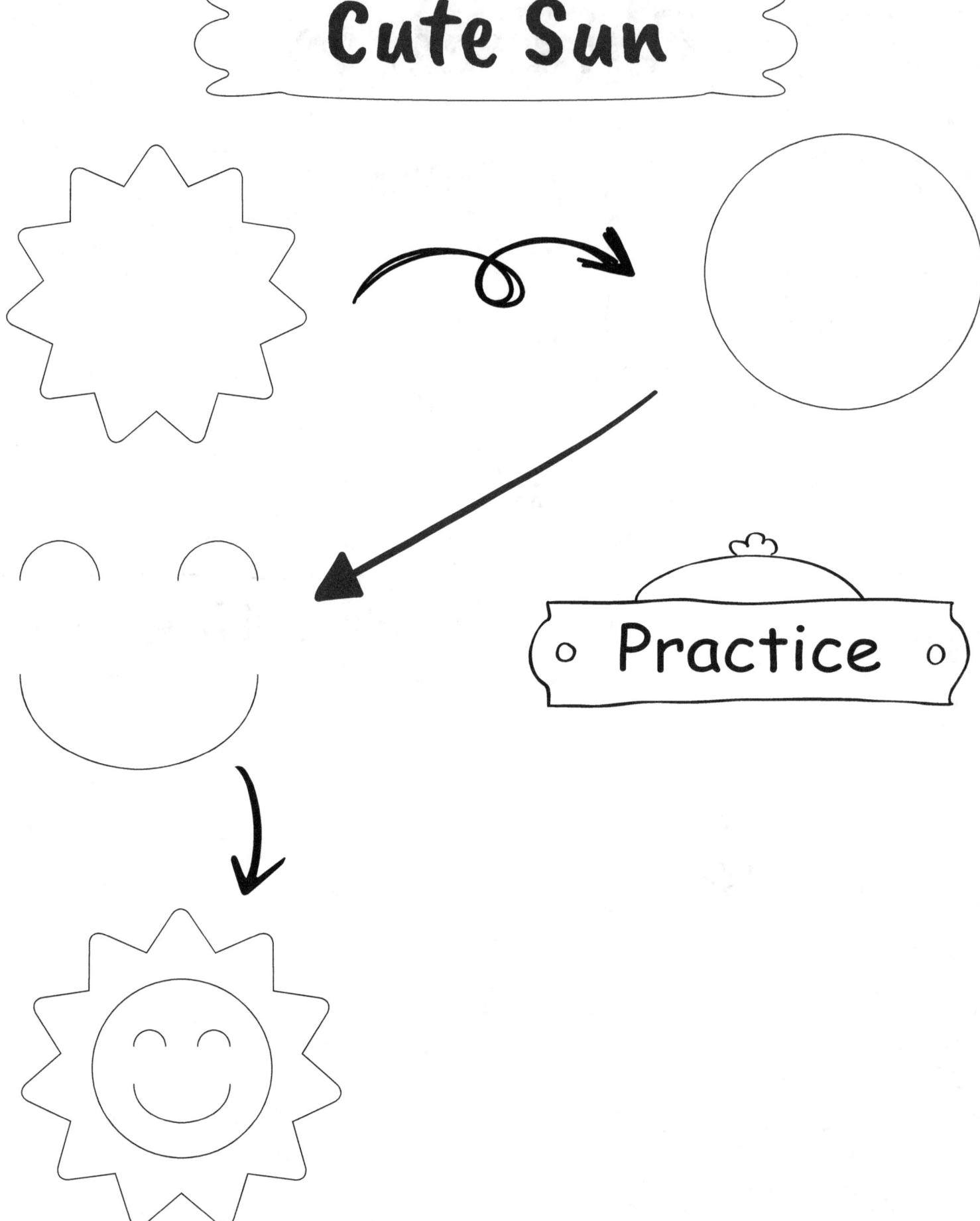

Practice

Jug

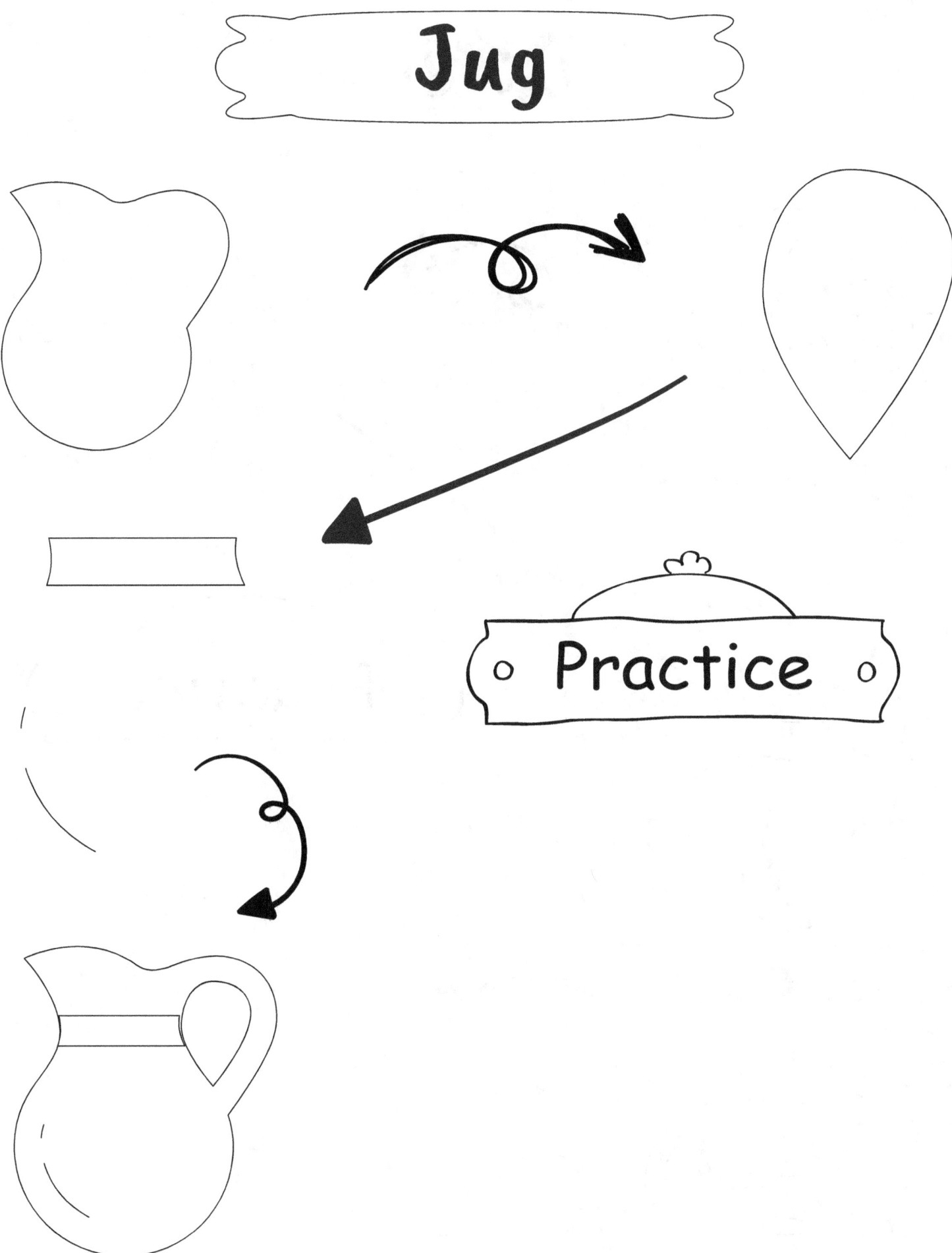

Practice

Otter

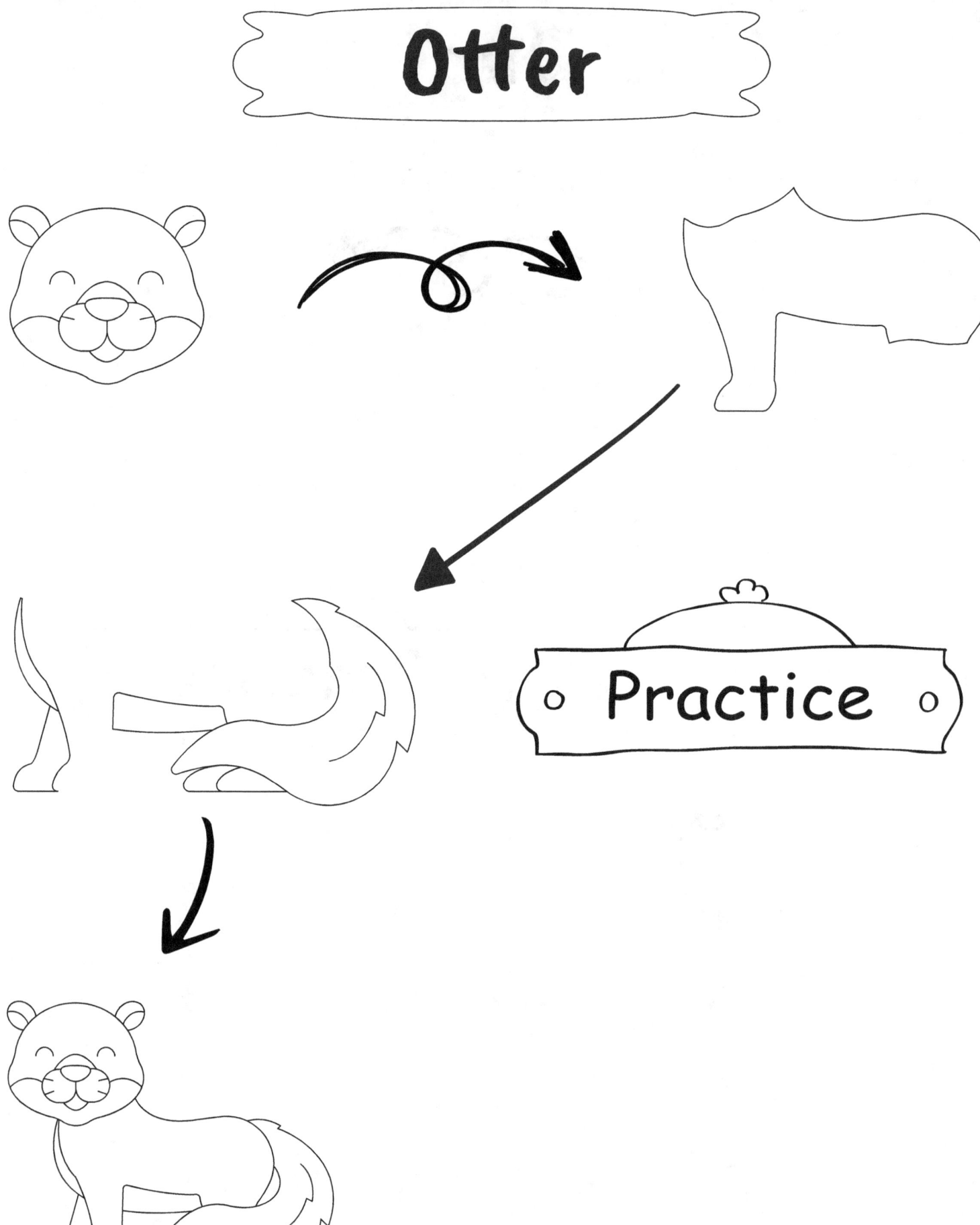

Practice

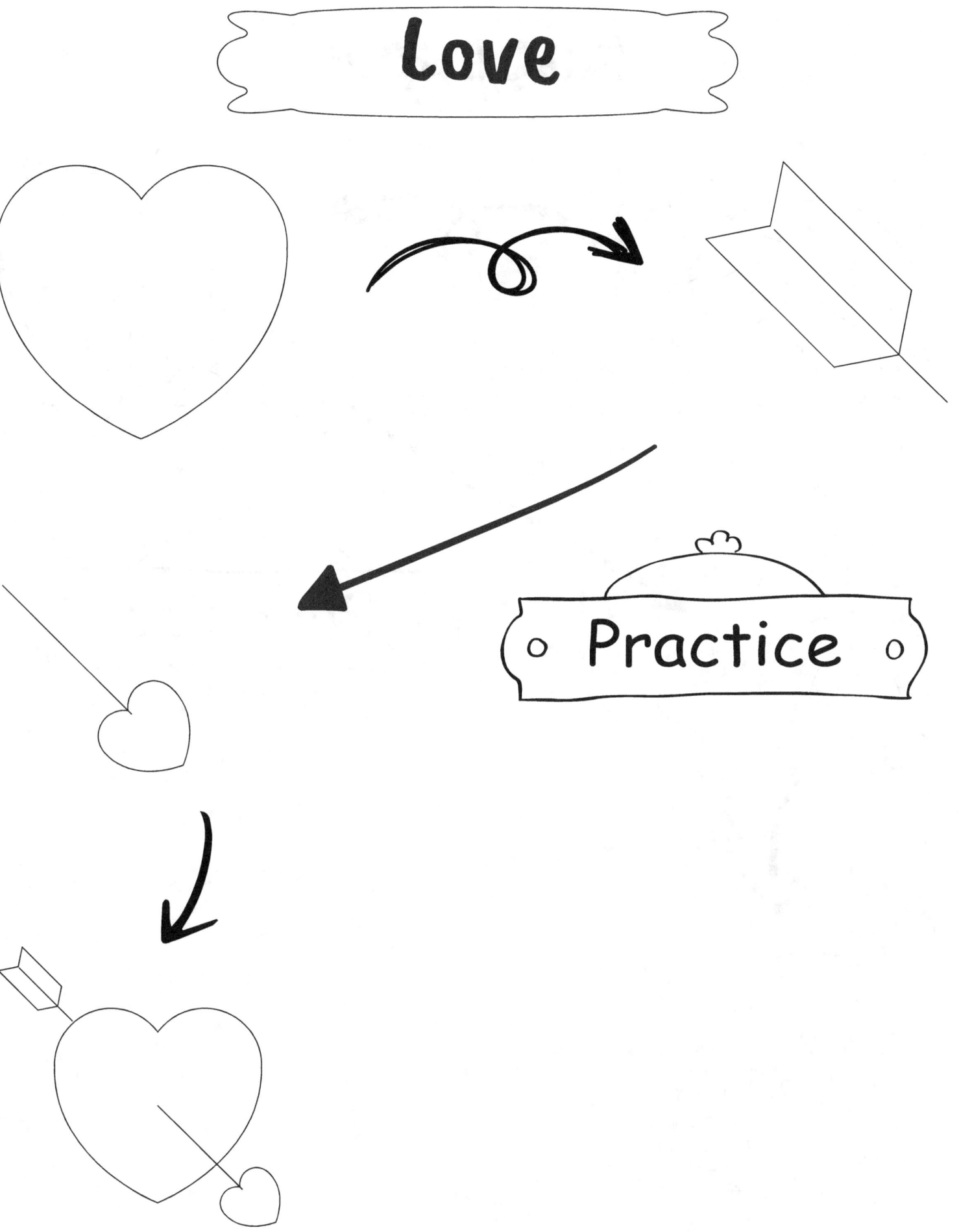

Raccoon

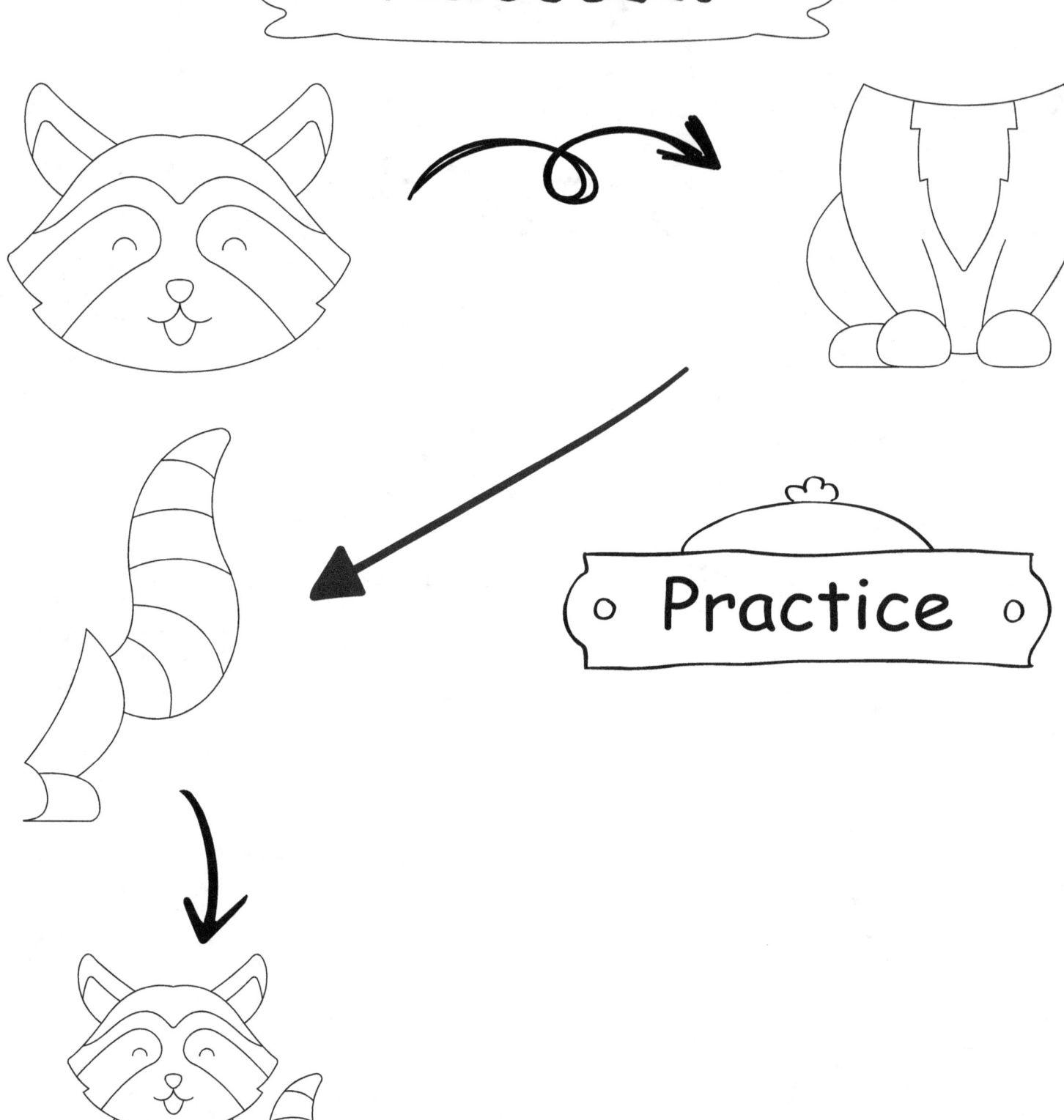

Practice

Goat

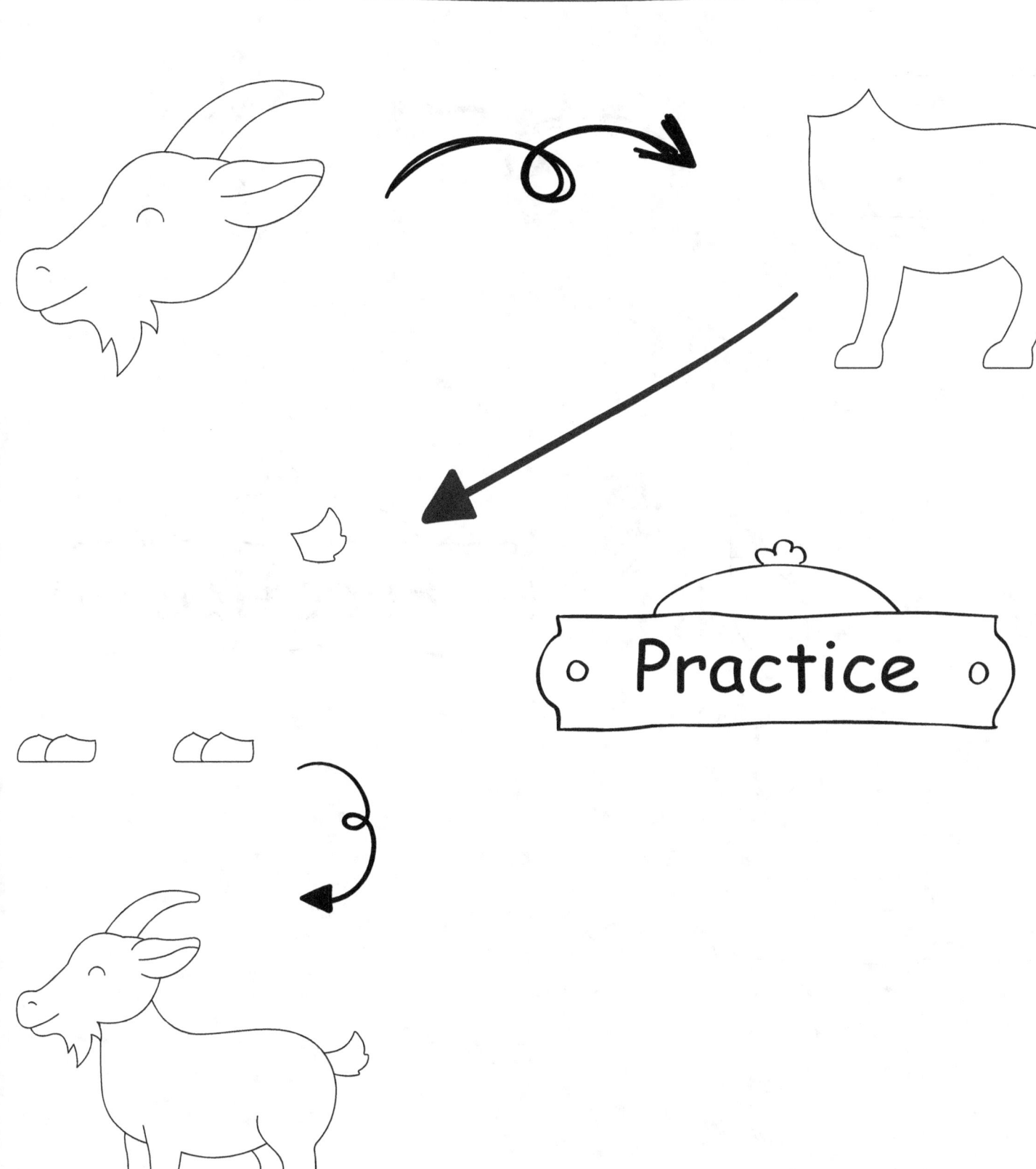

Practice

Socks

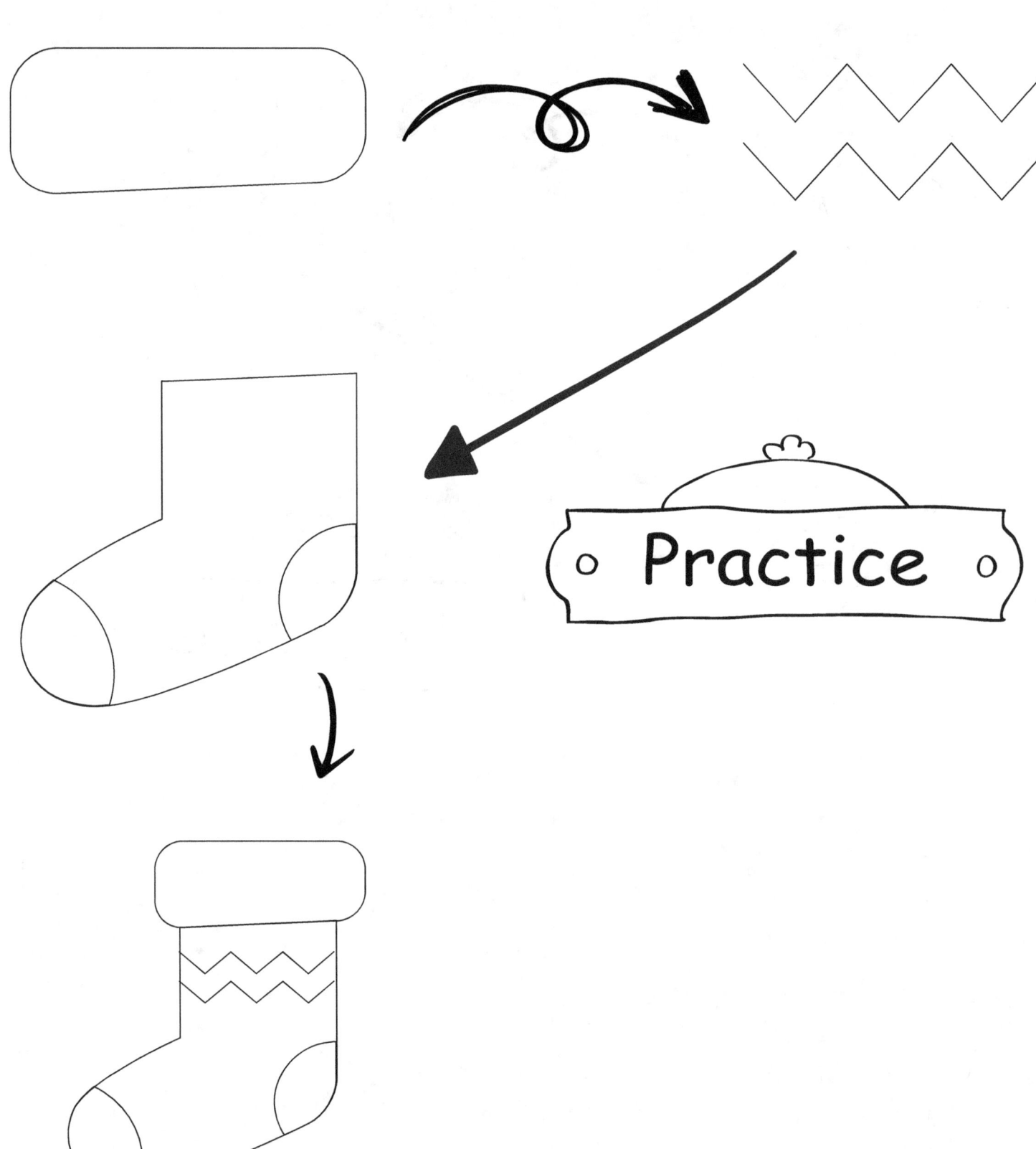

Practice

Hedgehog

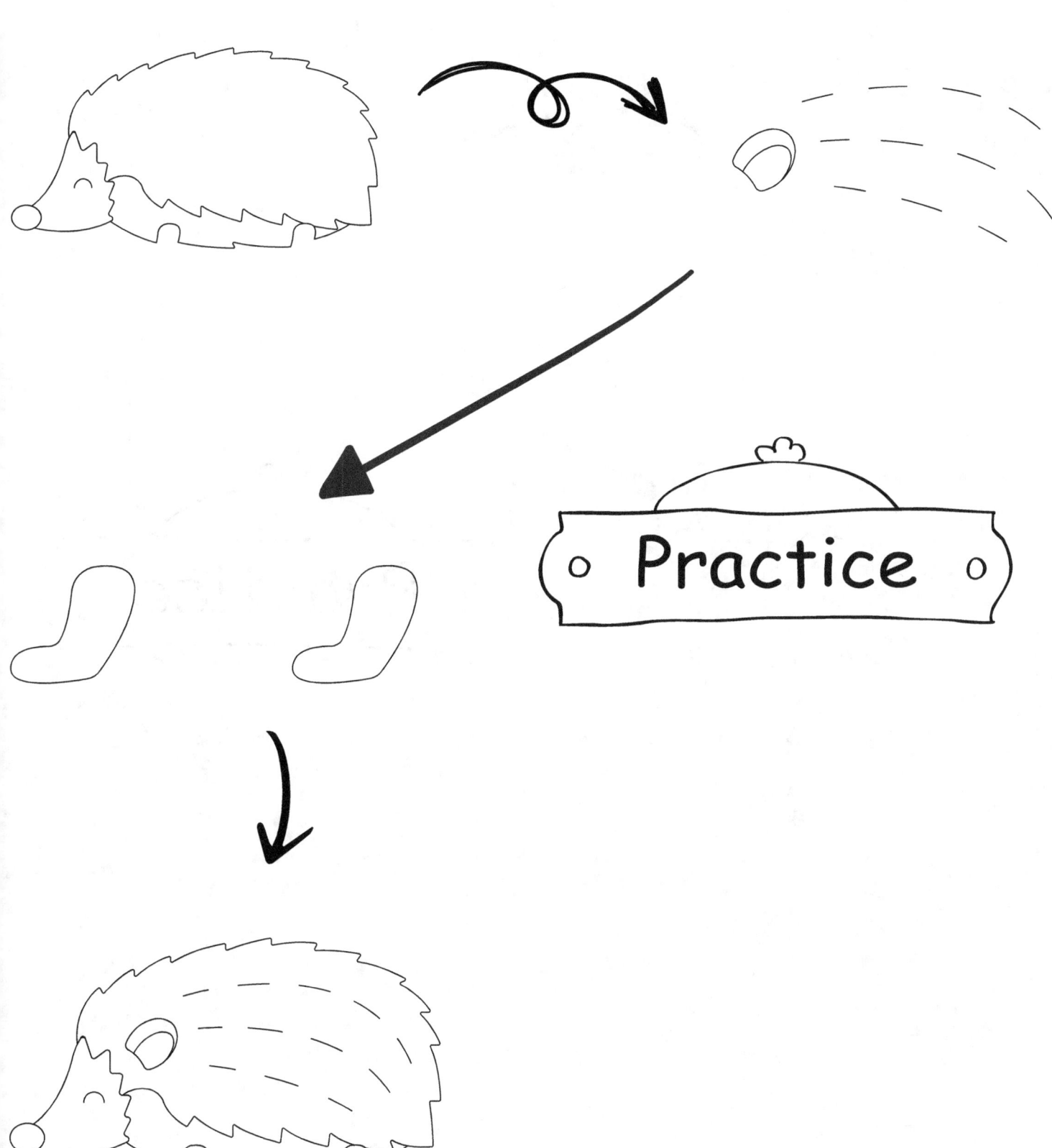

Practice

Ballon

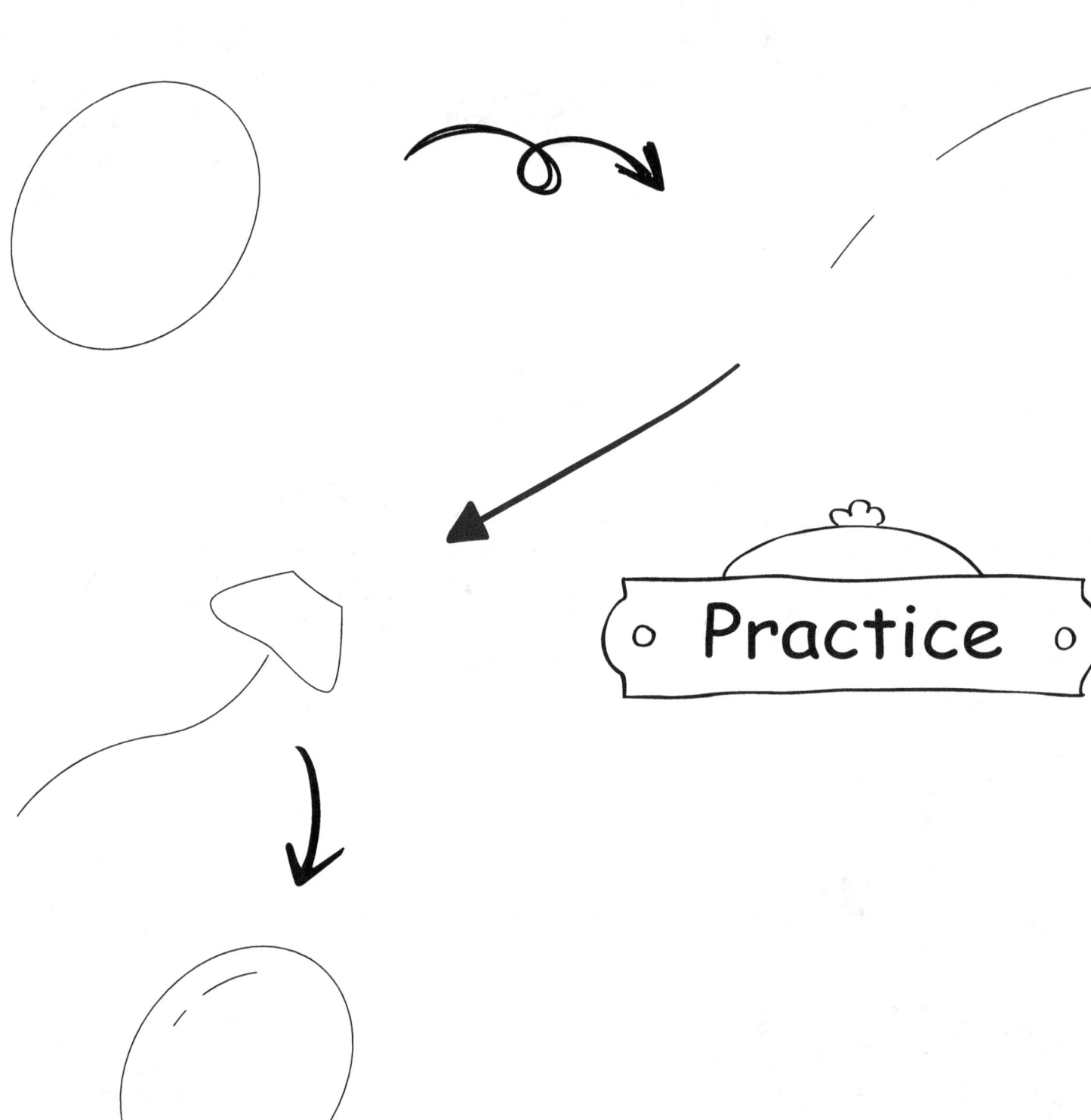

Practice

Gift box

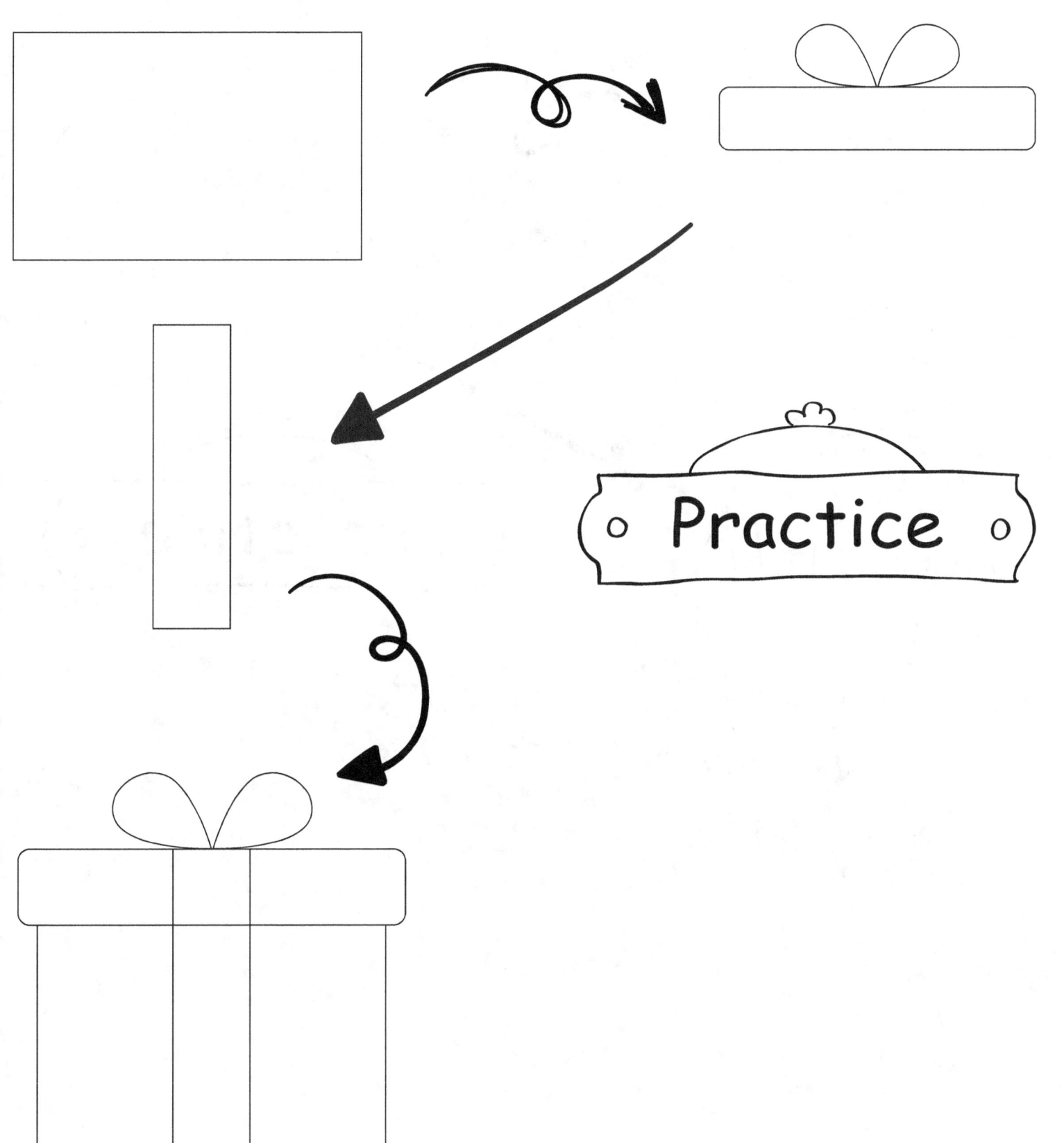

Practice

Pig

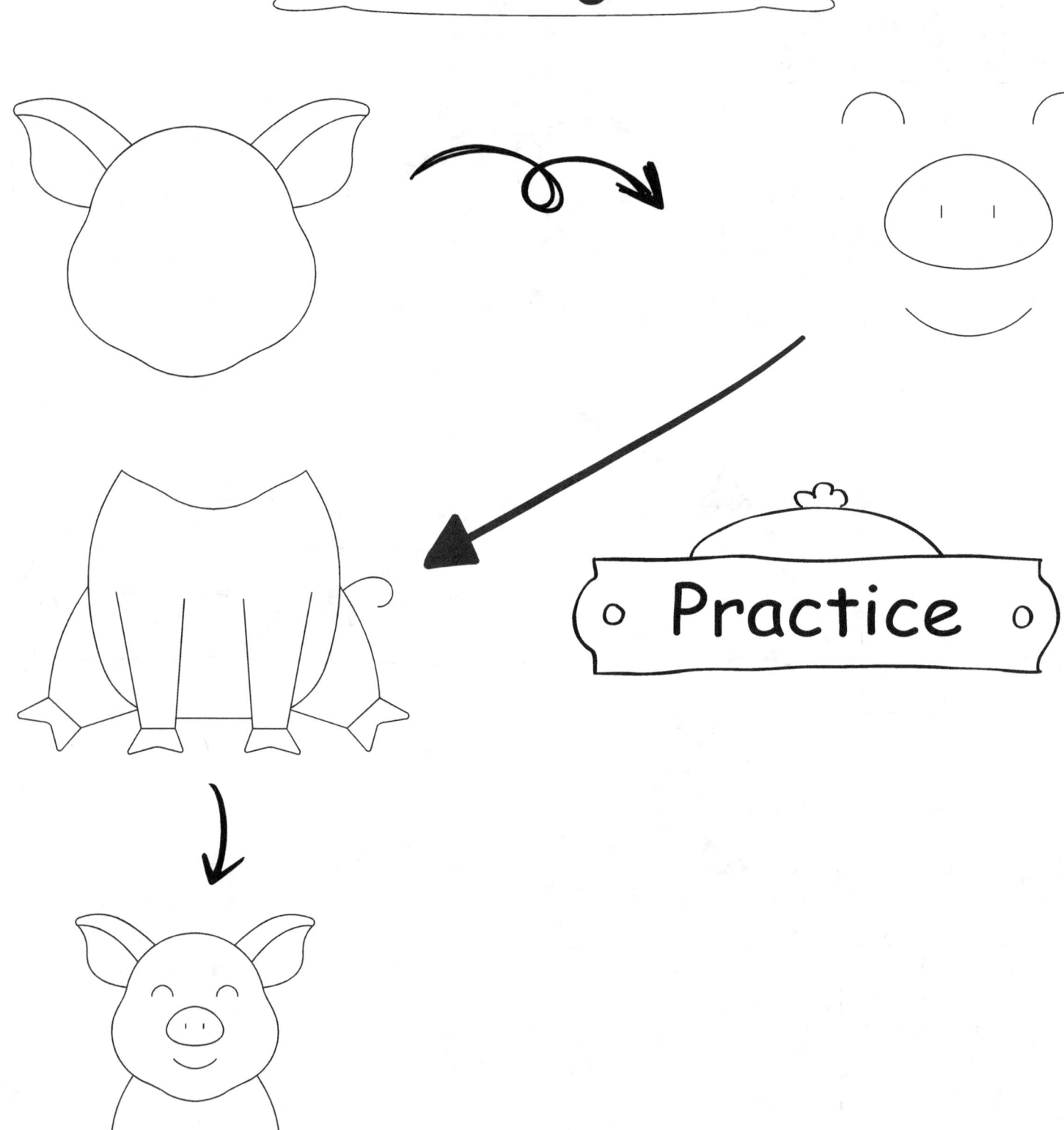

Candle

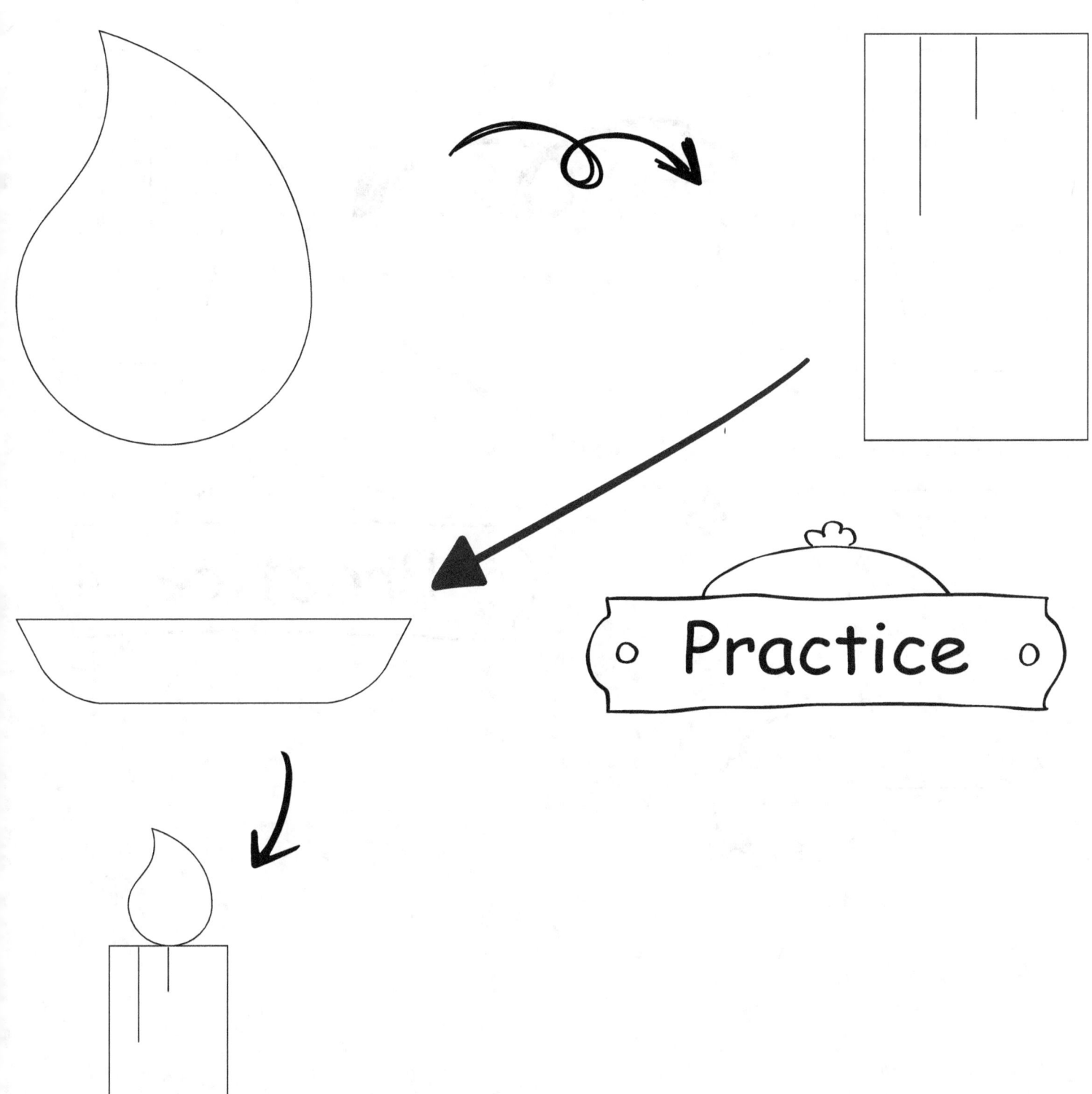

Coffin

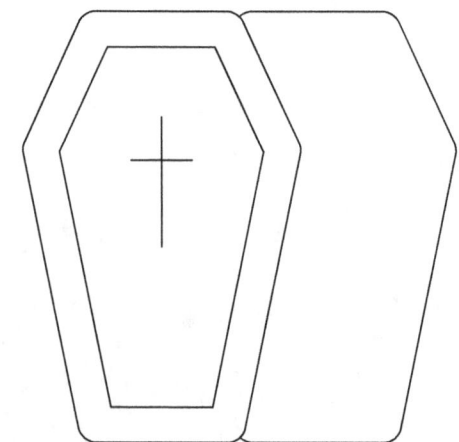

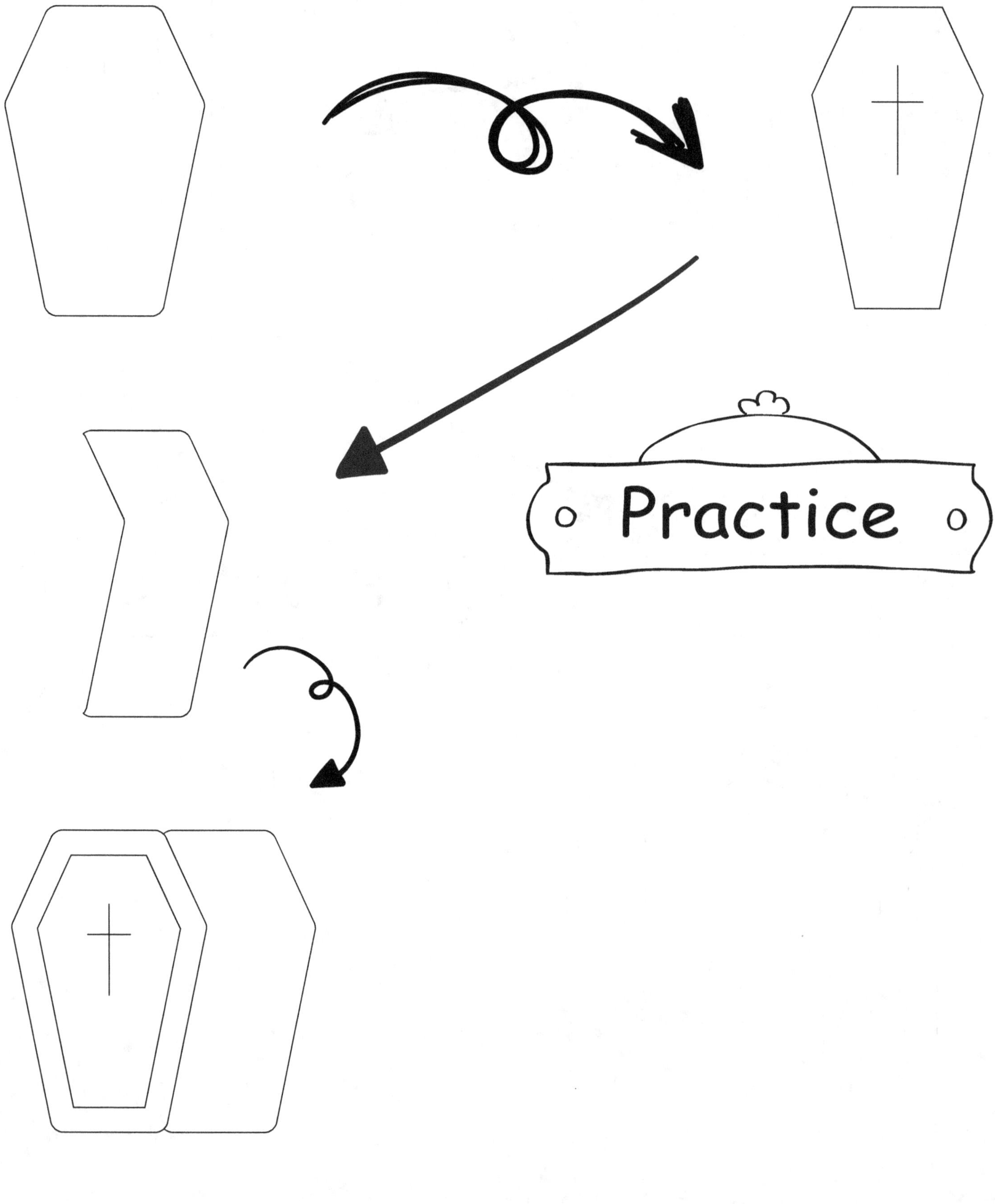

Practice

Tortoise

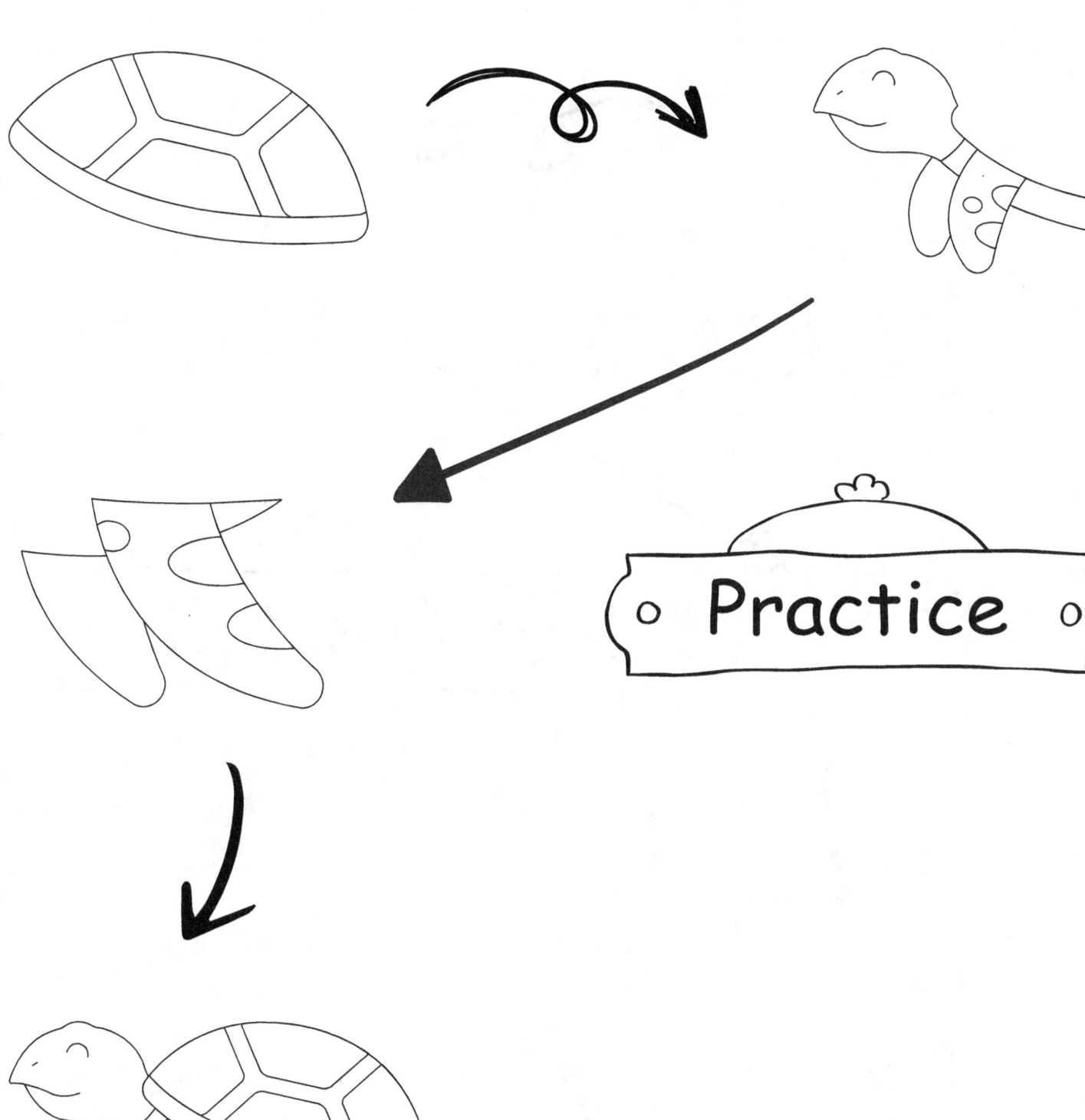

Practice

Lollipop

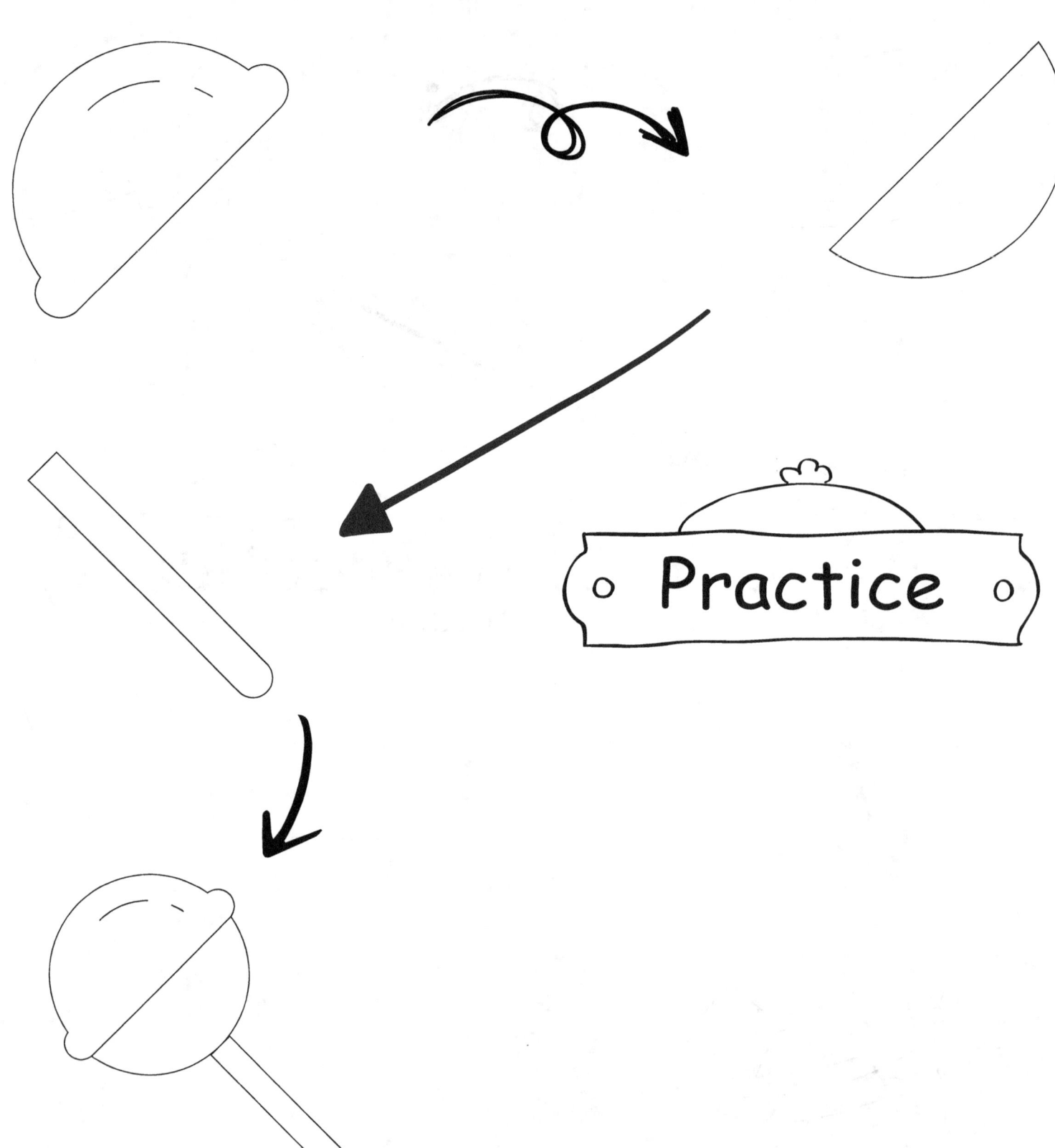

Practice

Toucan

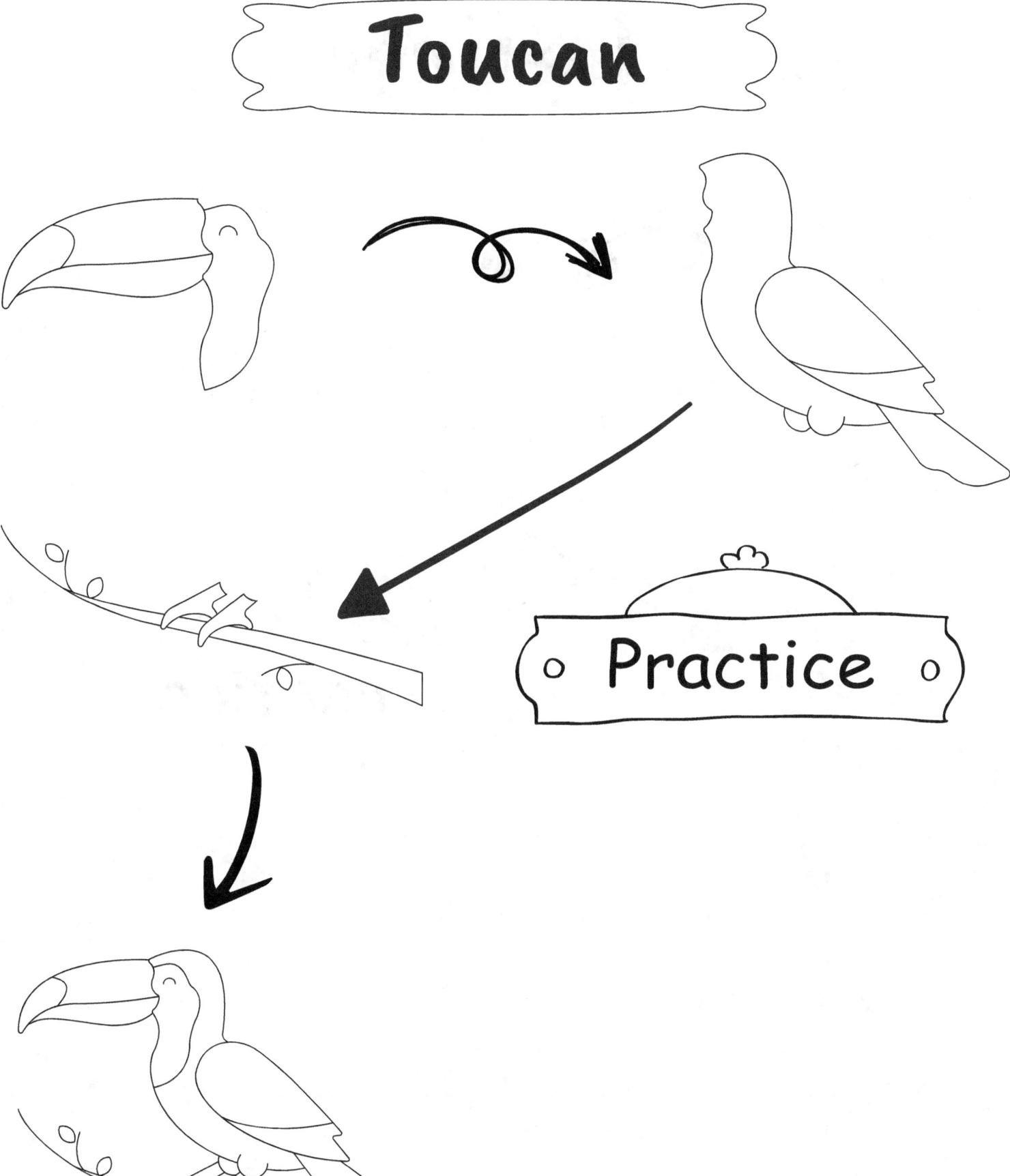

Practice

Flamingo

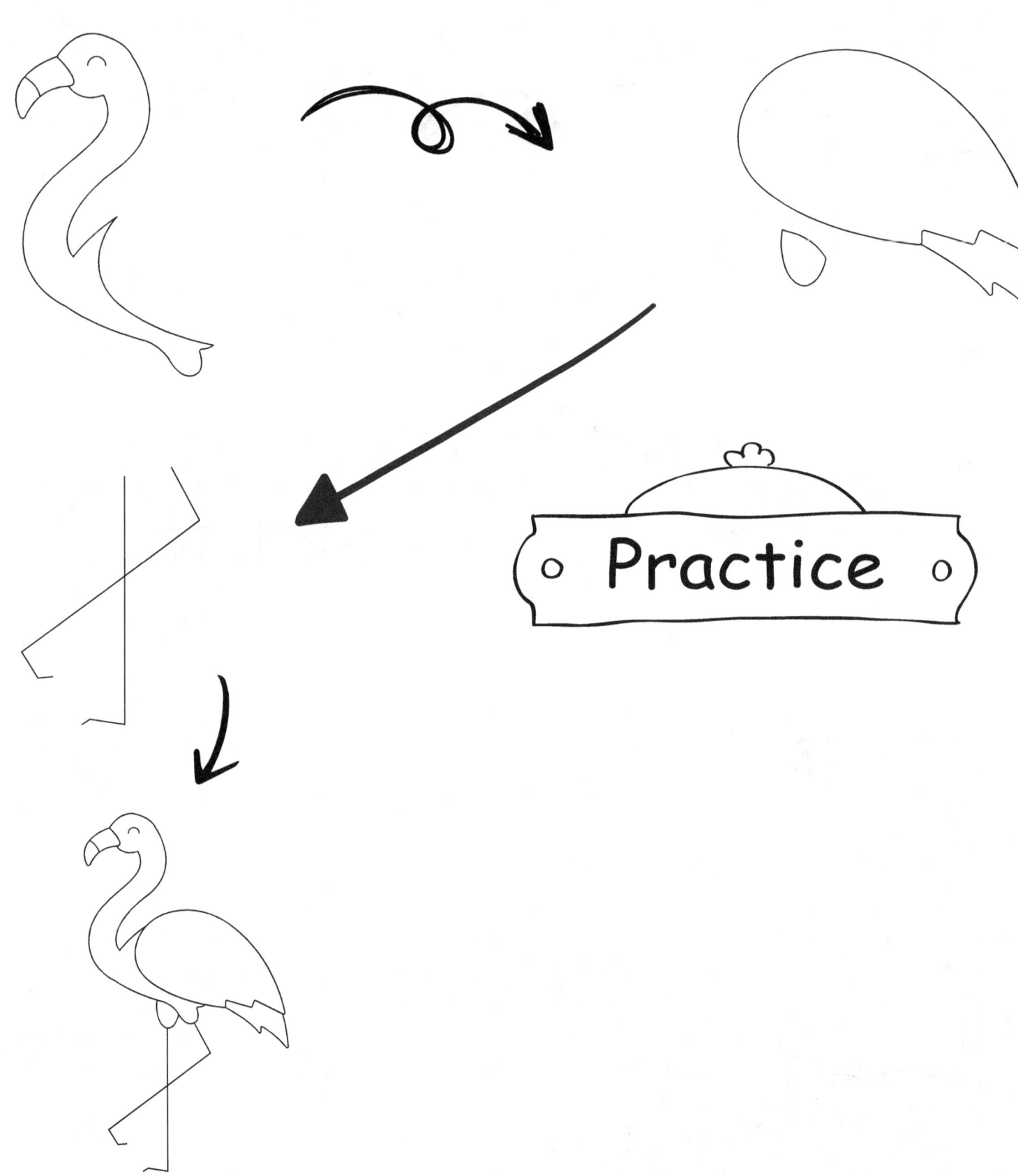

Practice

Football

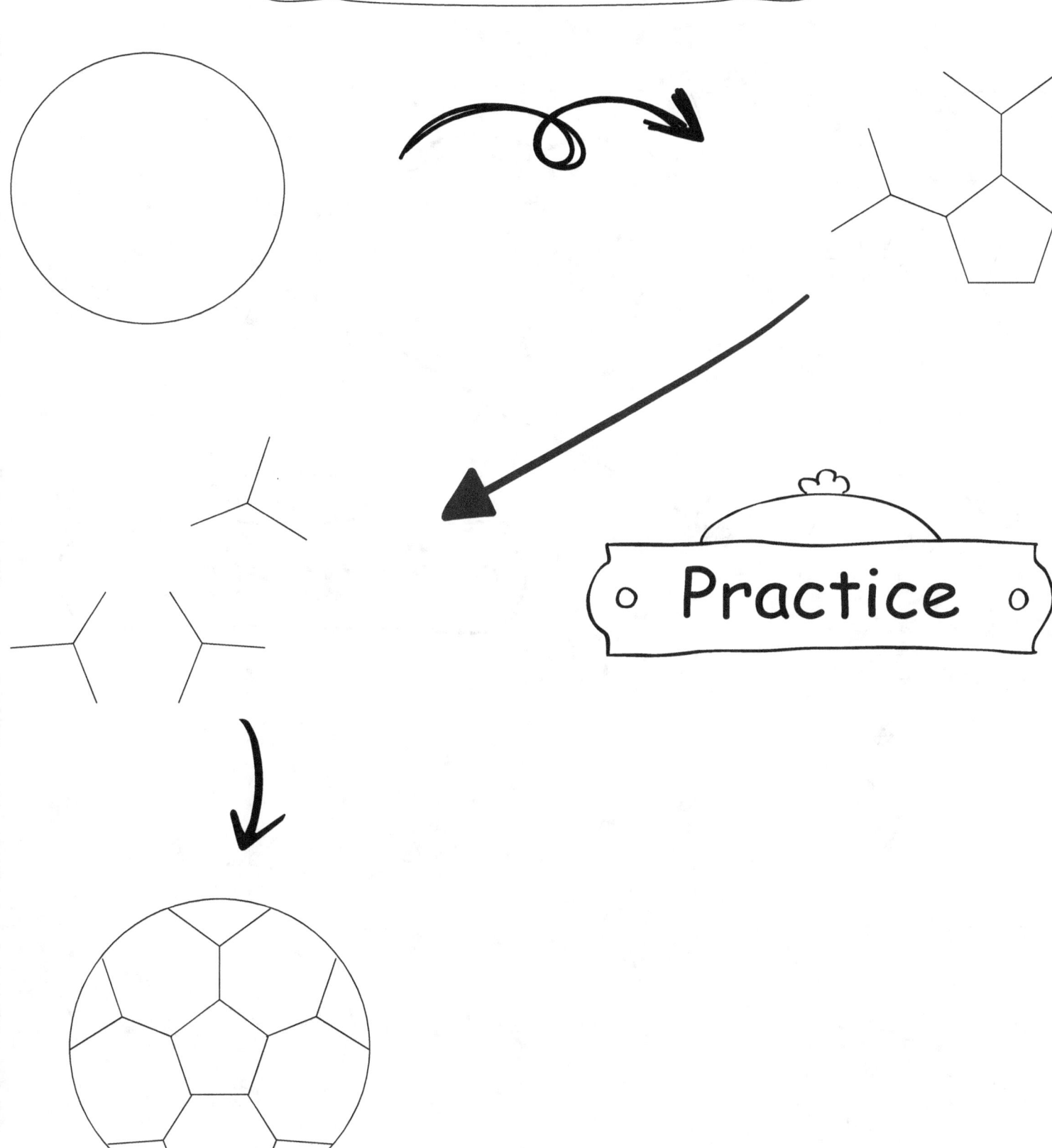

Practice

Madel

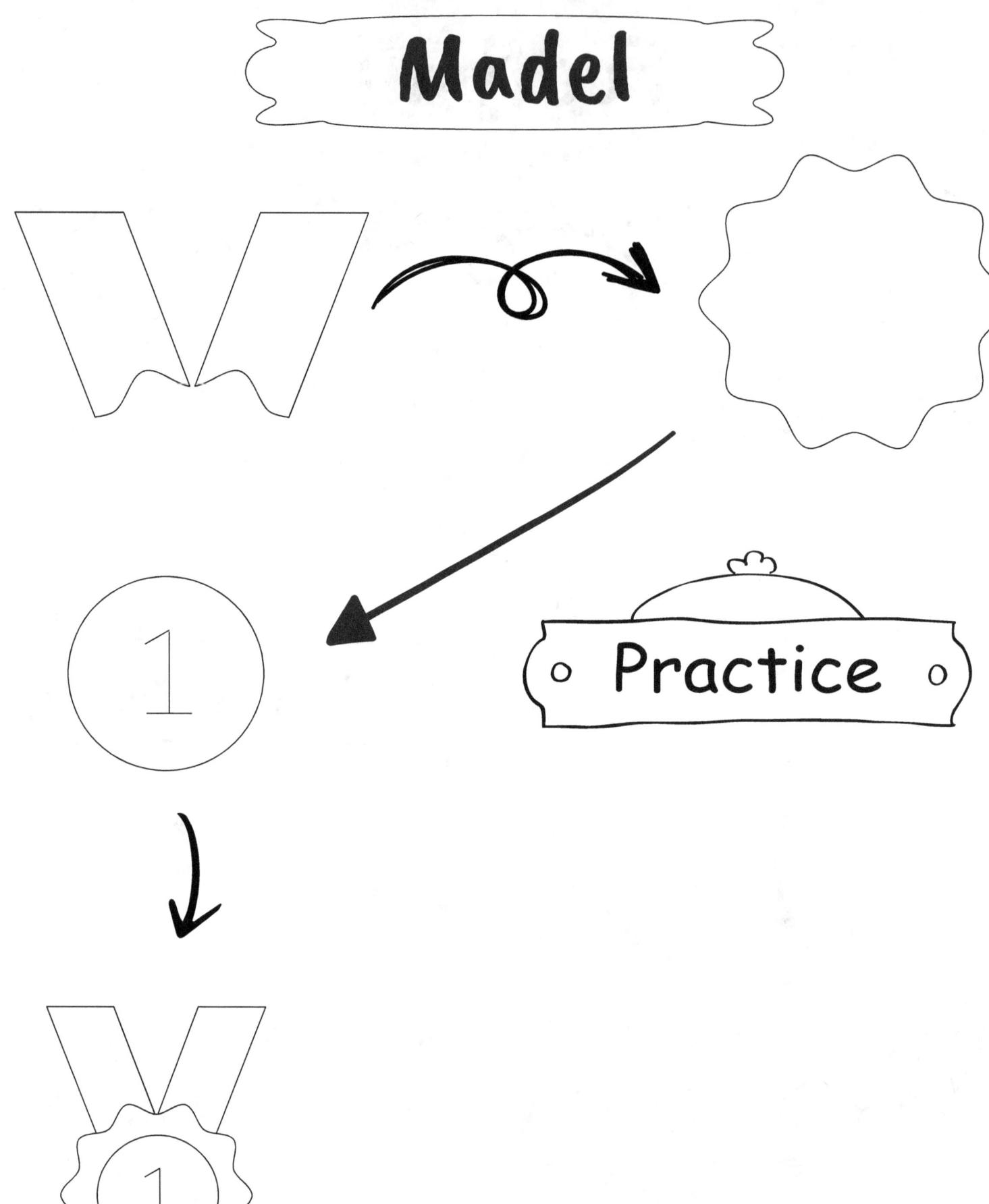

Crab

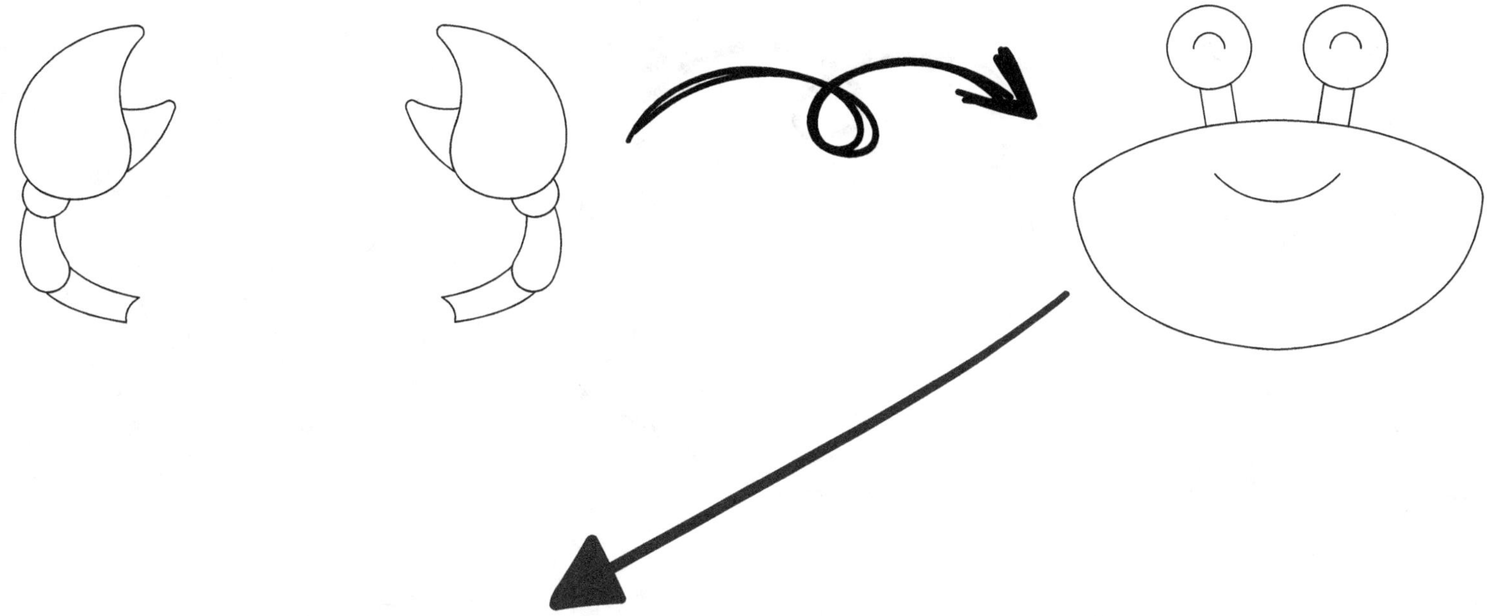

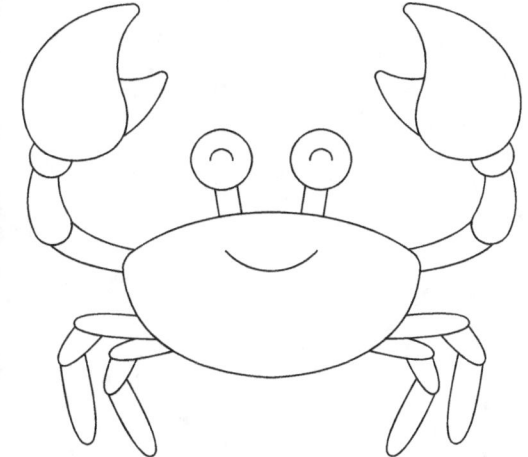

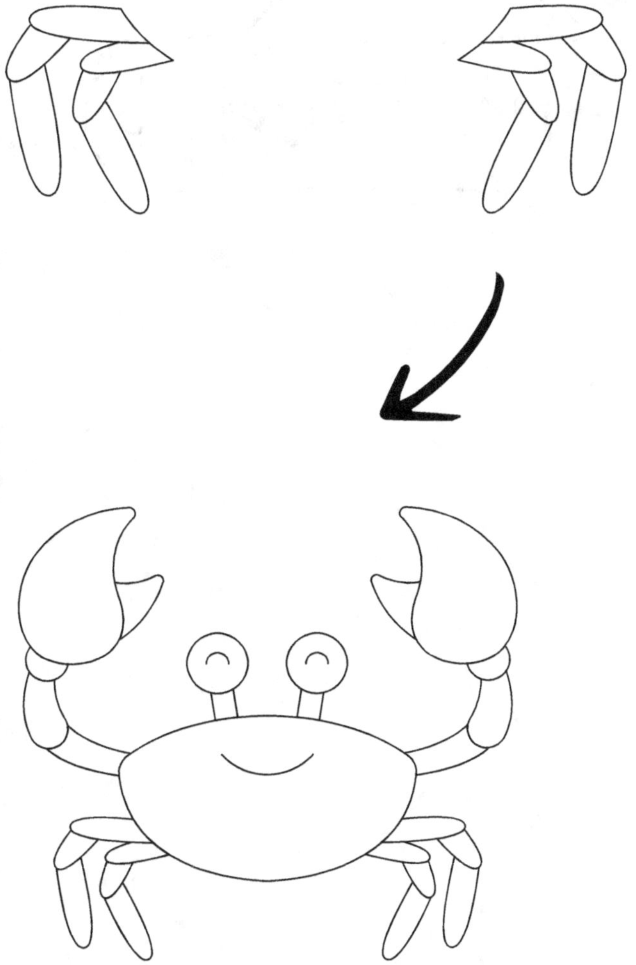

Eagle

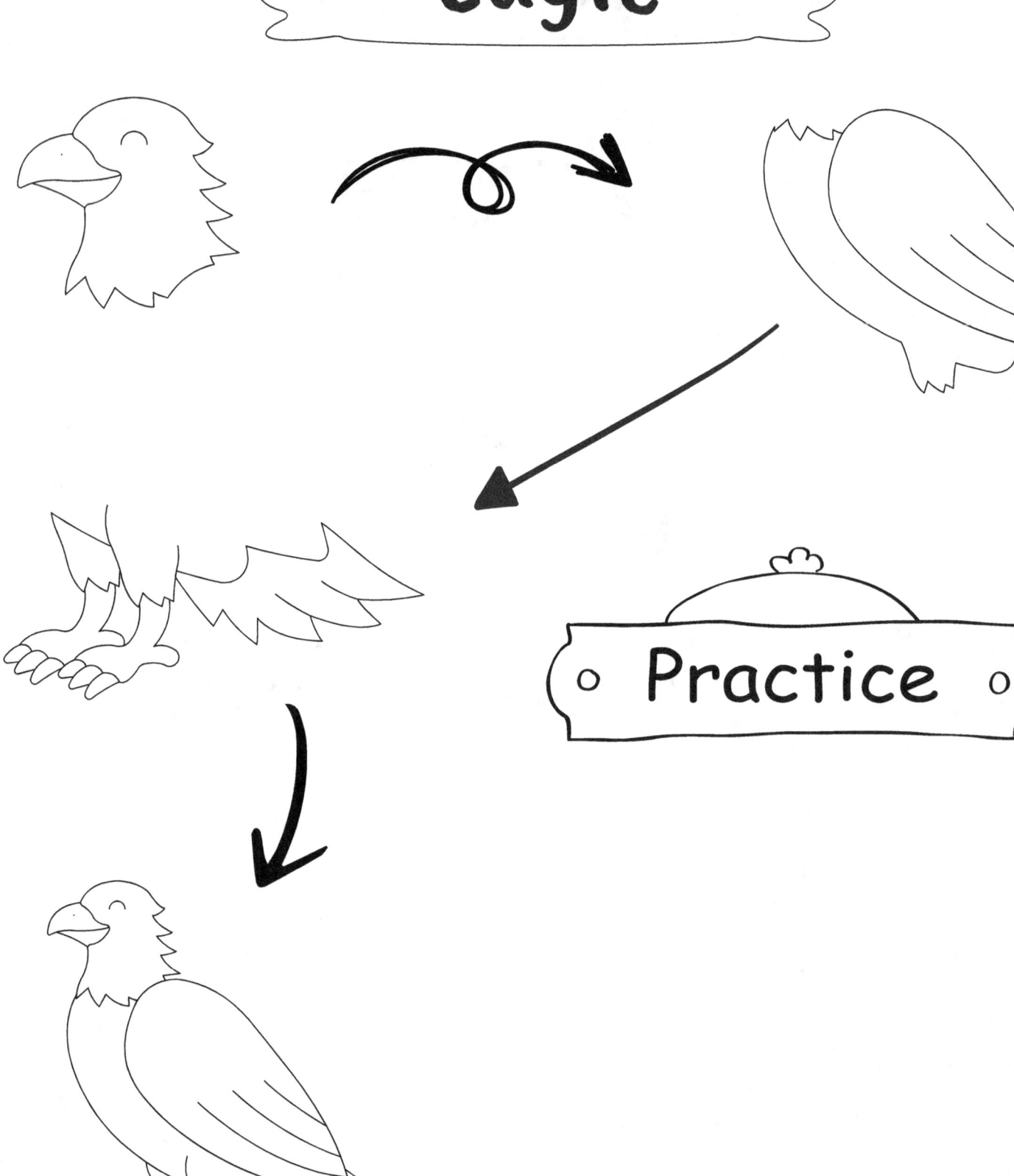

Whistle

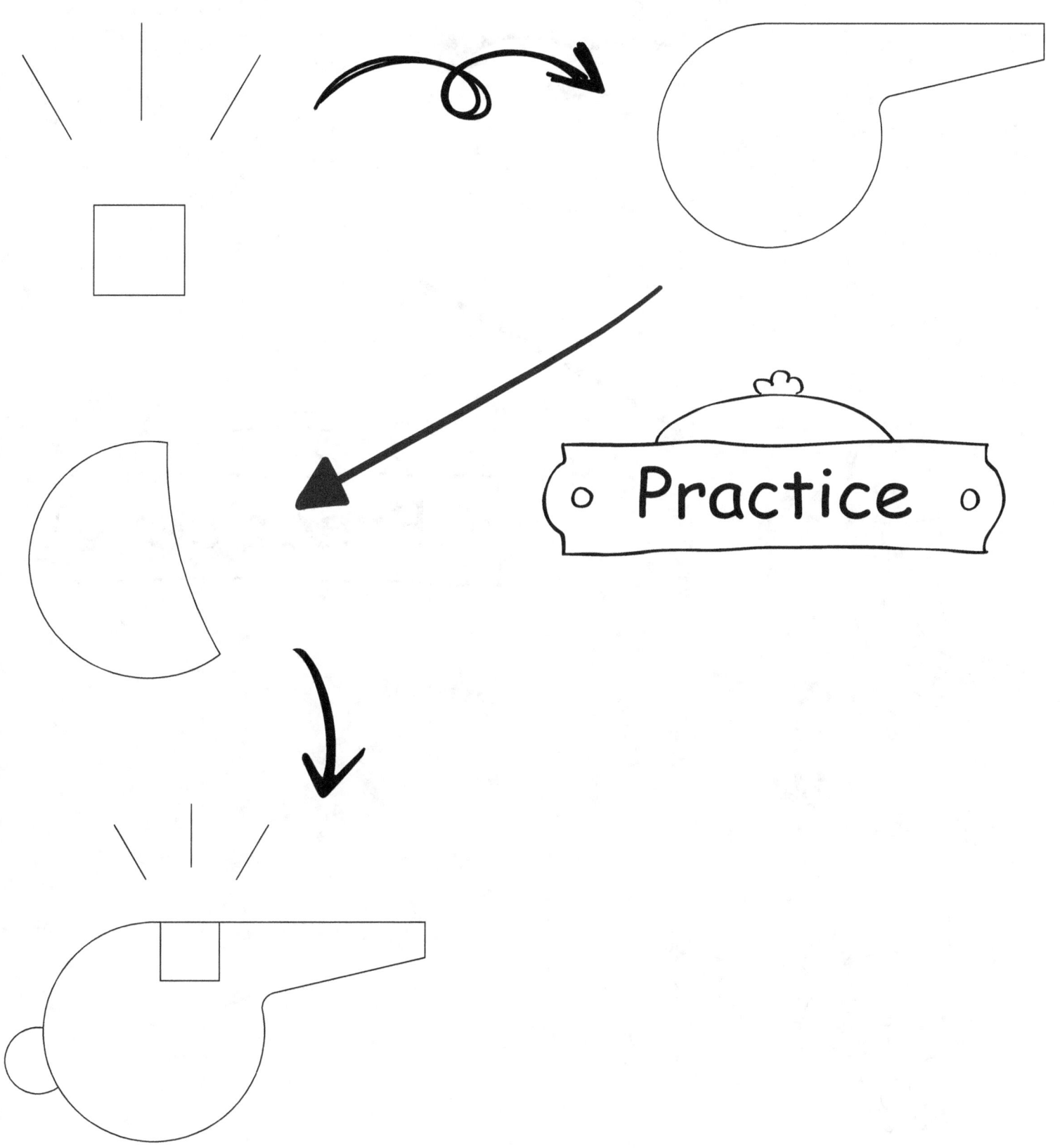

Practice

Peacock

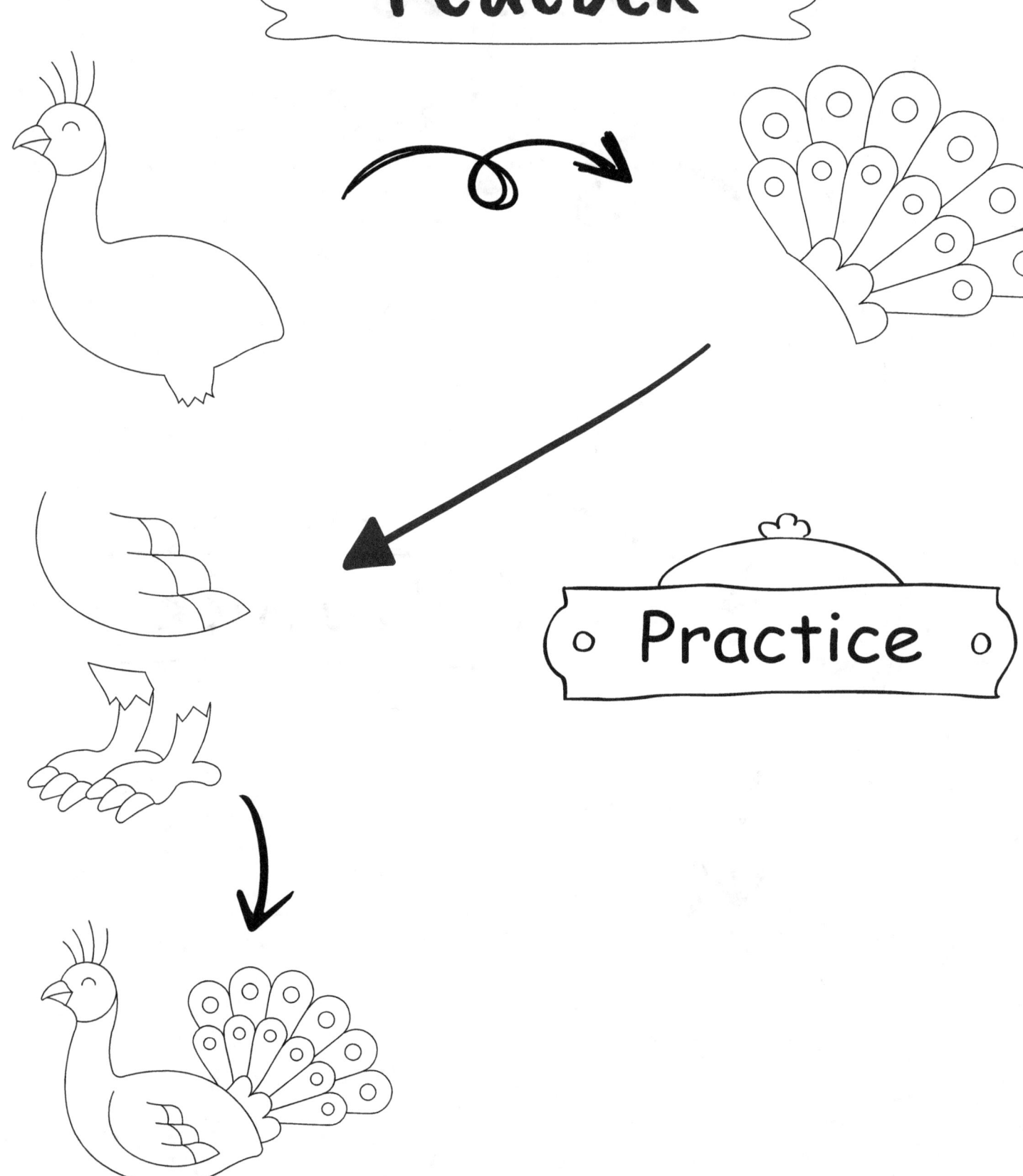

Practice

Camera

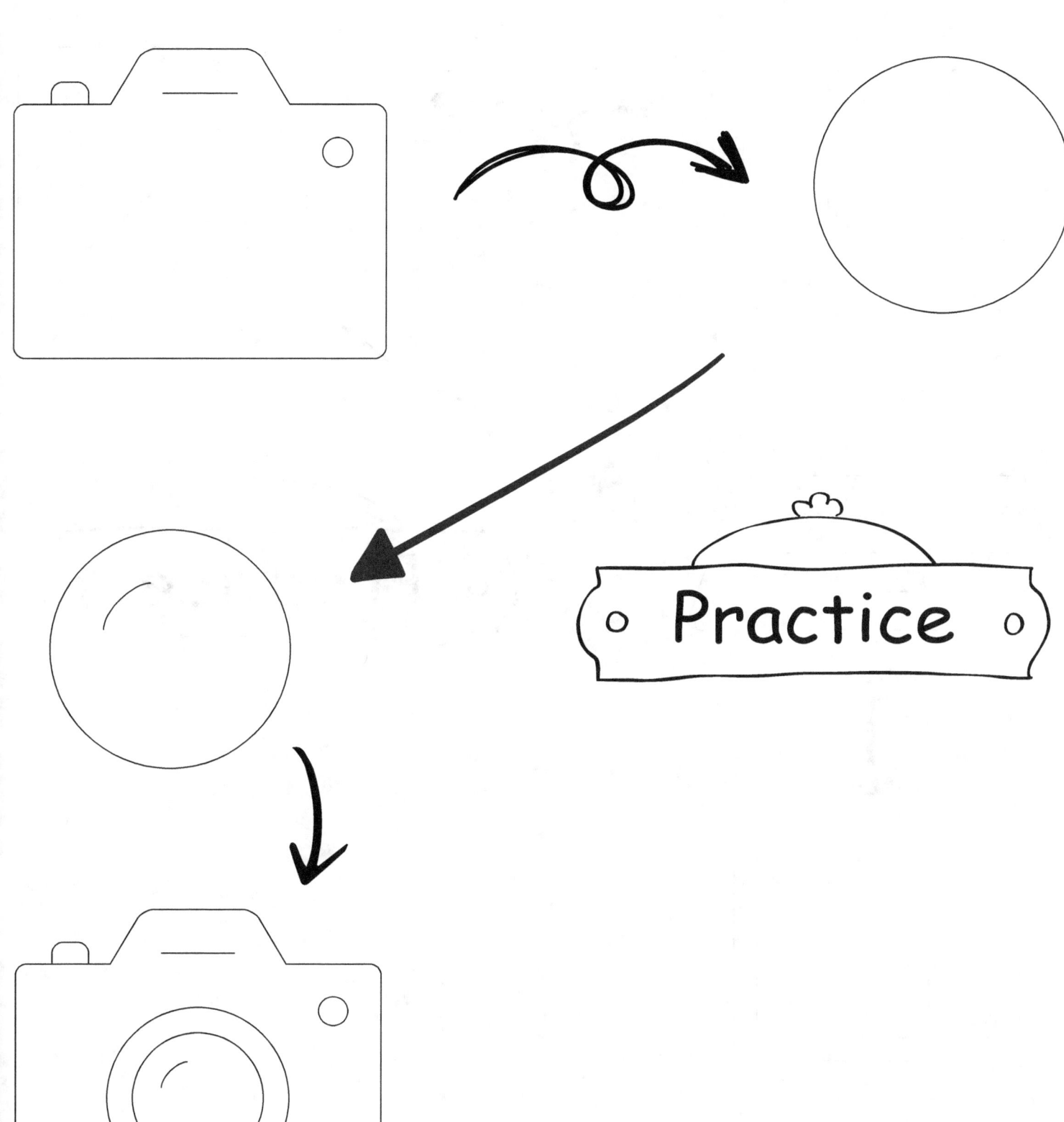

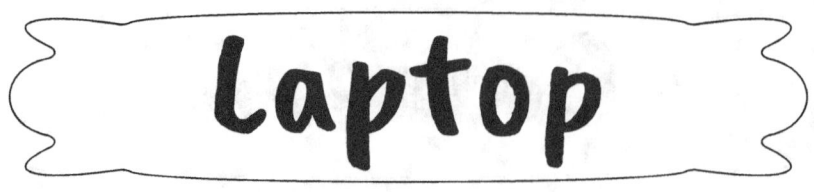

Laptop

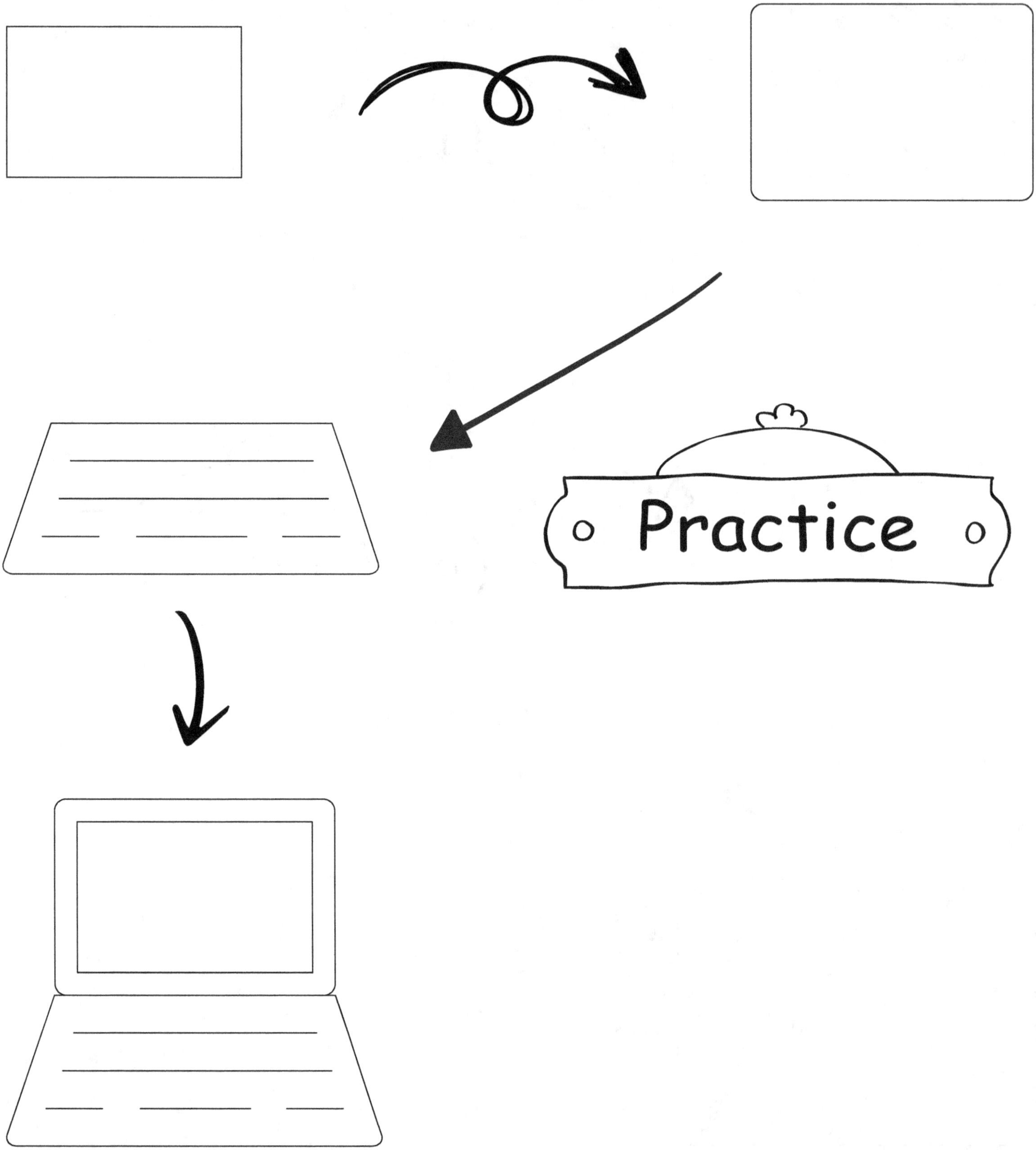

Practice

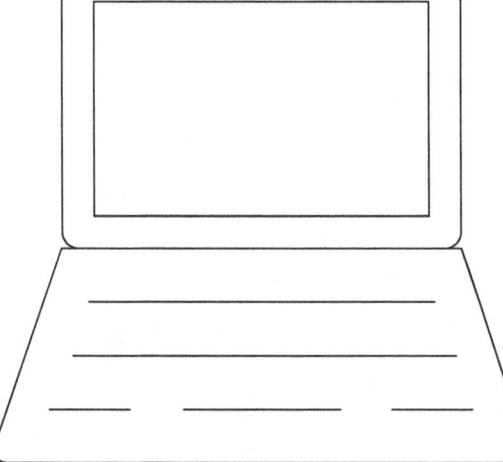

Starfish

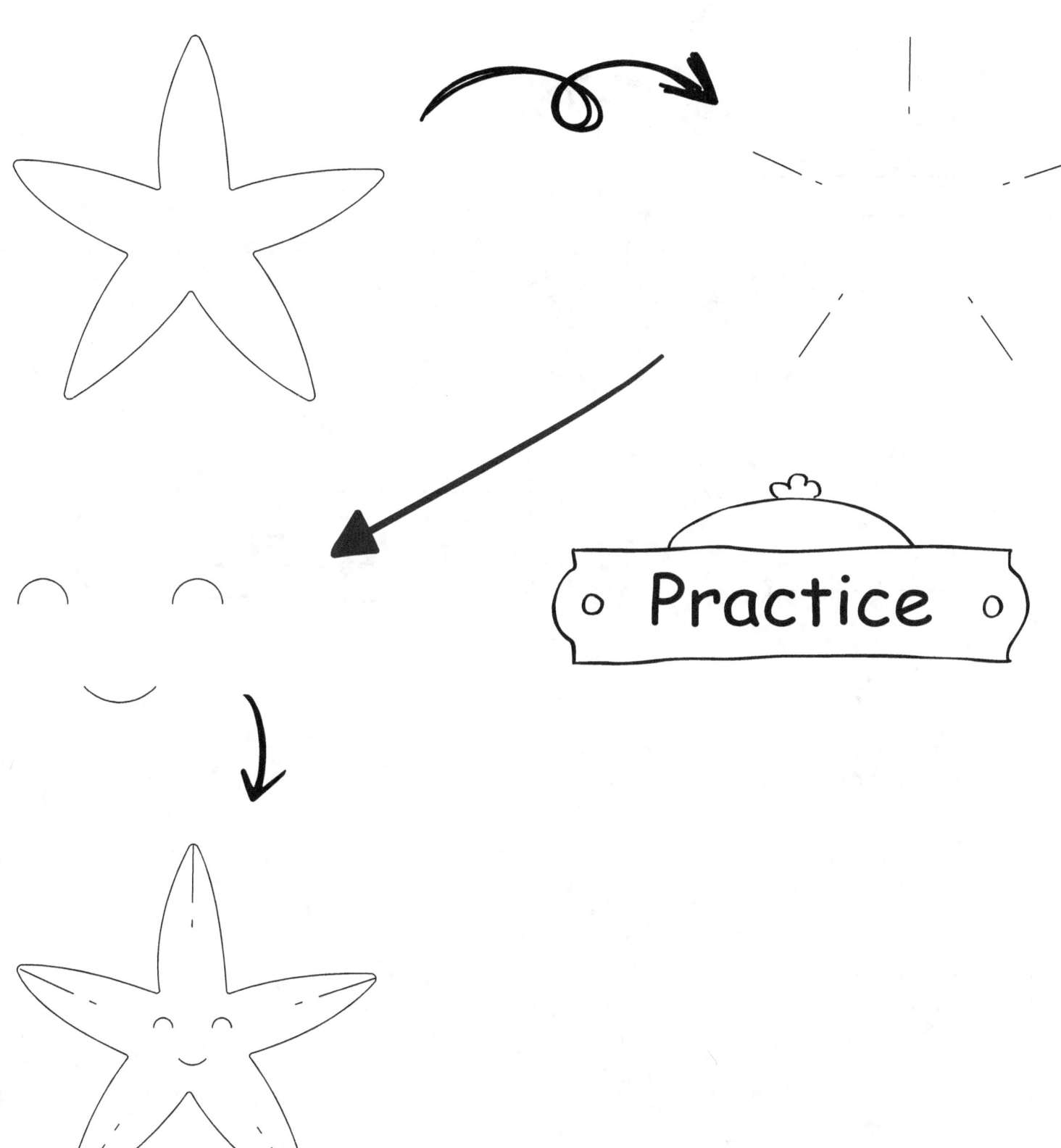

Practice

Cup

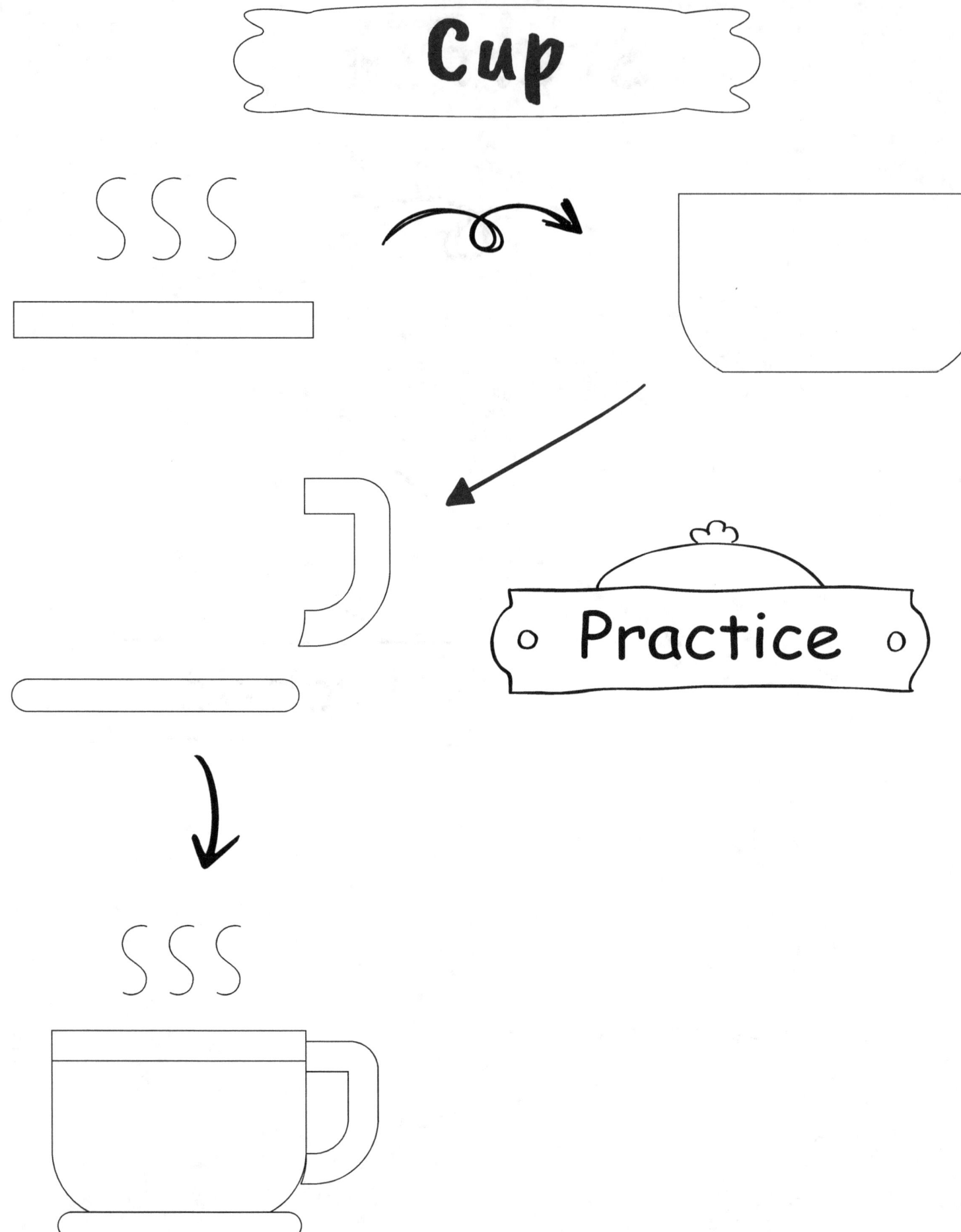

Practice

Swan

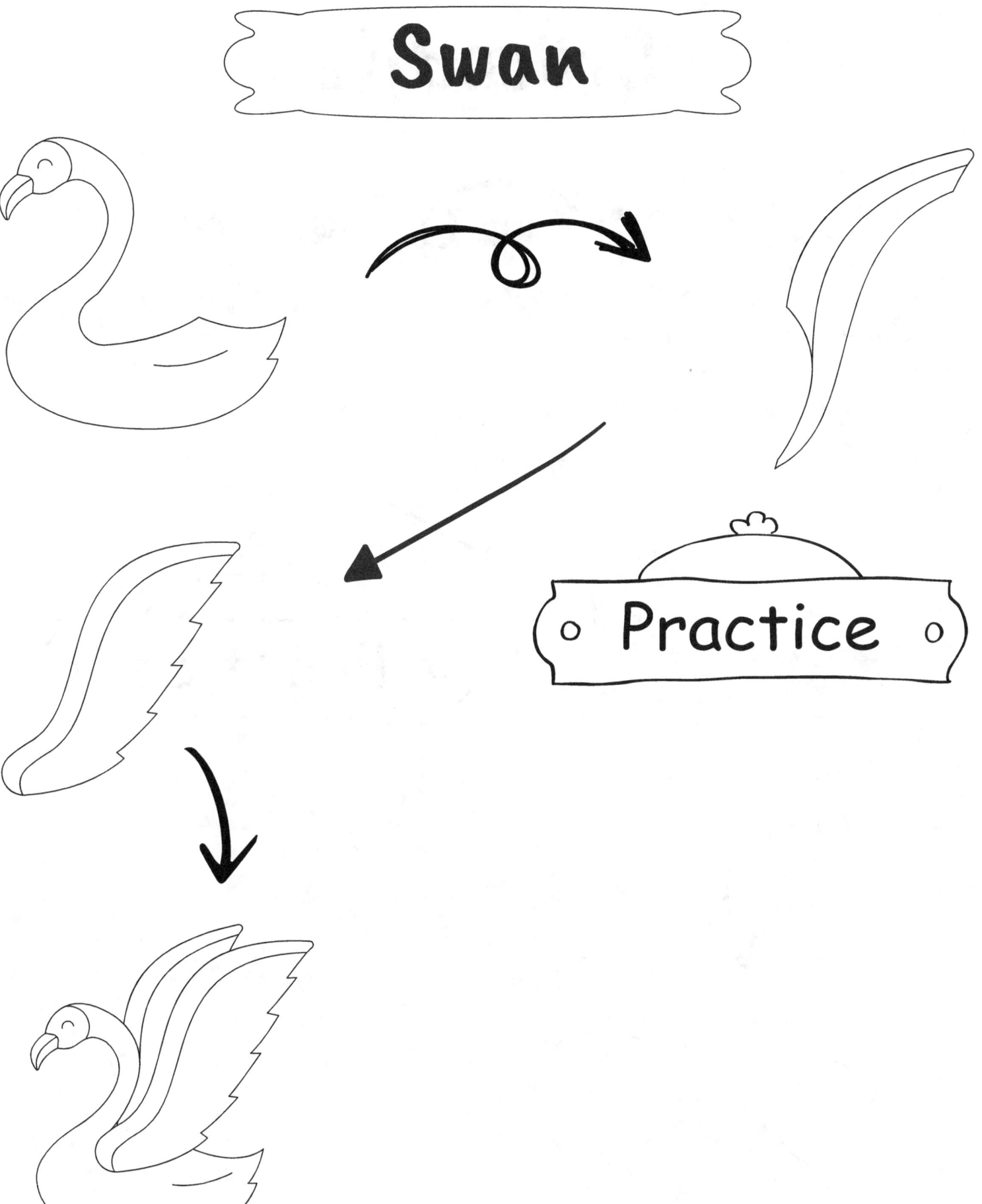

Practice

Crocodile

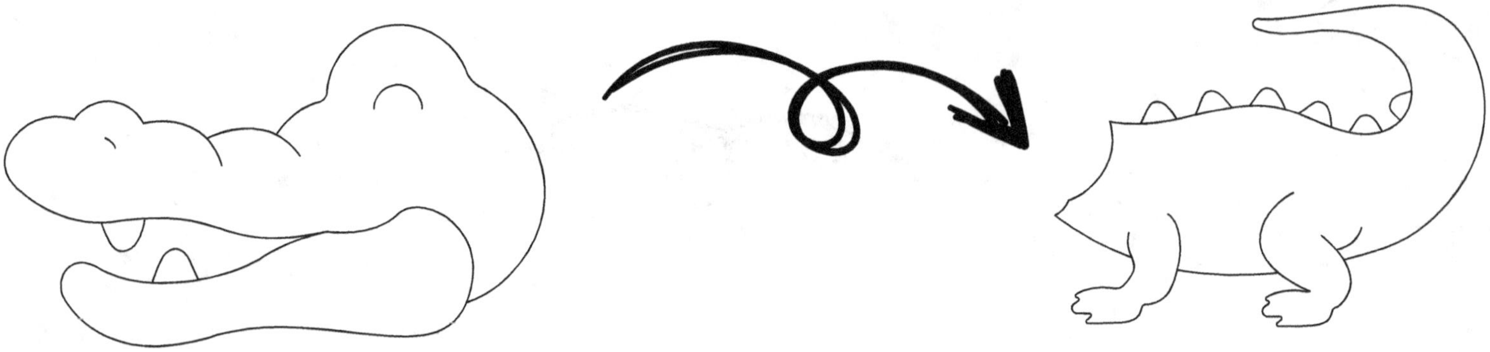

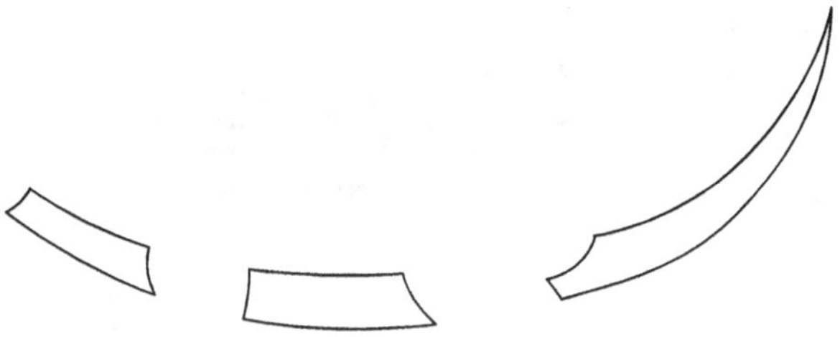

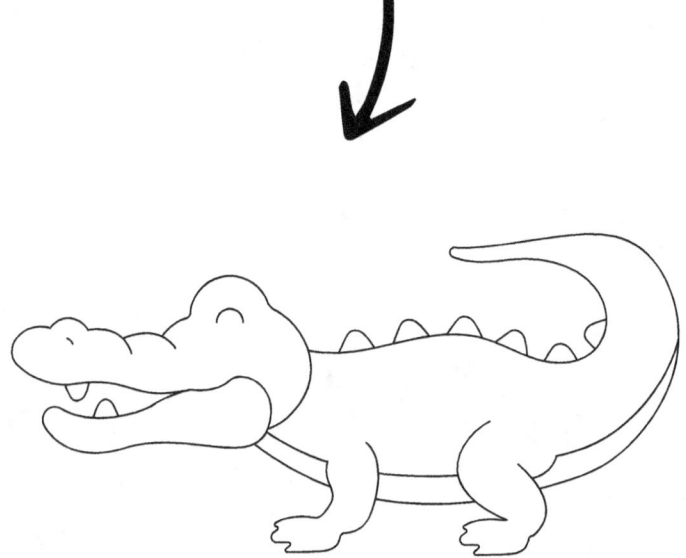

Practice

Ice cream

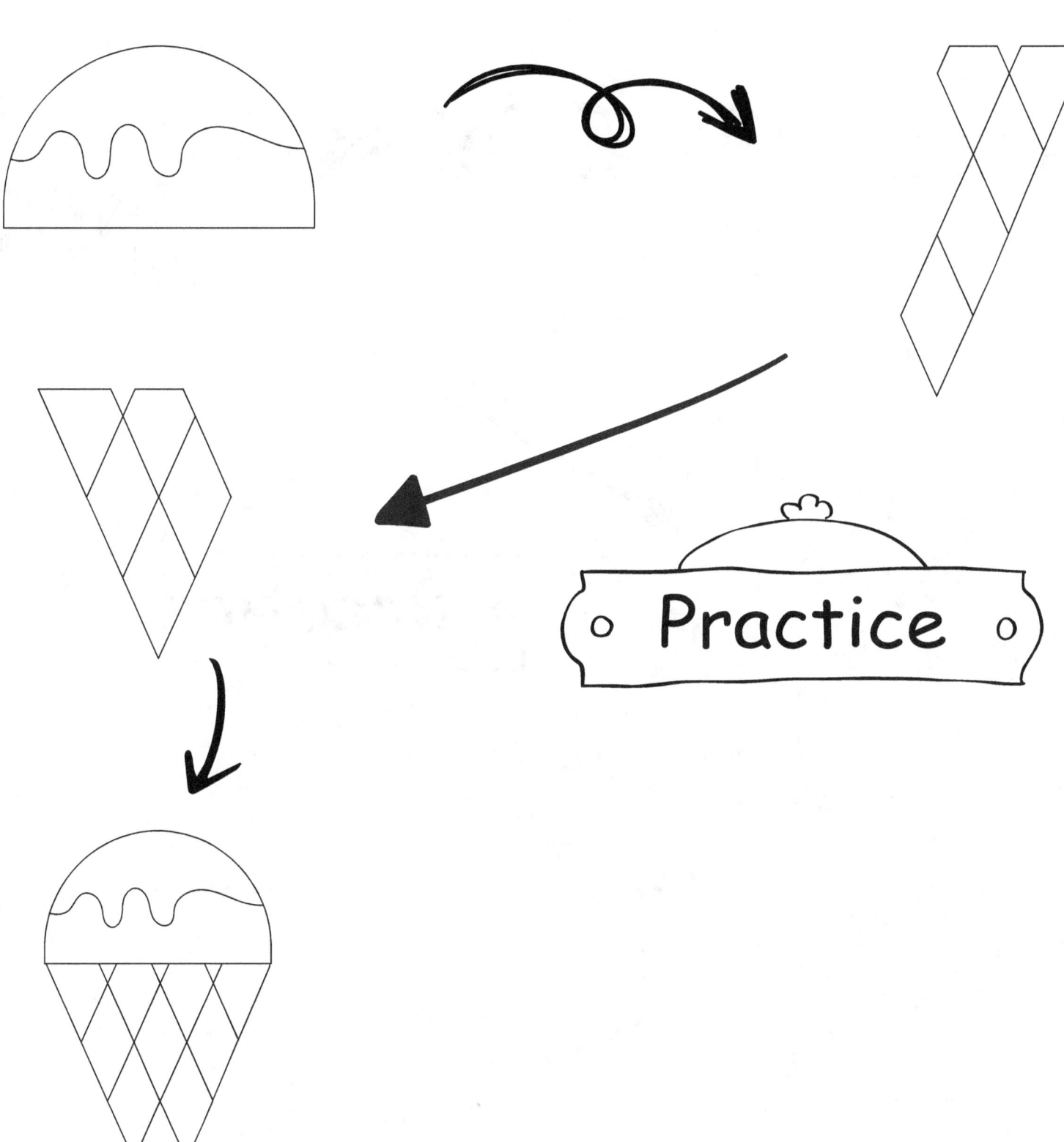

Beetle

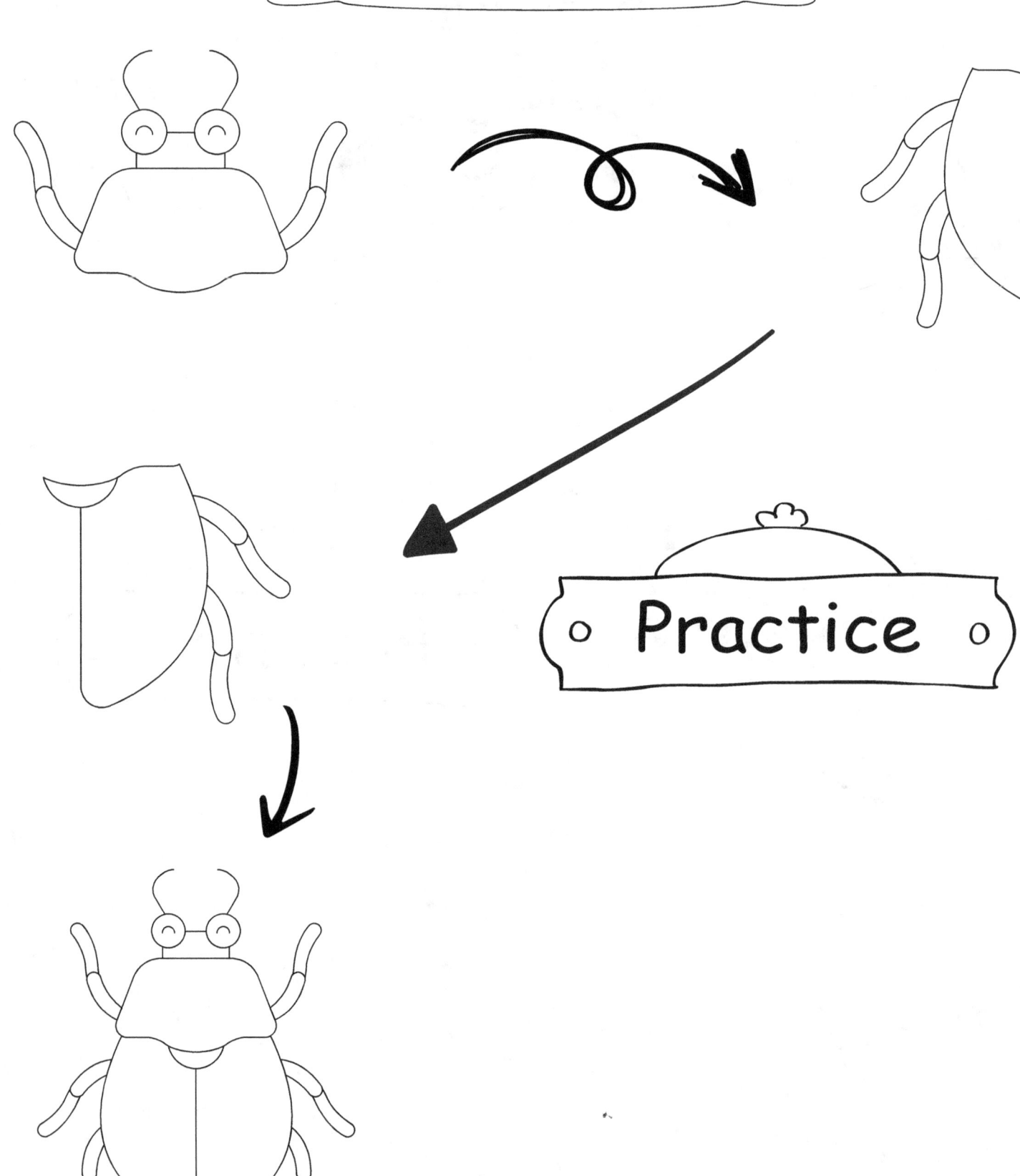

Practice

Tree

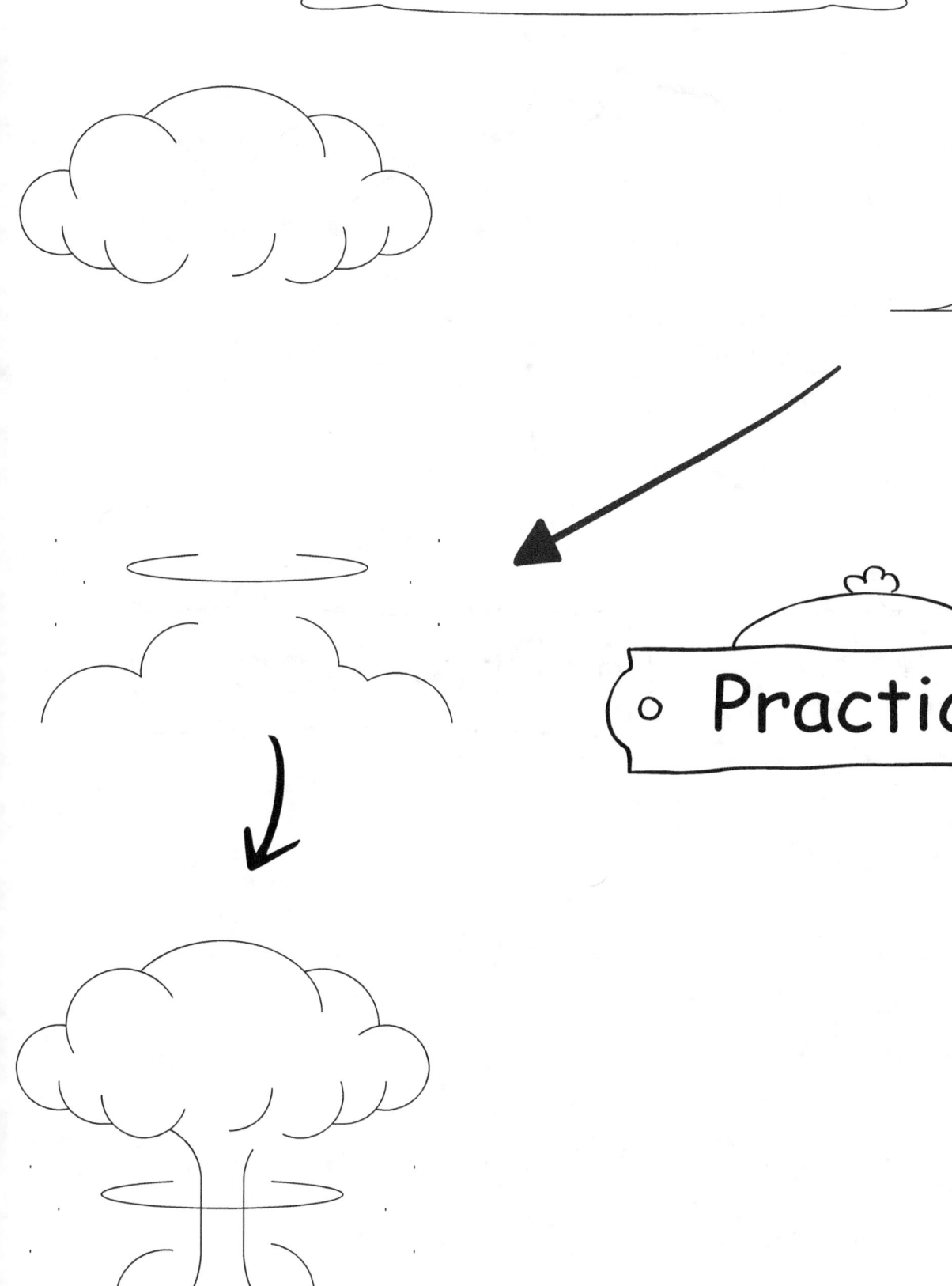

Practice

Flower

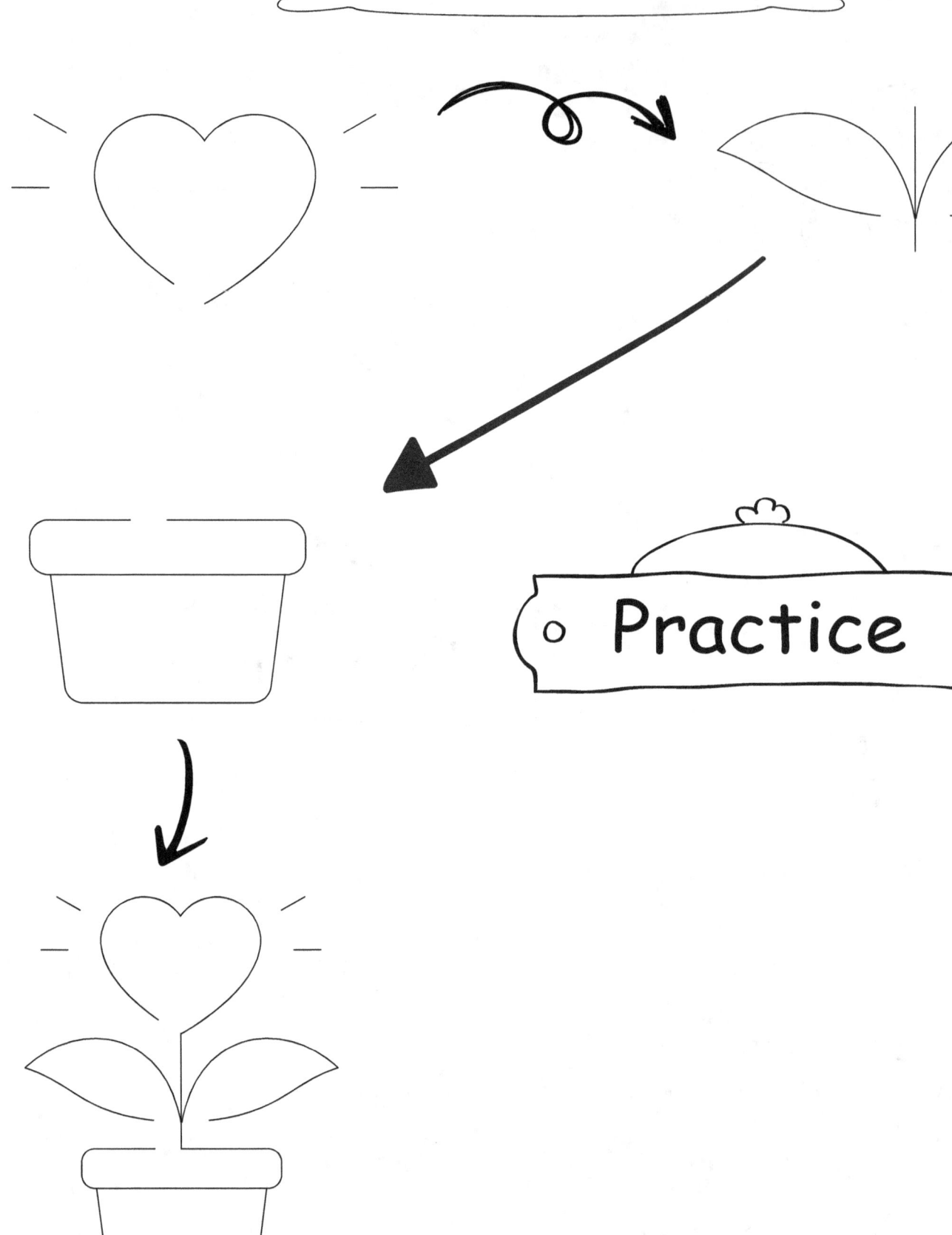

Practice

Rocket

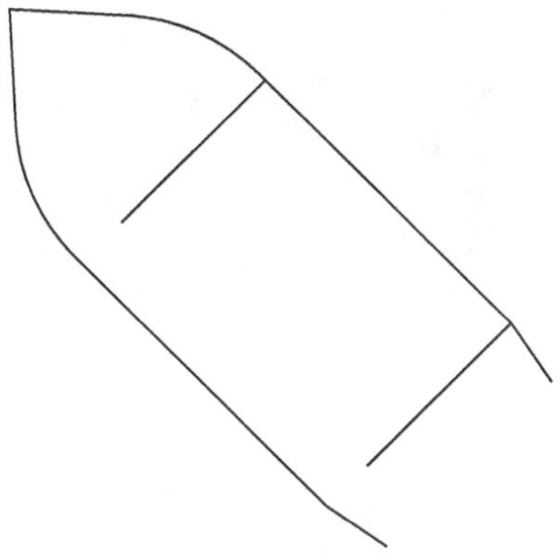

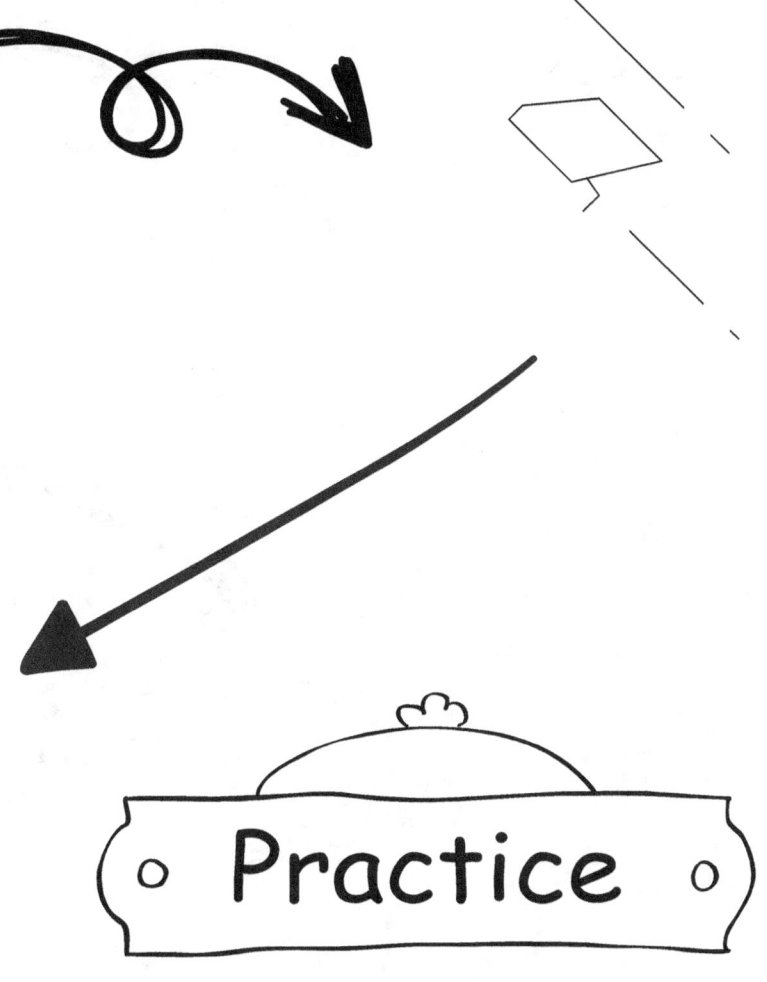

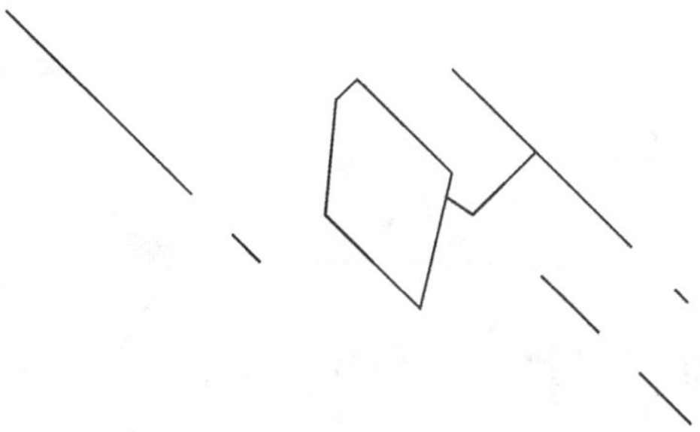

Practice

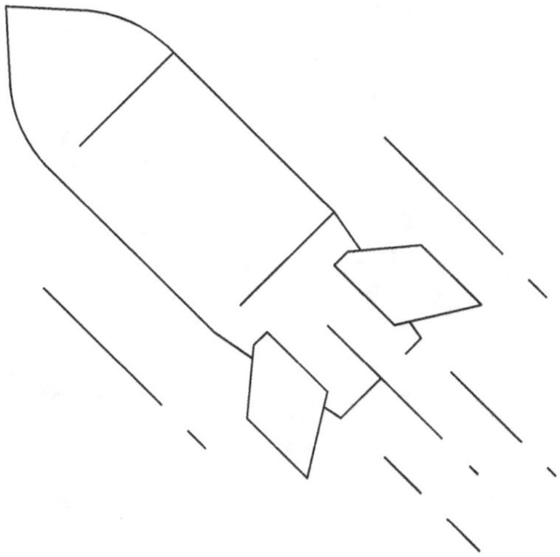

Running Man

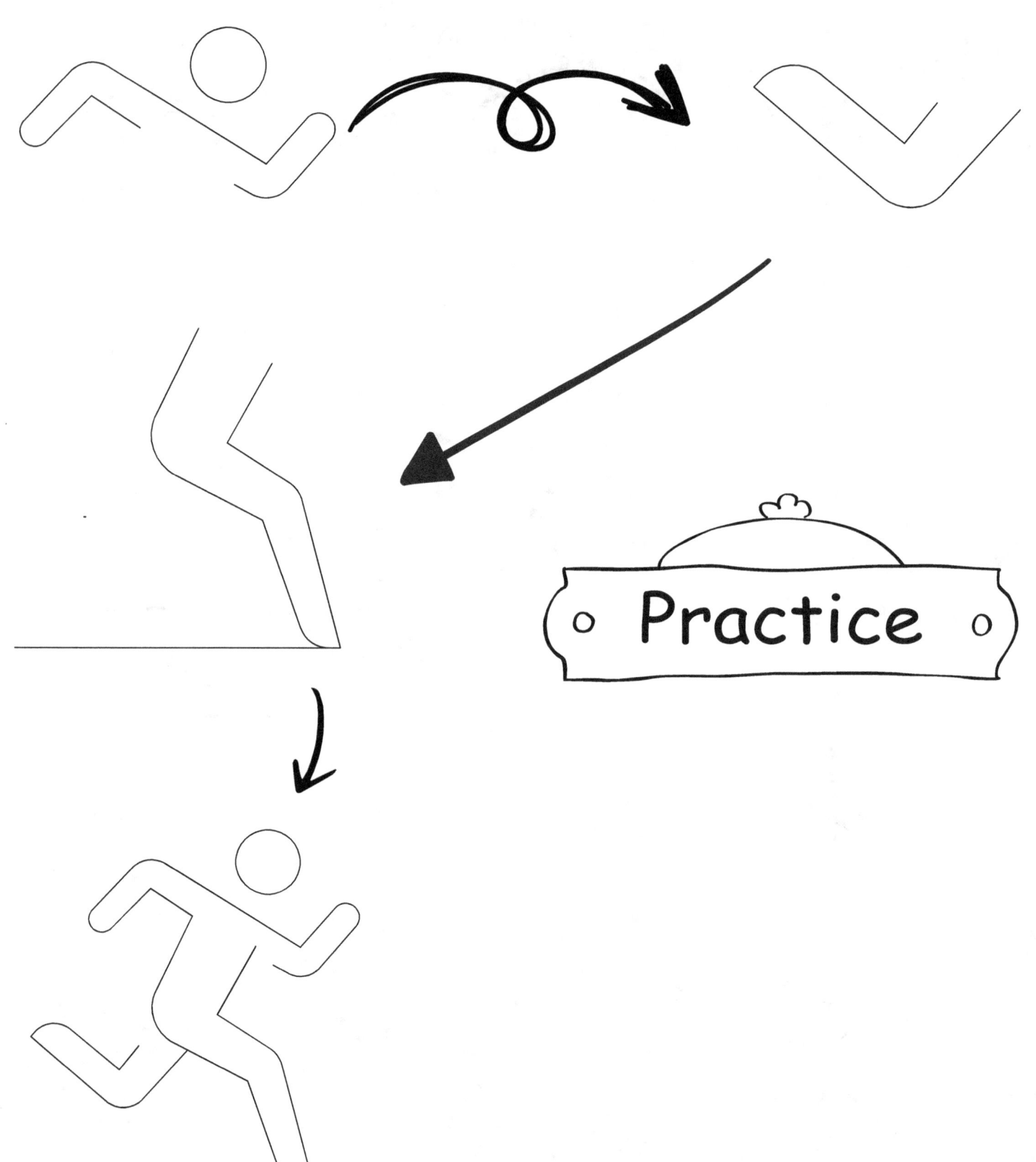

Practice

Help Hand

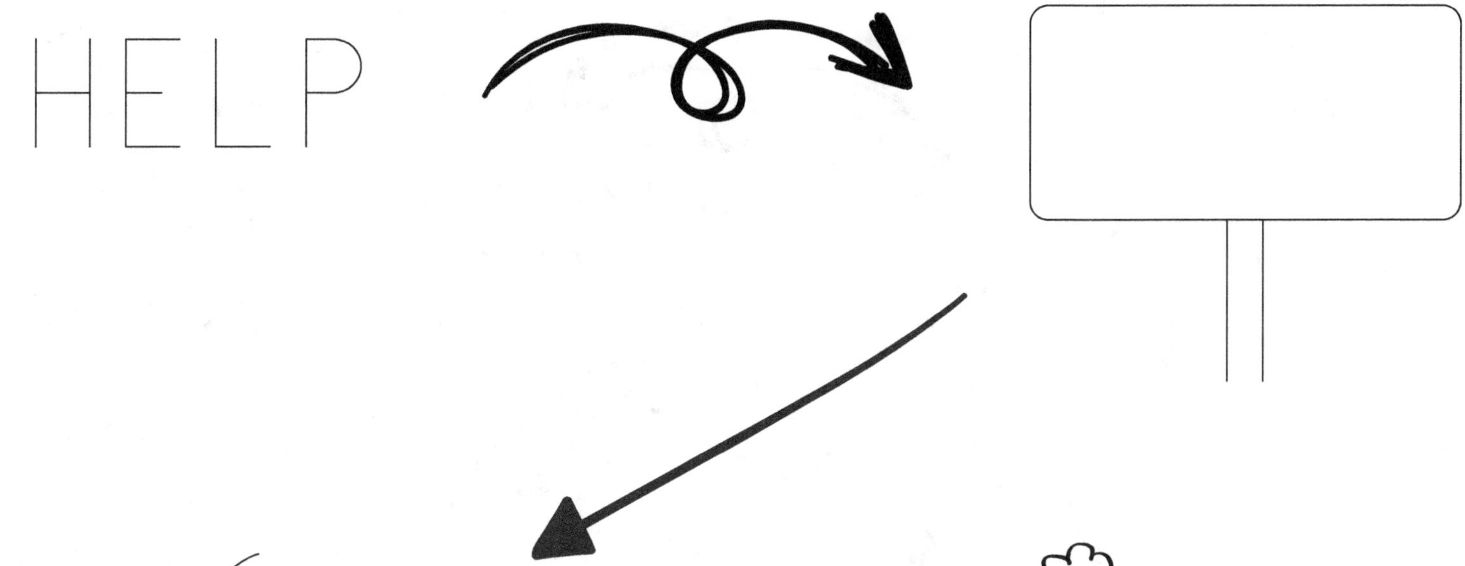

HELP

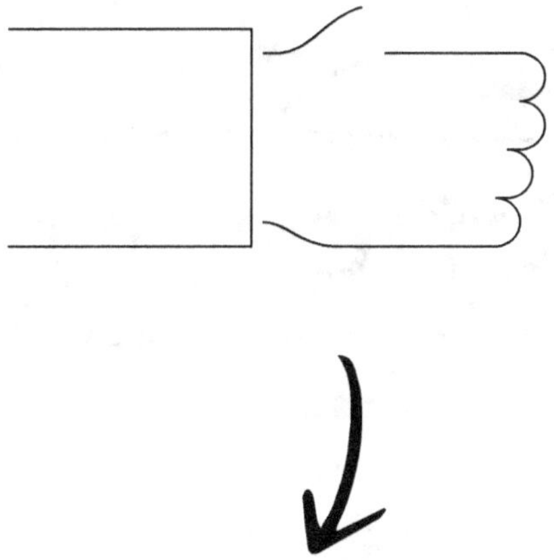

Practice

HELP

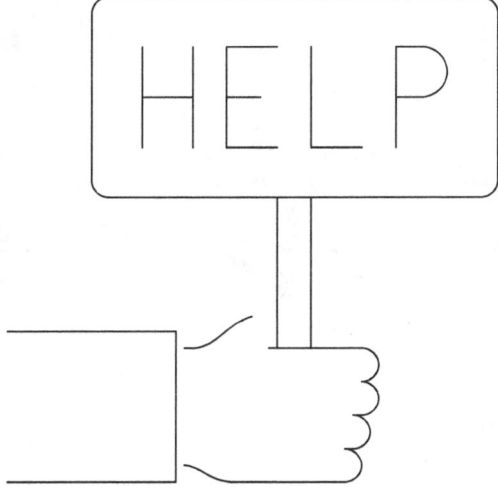

Yak

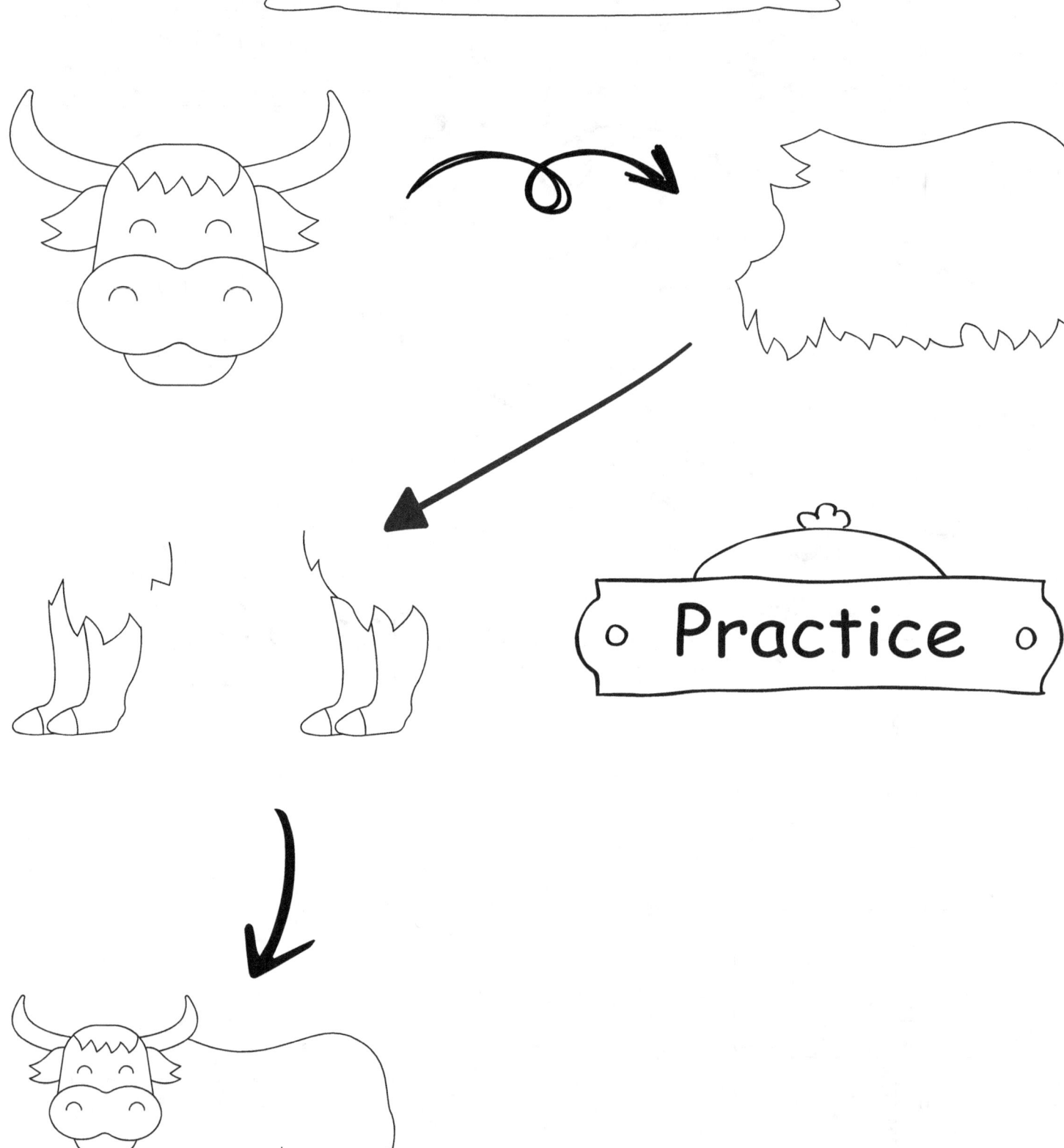

Practice

Snail

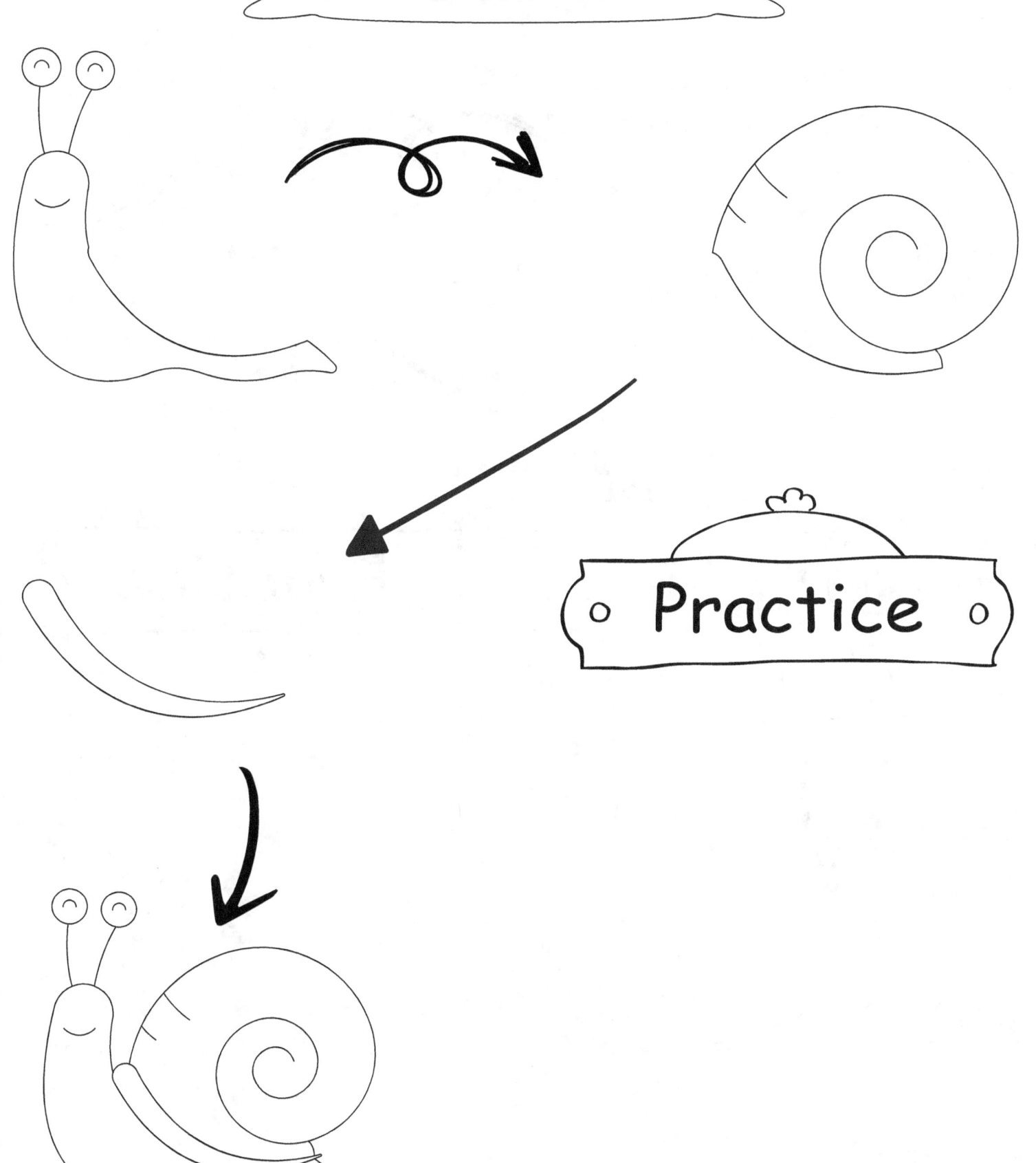

Kiwi

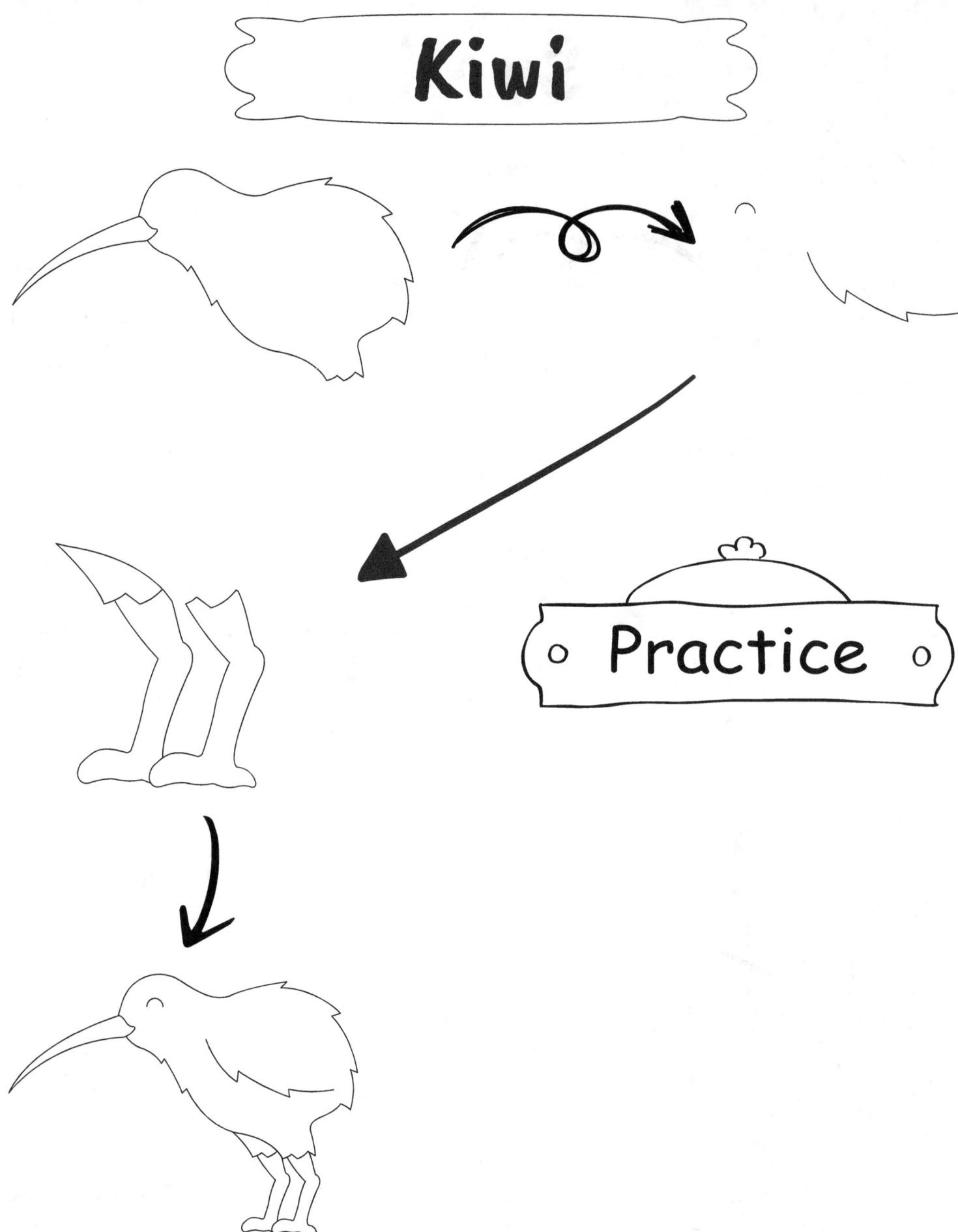

Practice

Cake

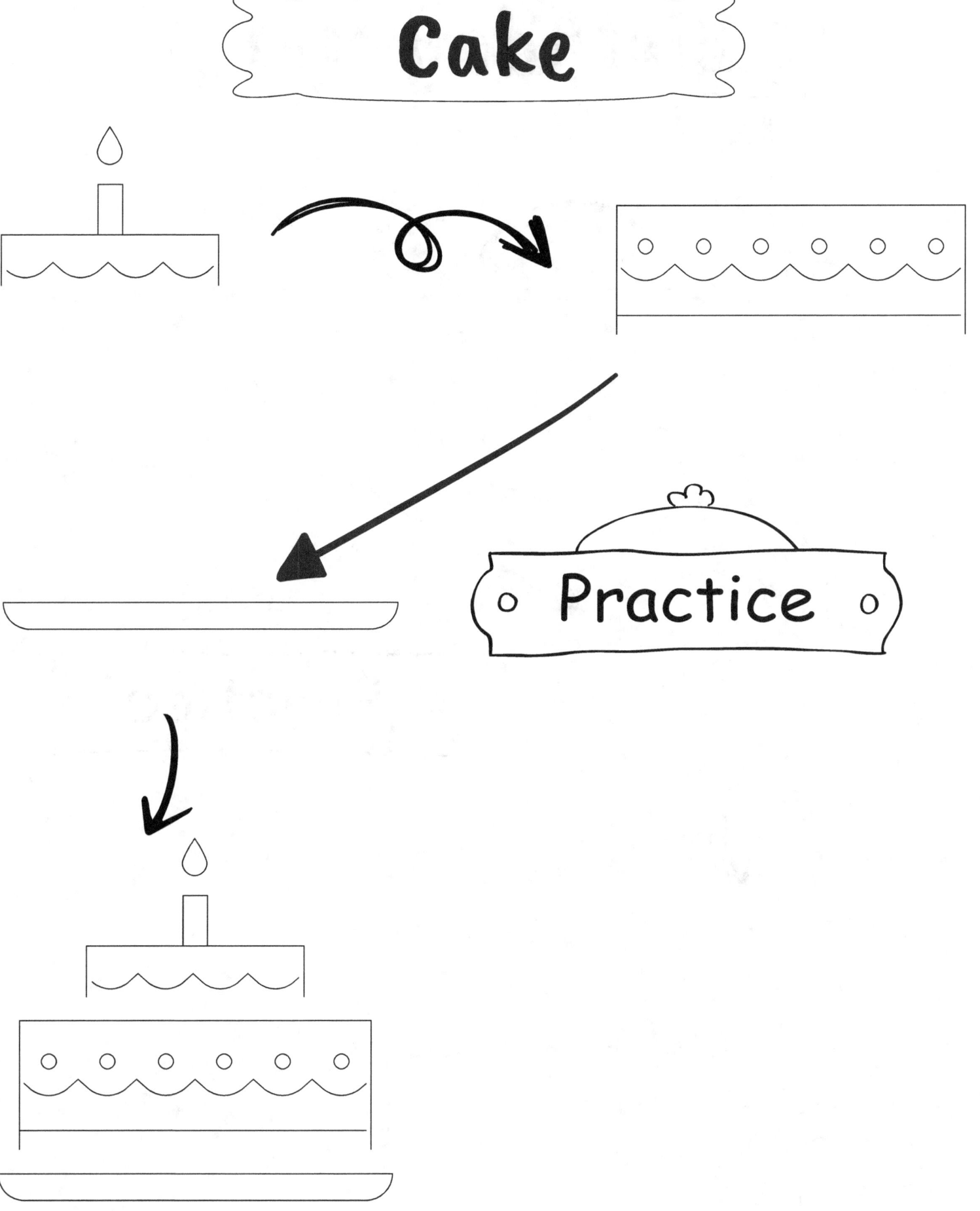

Practice

Birthday Hat

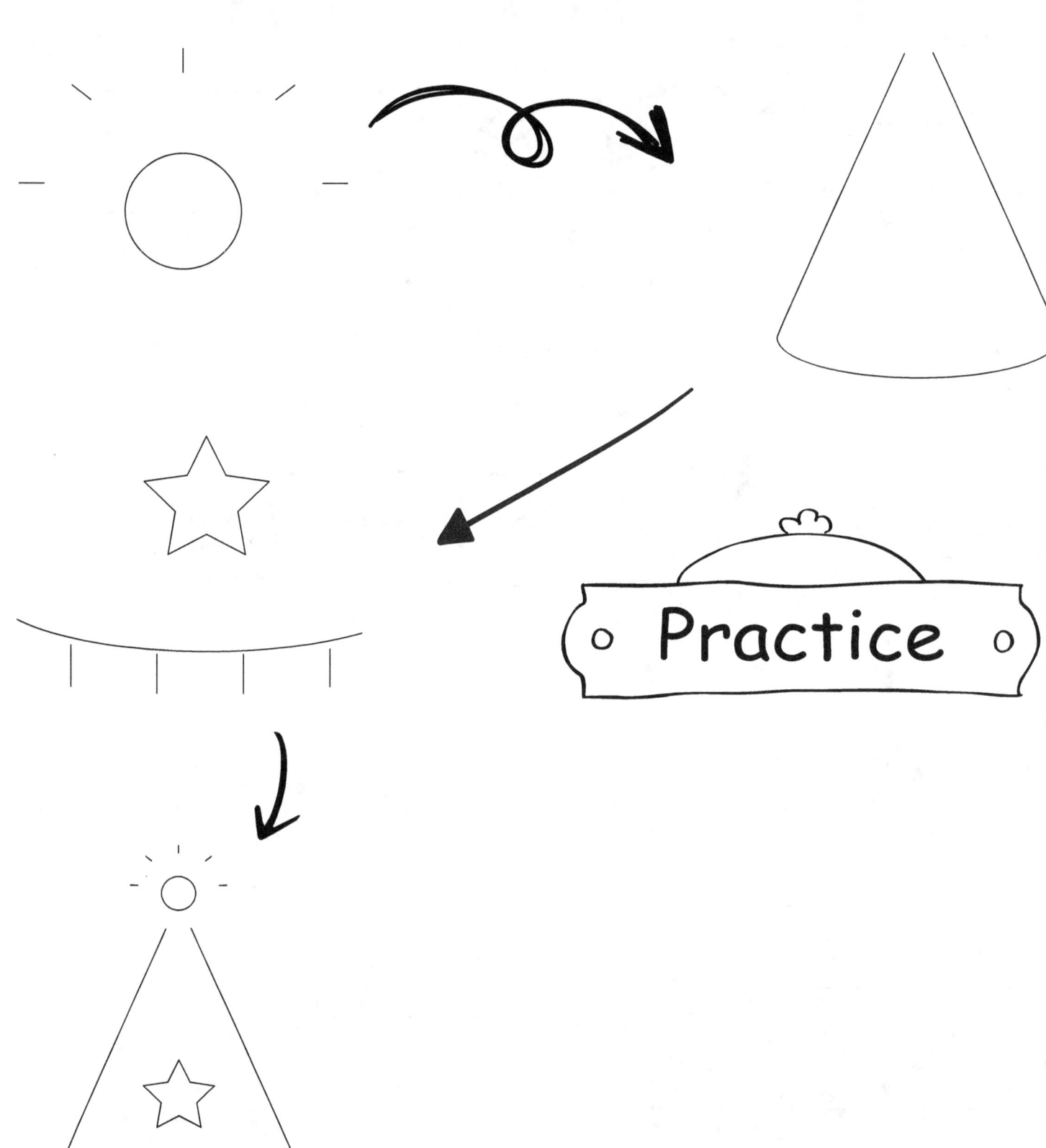

Practice

DJ Mixer

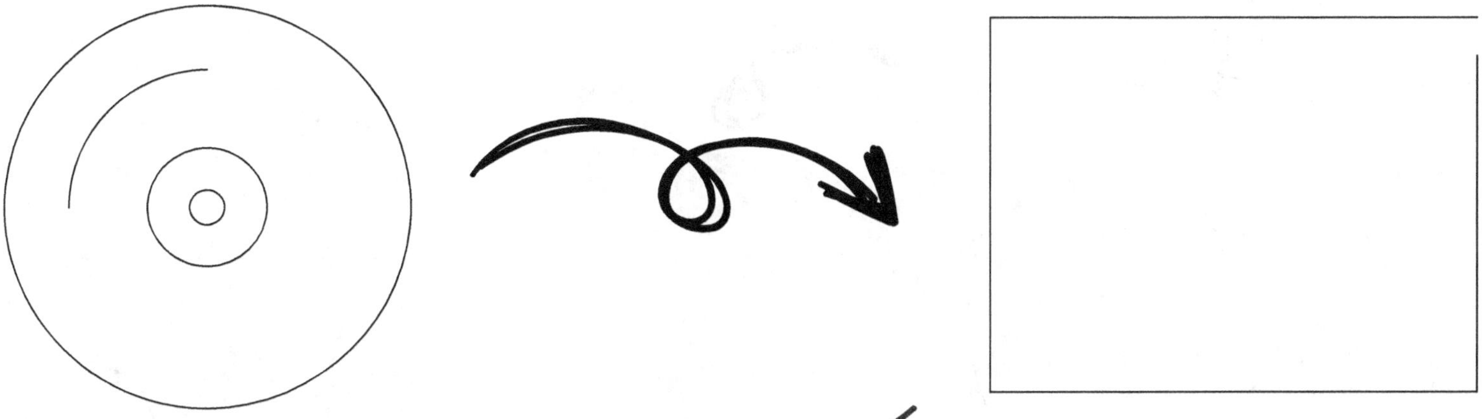

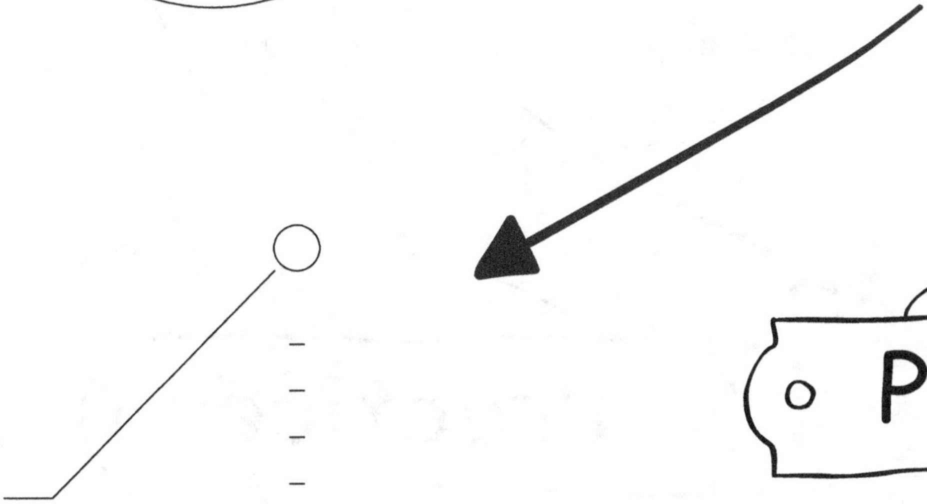

Practice

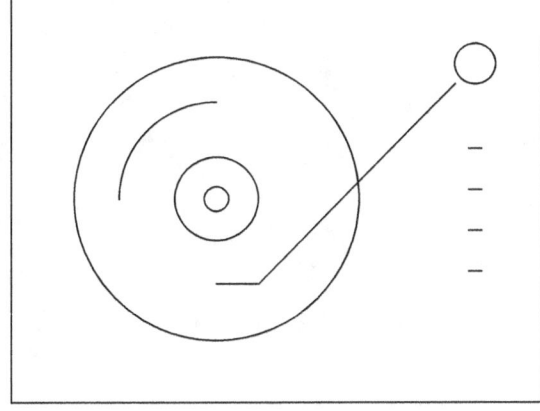

Disco Ball

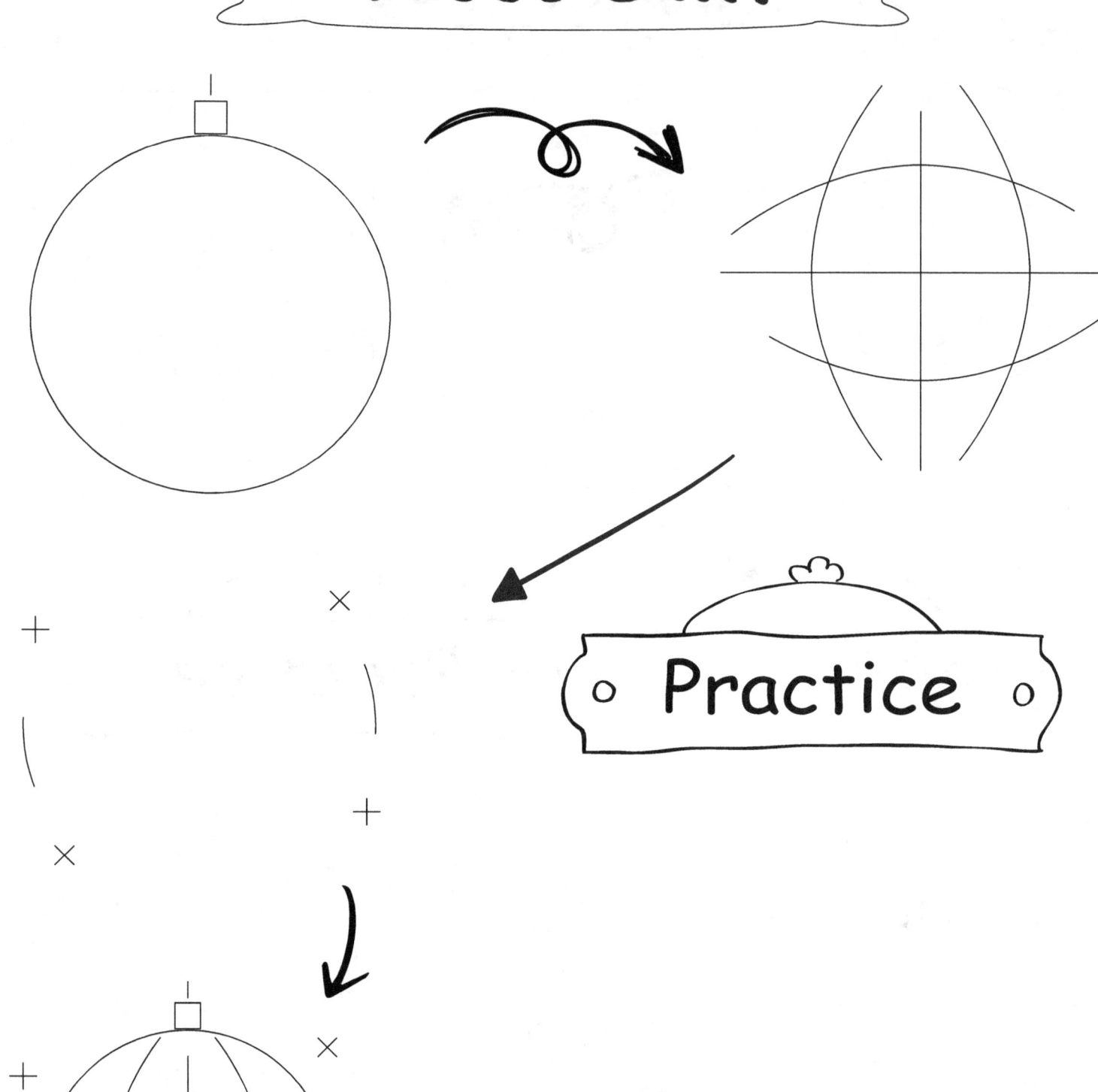

Practice

Frog

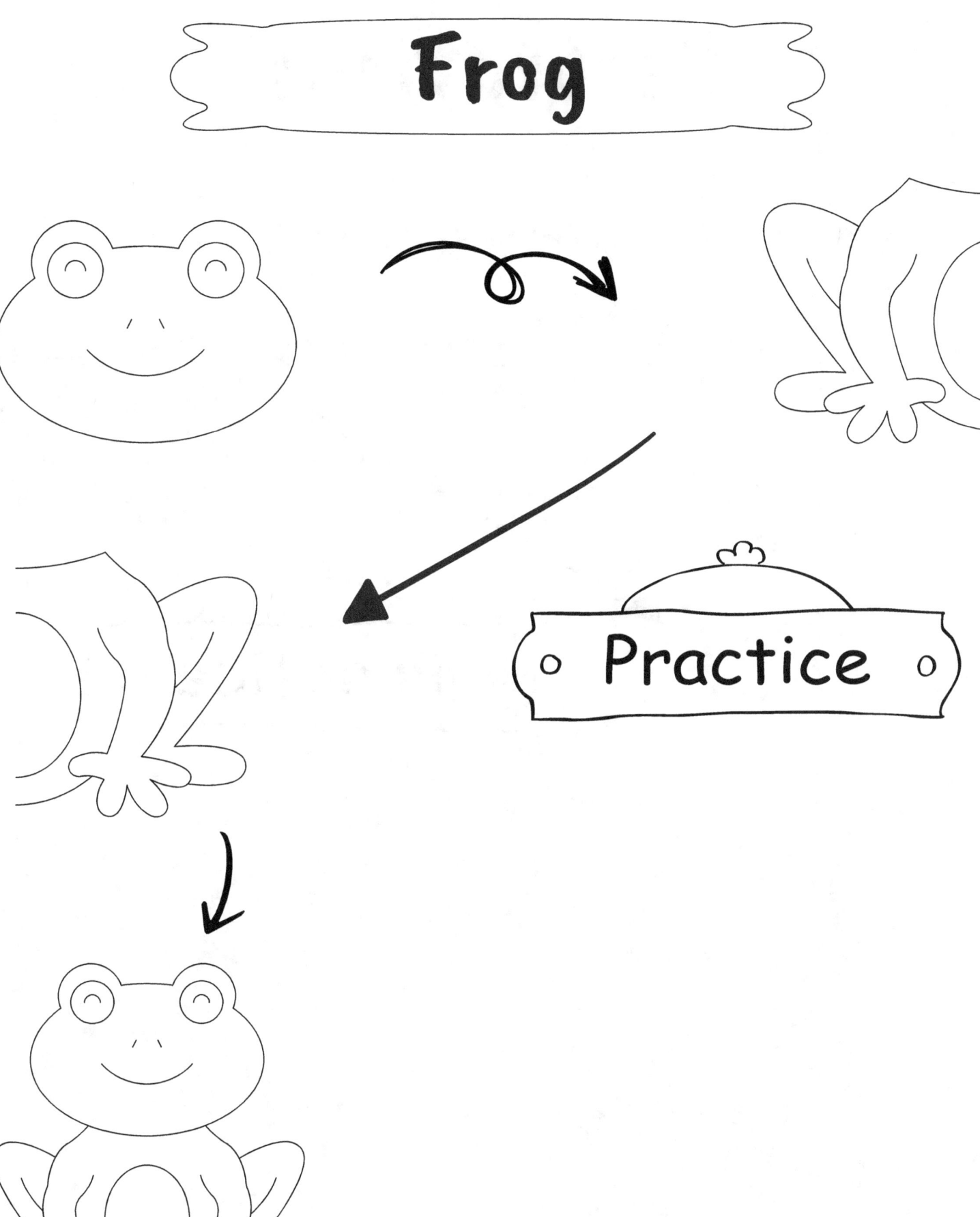

Practice

Decorations

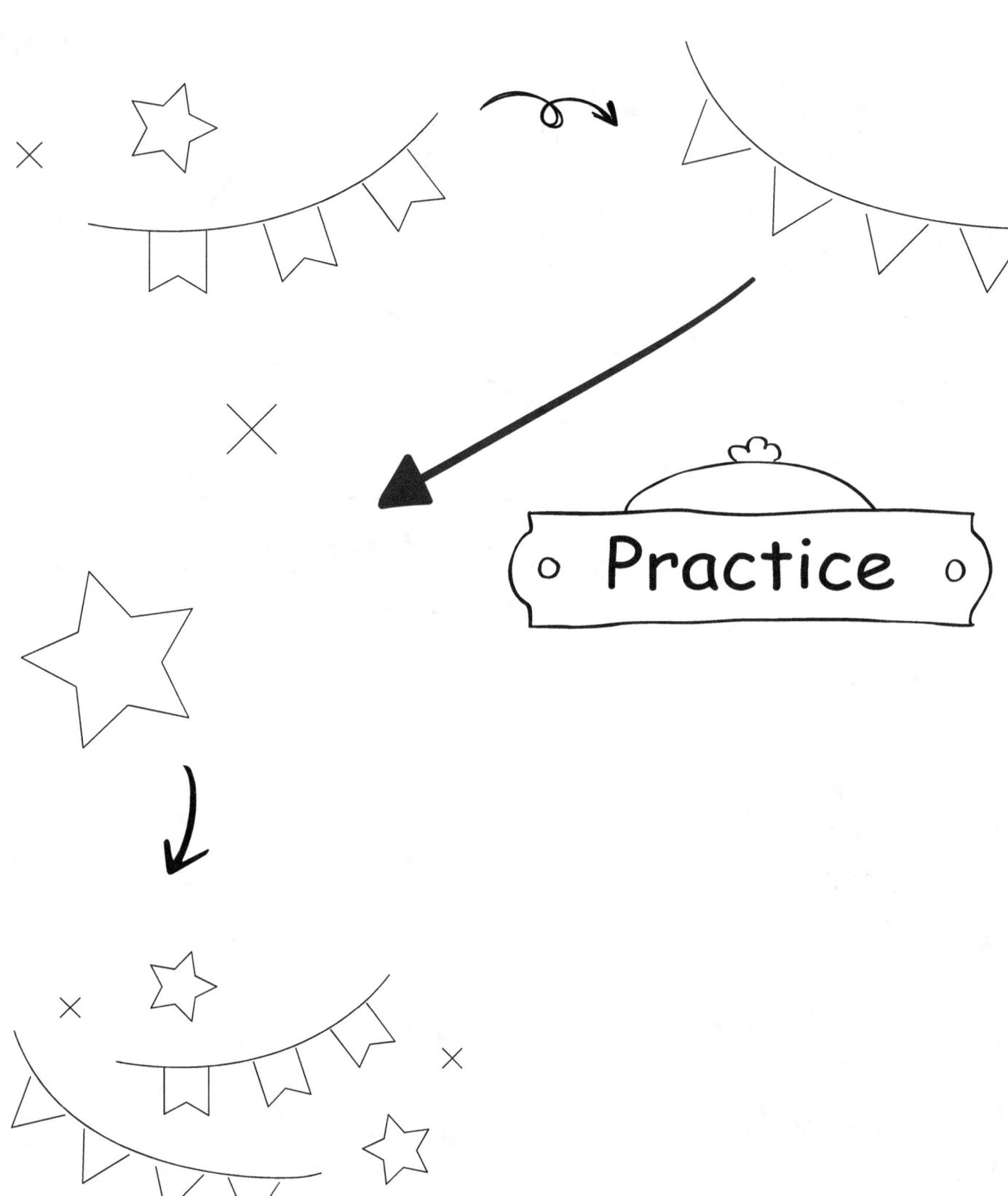

Practice

Guitar

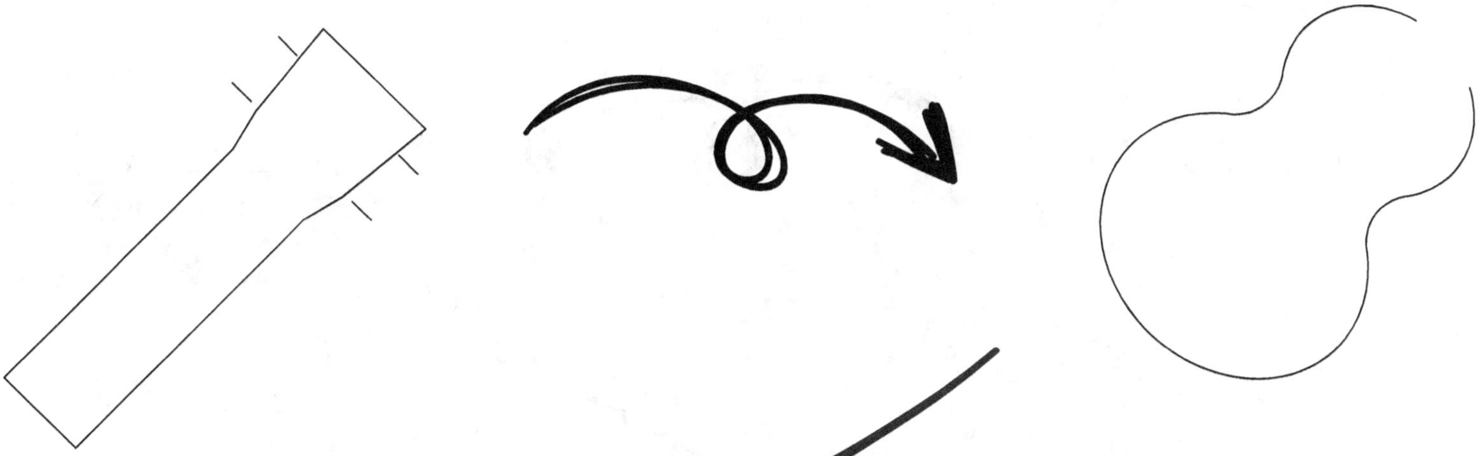

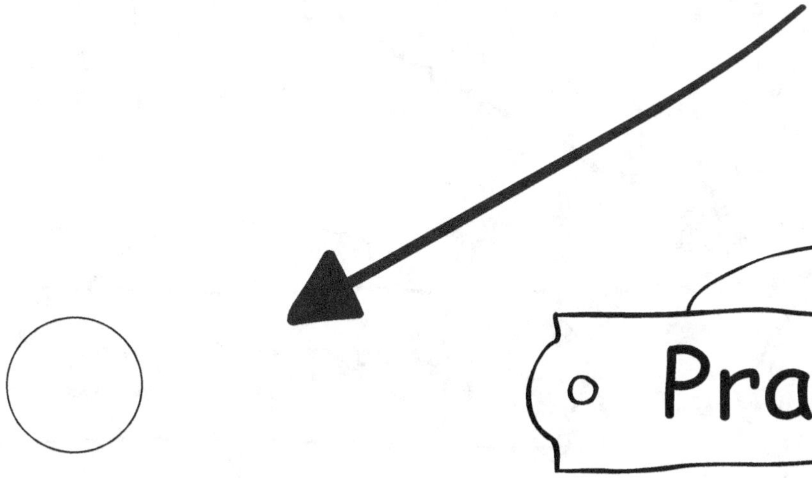

Practice

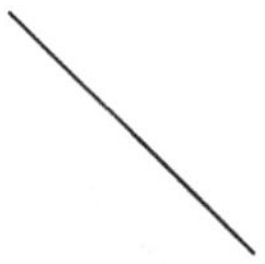

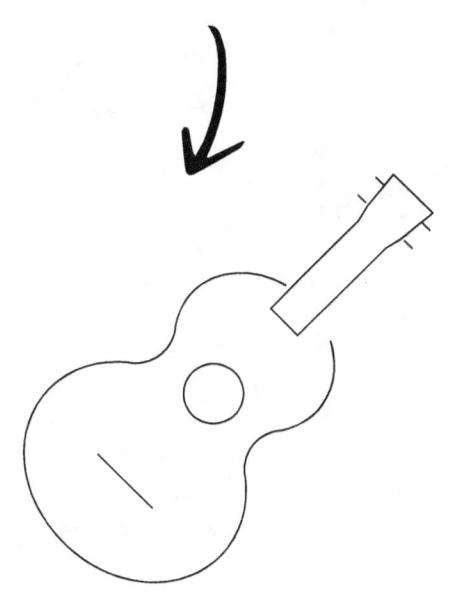

Chameleon

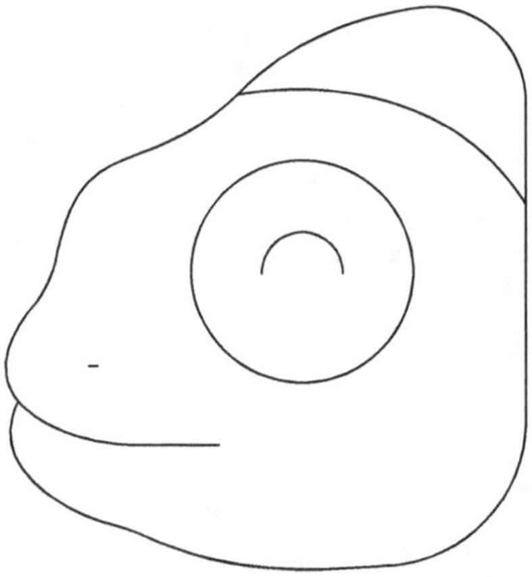

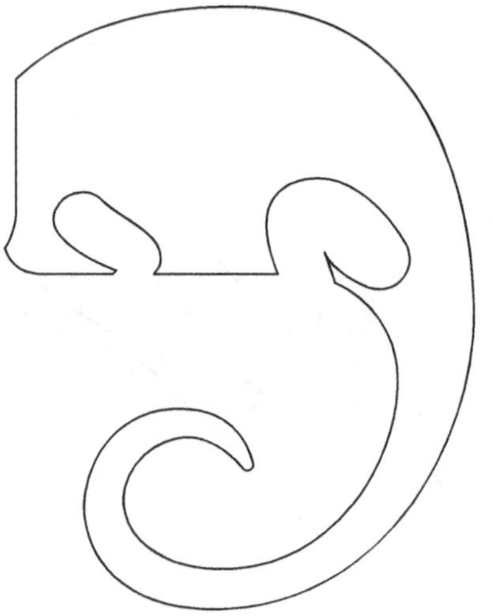

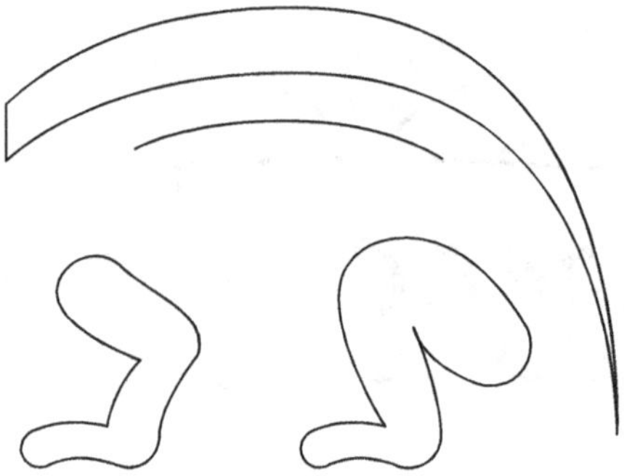

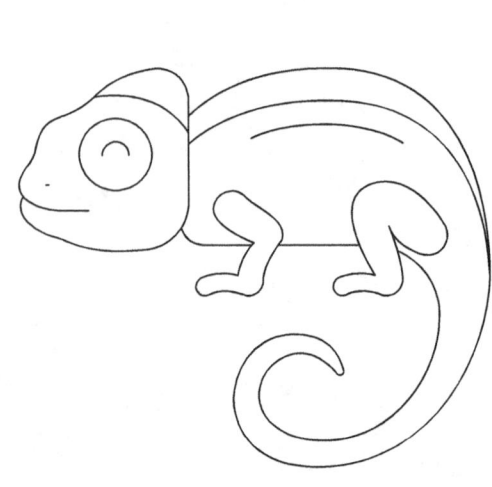

Ant

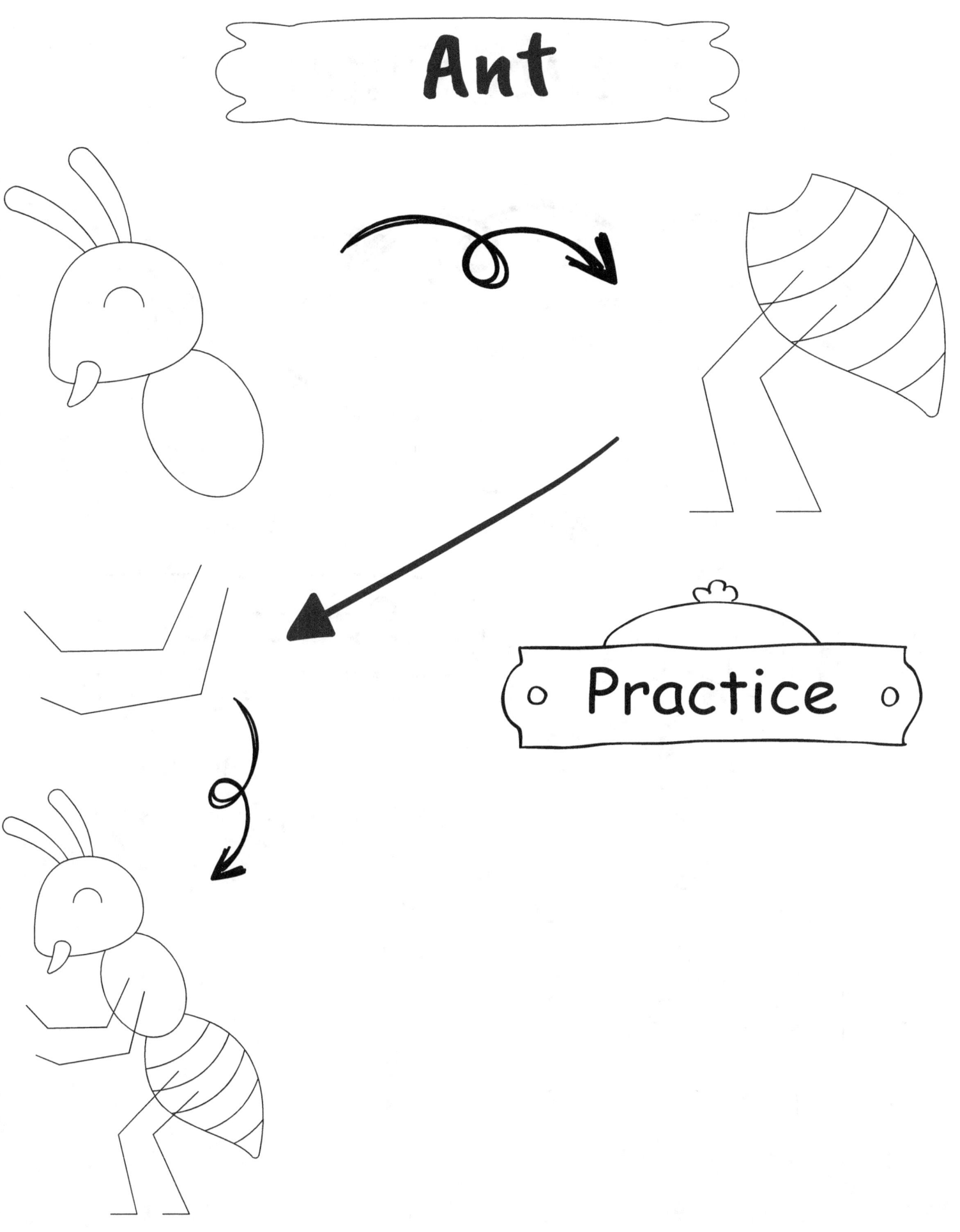

Firecracker

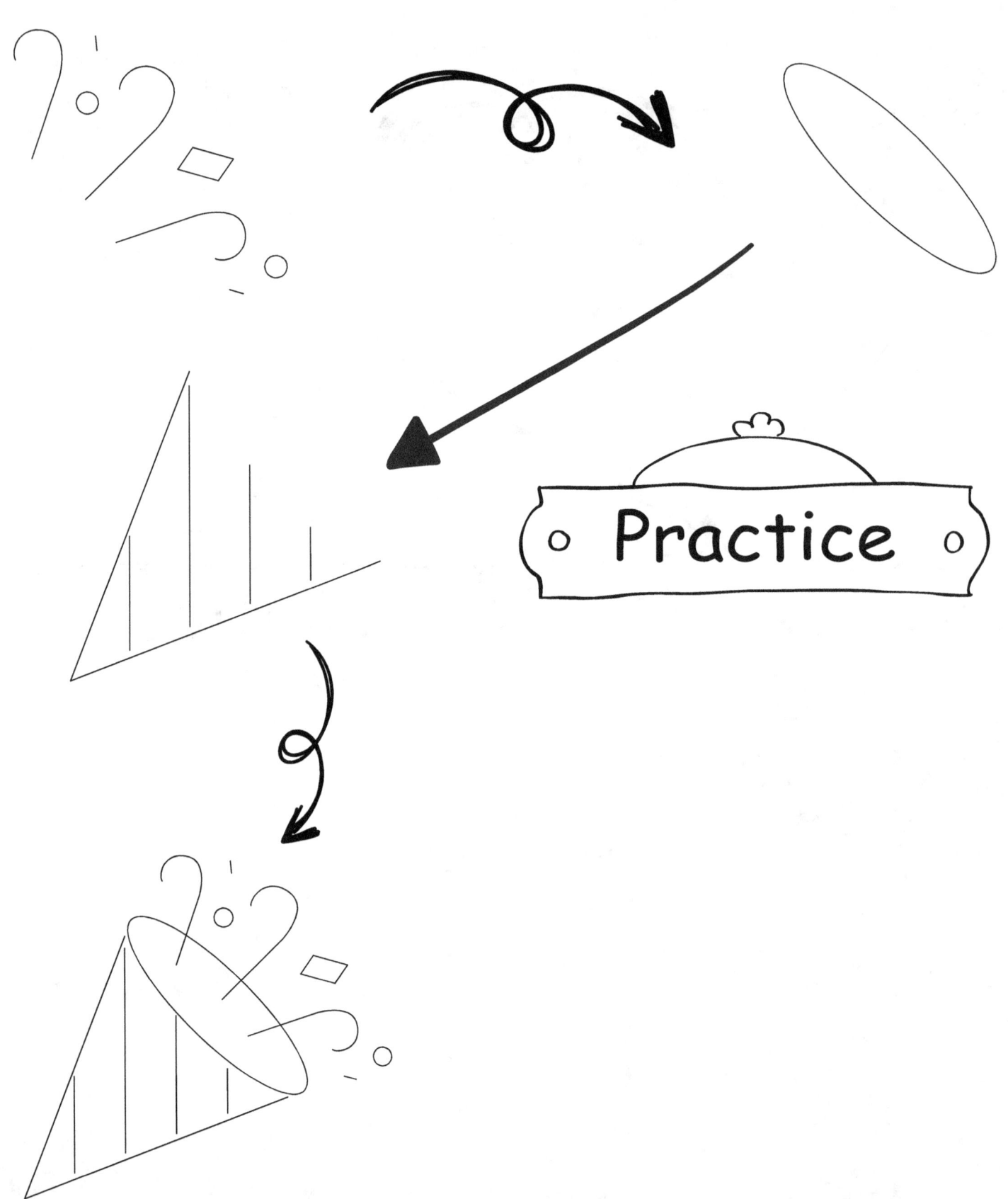

Practice

Pizza Slice

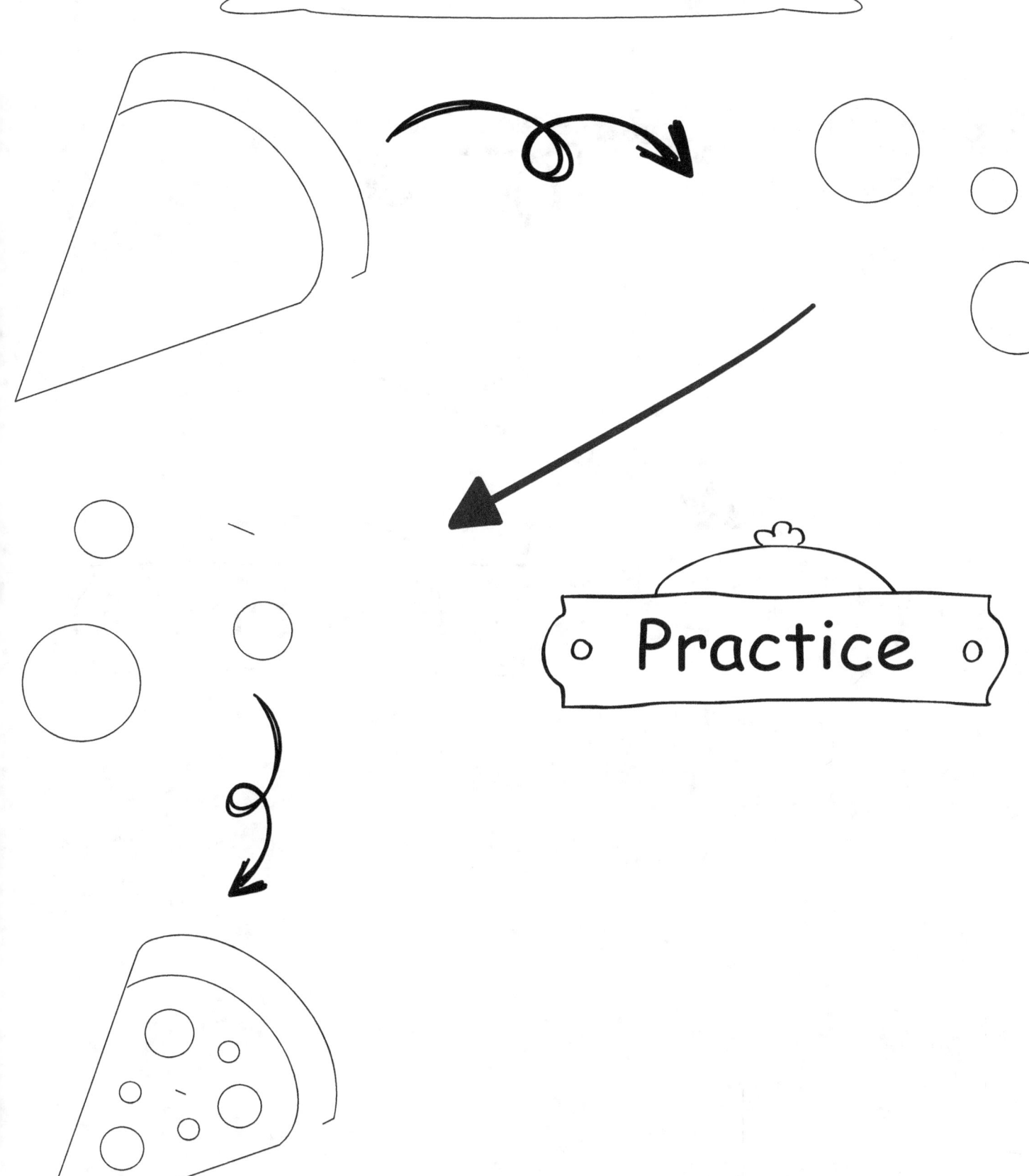

Practice

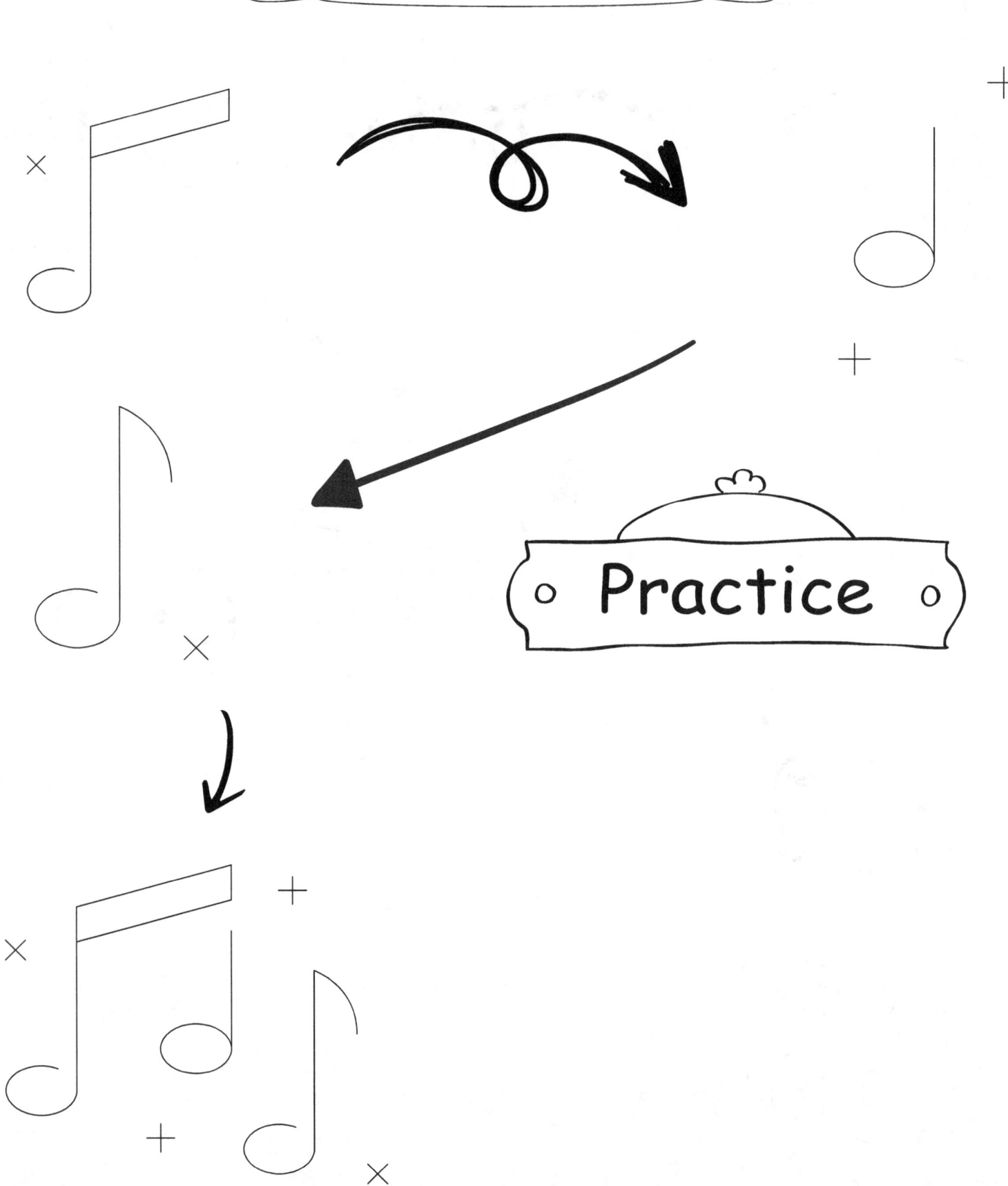

Anteater

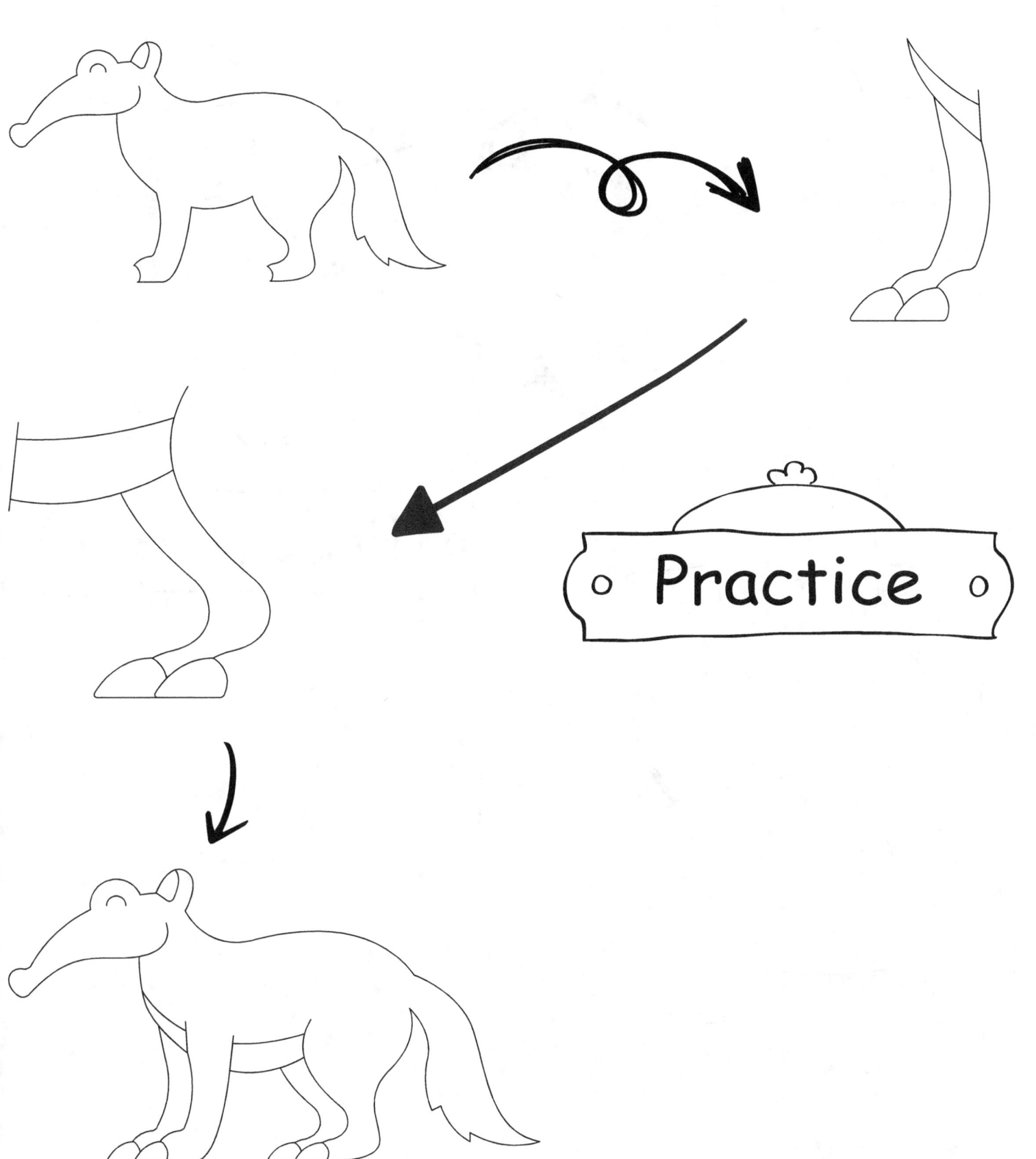

Practice

Bee

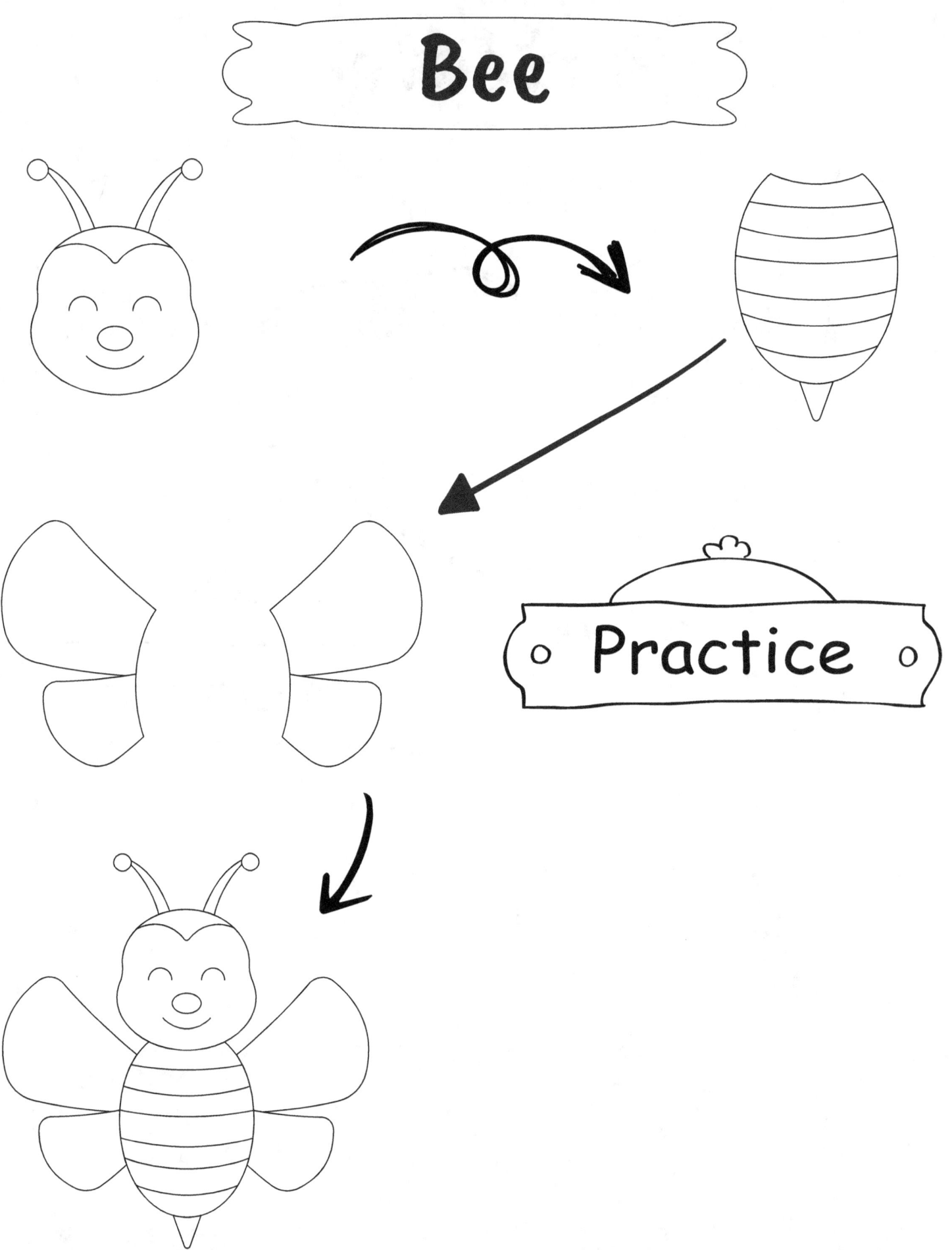

Practice

Loudspeakers

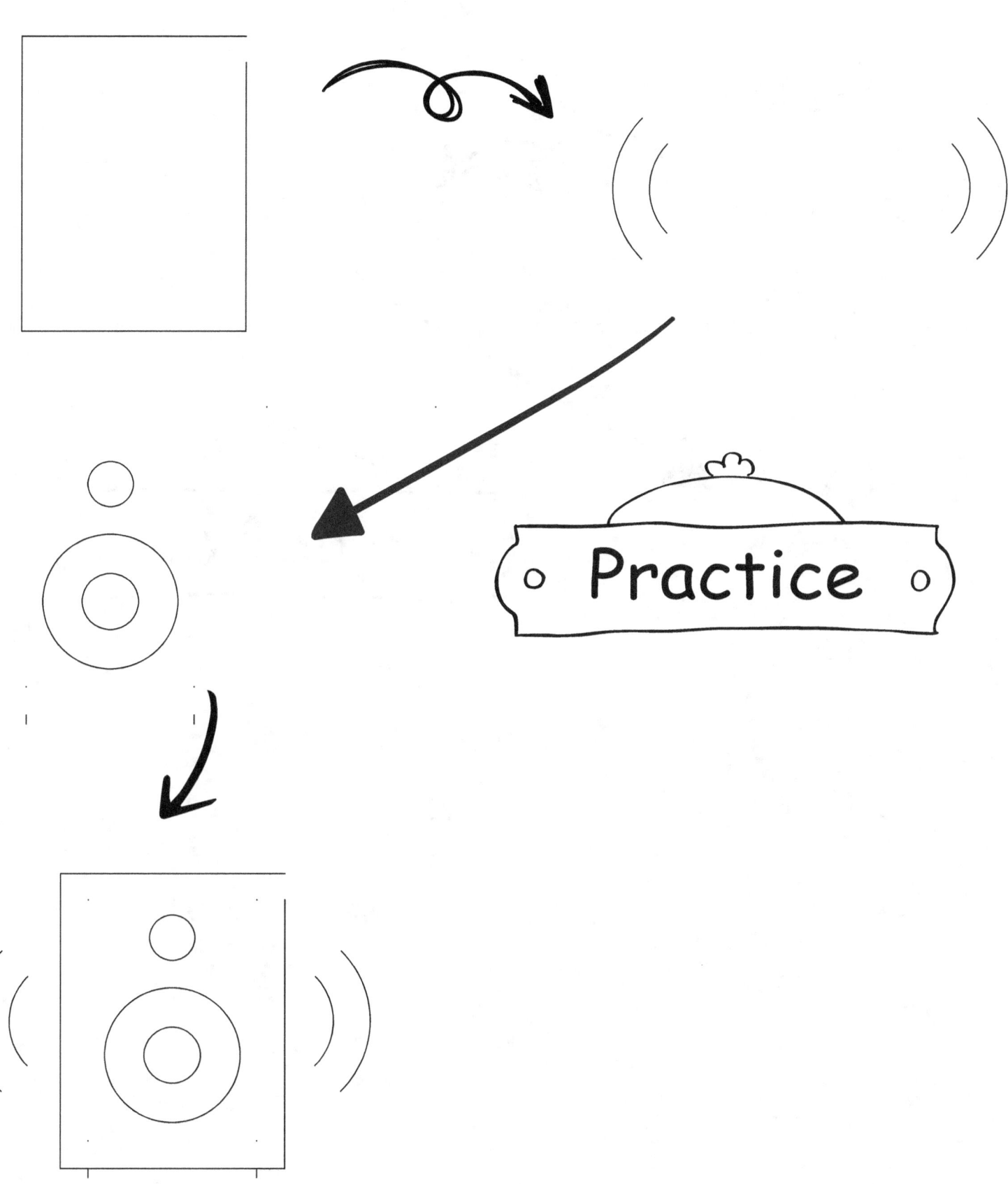

Practice

Christmass

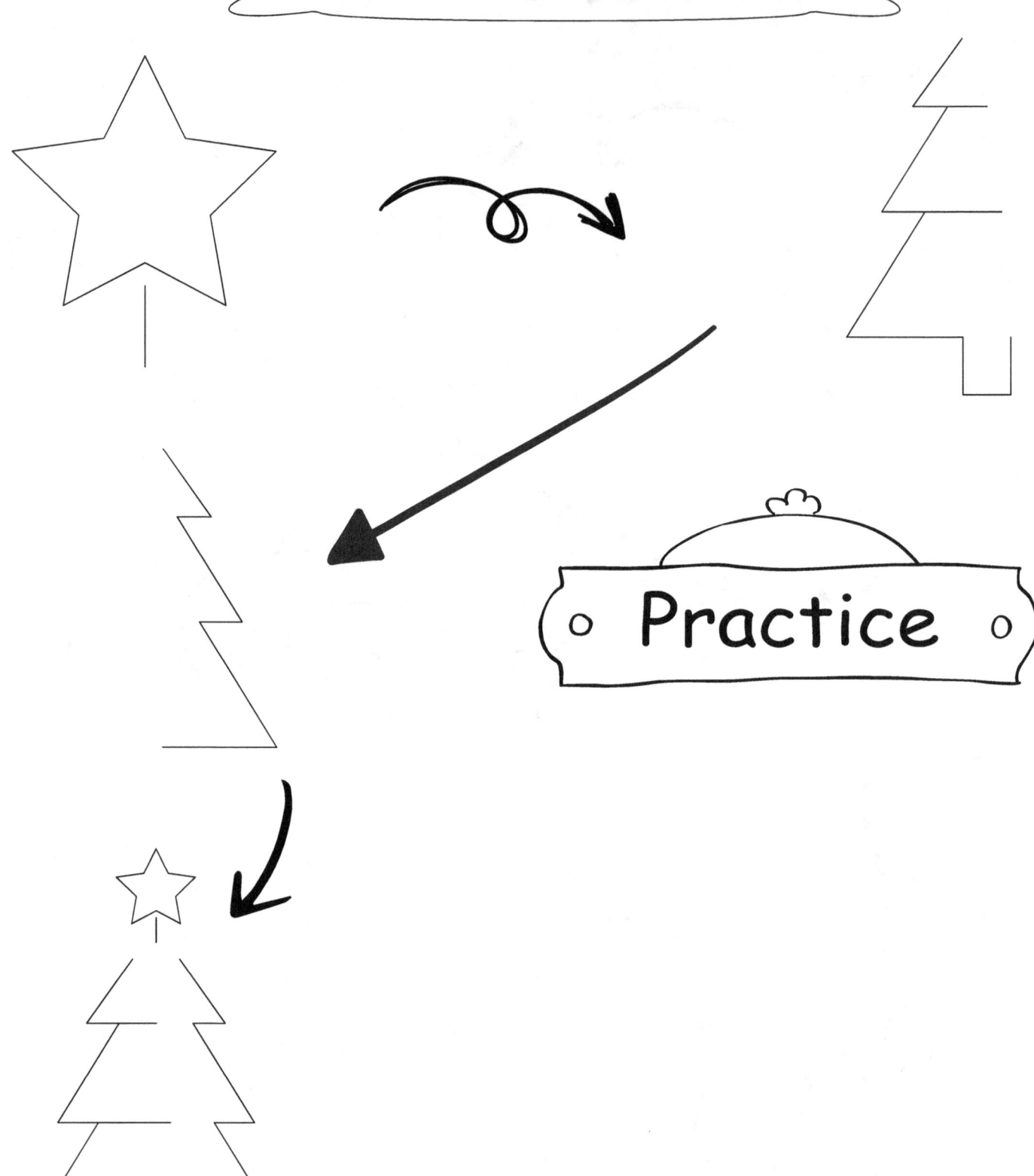

Practice

Cocktail

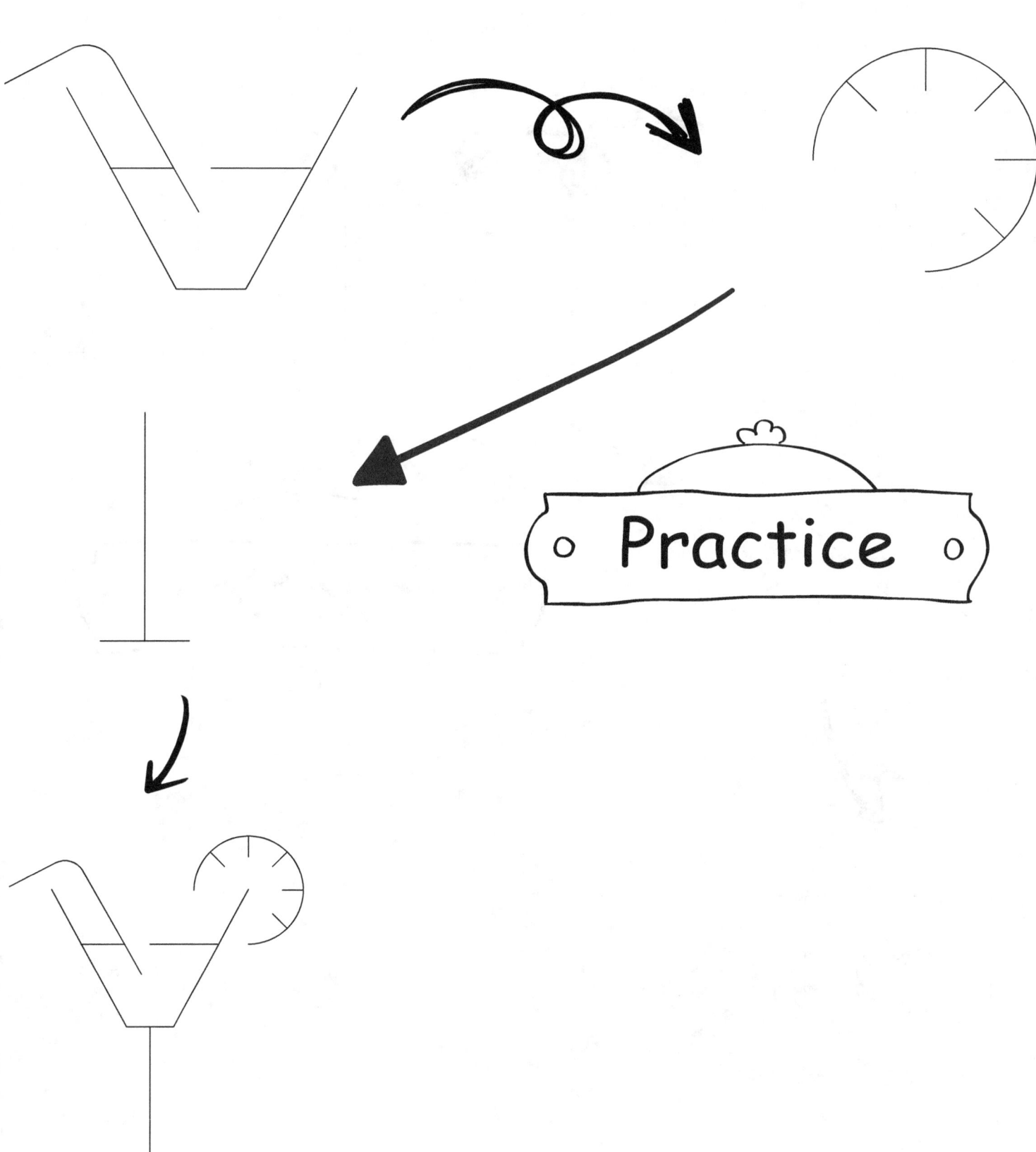

Practice

Valentine's Day

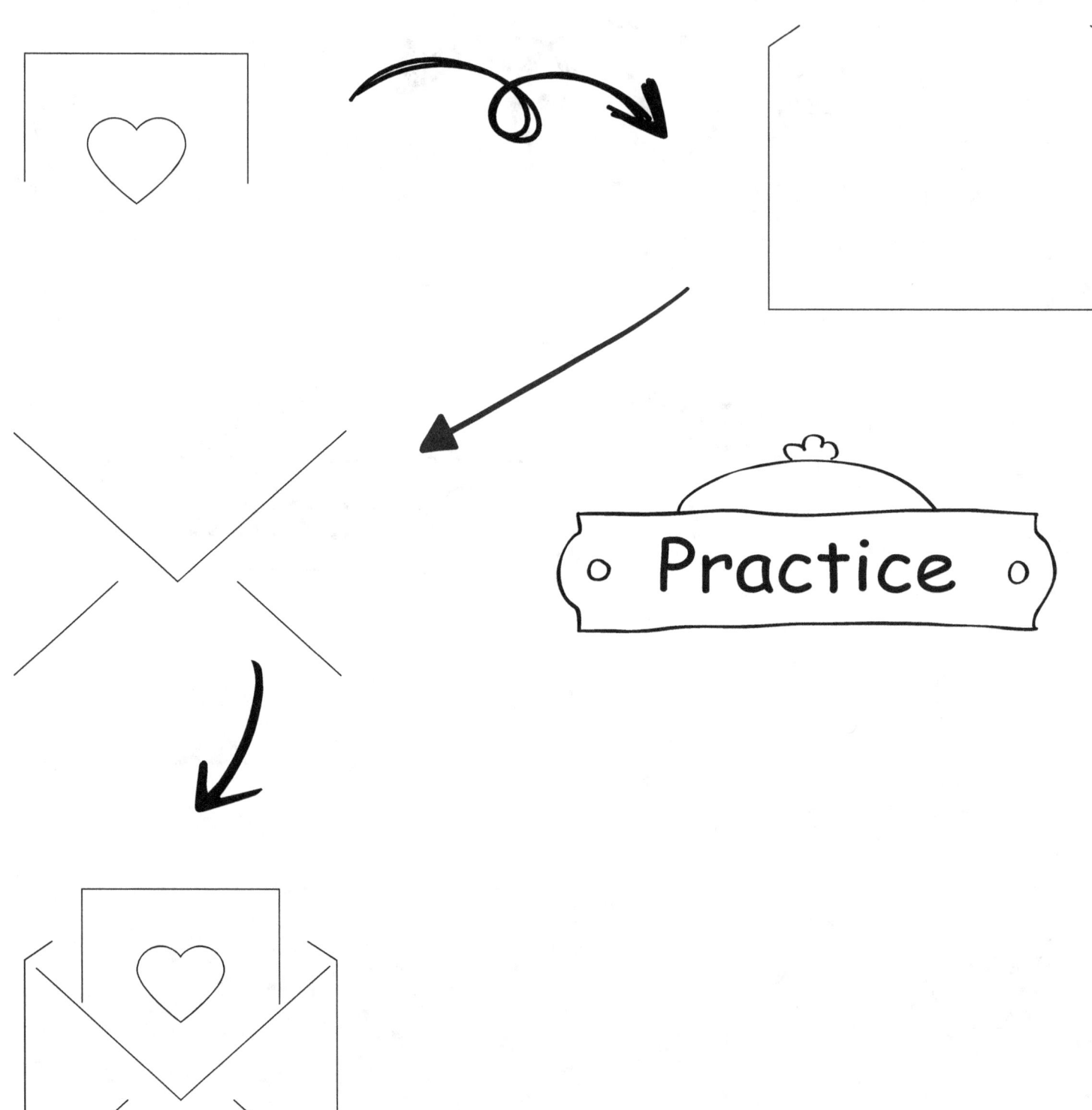

Practice

Snake

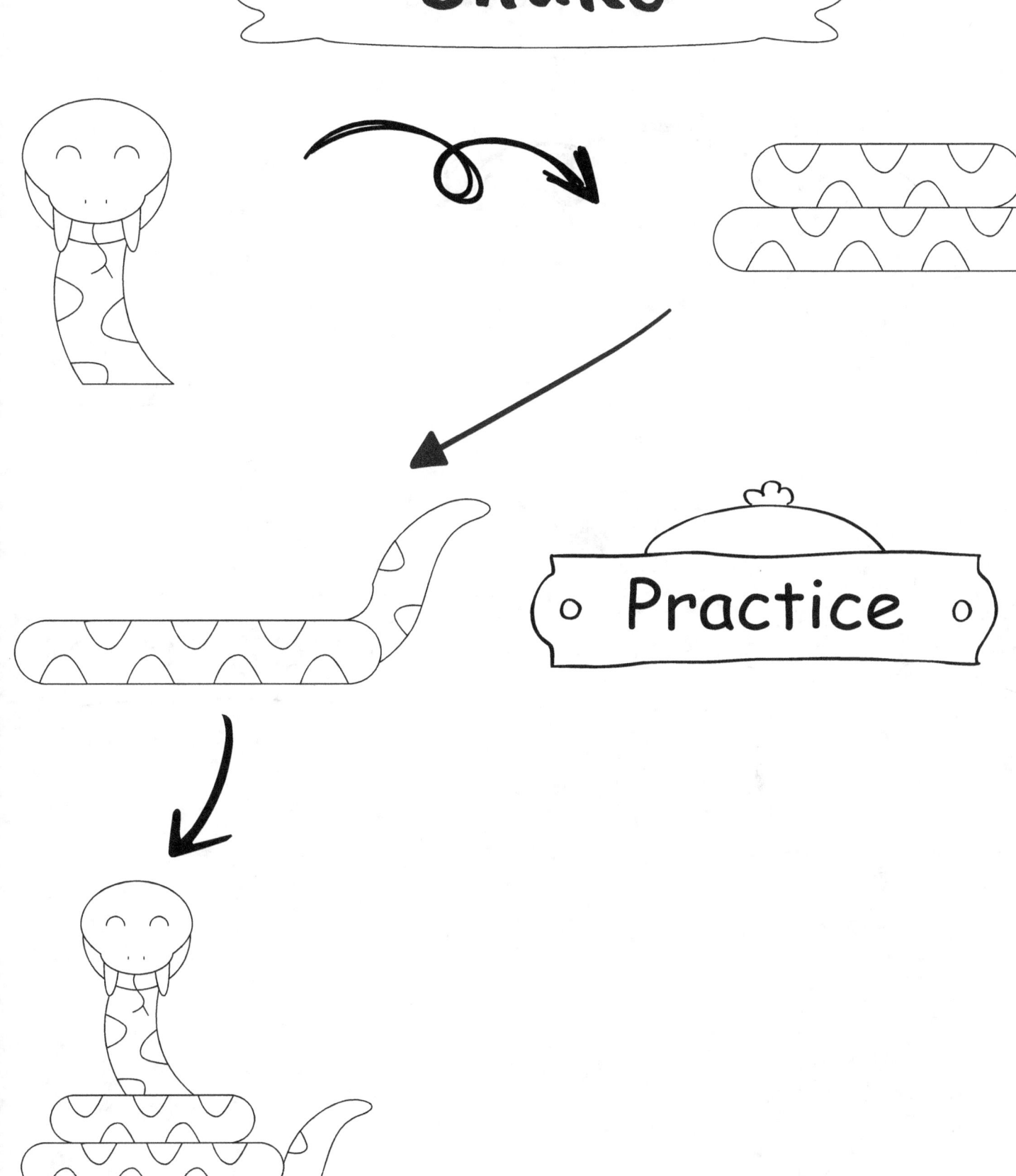

Practice

Gorilla

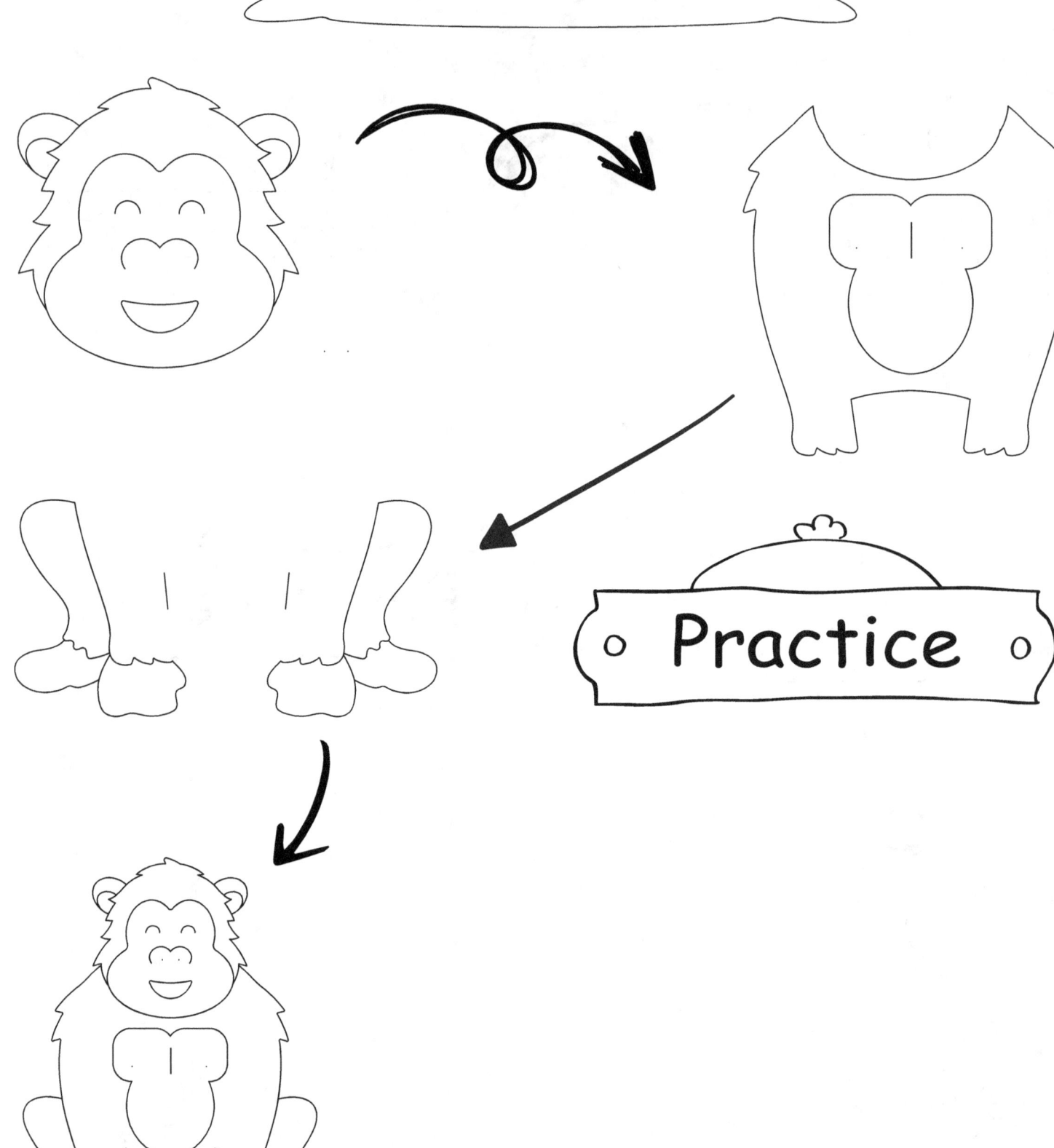

Practice

Polar Bear

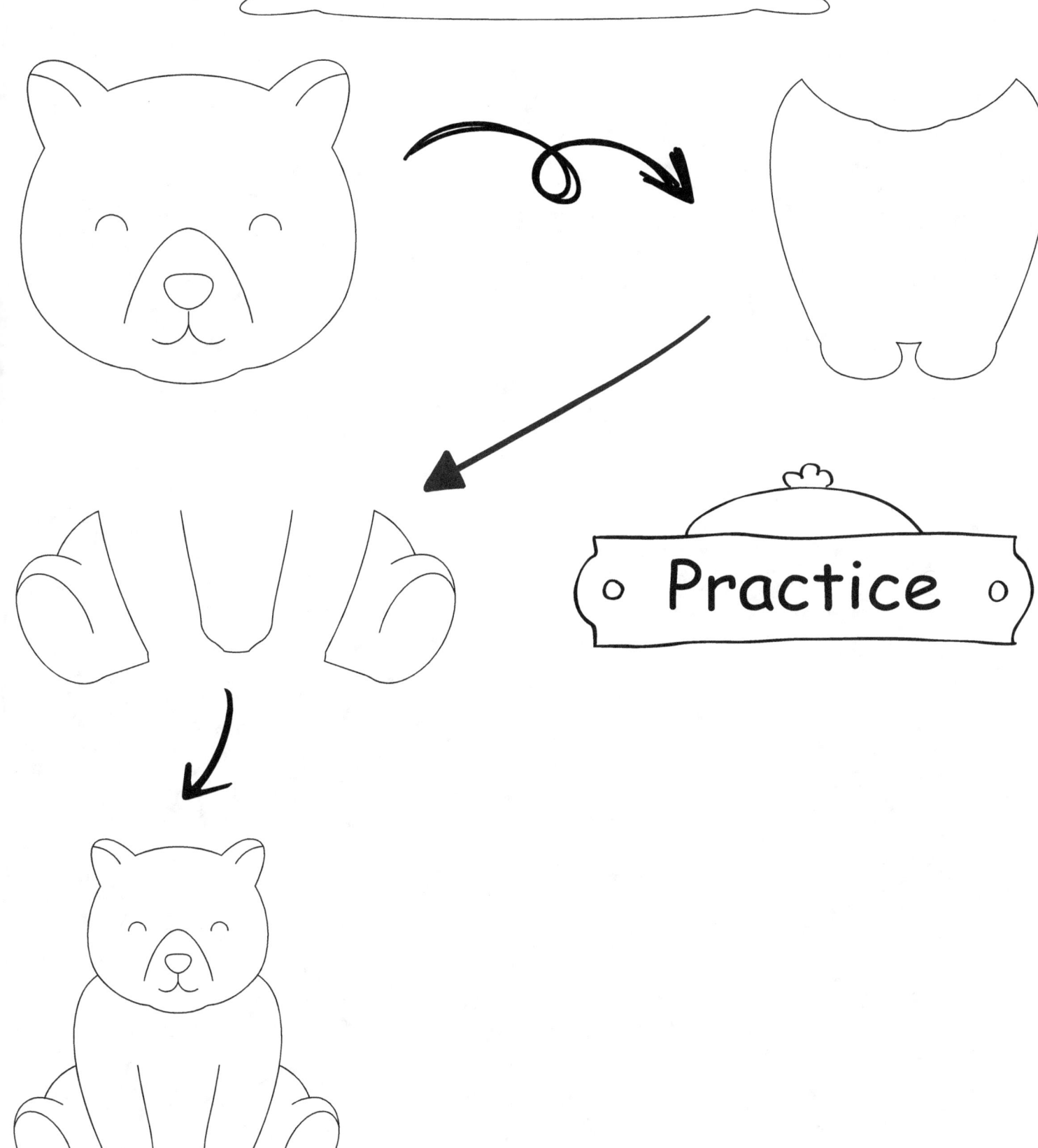

Practice